Read Write Inc.
PHONICS

C000225461

Get Writing!

Handbook

and CD-ROM

Series developed by **Ruth Miskin**

OXFORD
UNIVERSITY PRESS

OXFORD
UNIVERSITY PRESS

Great Clarendon Street, Oxford OX2 6DP

Oxford University Press is a department of the University of Oxford.
It furthers the University's objective of excellence in research, scholarship,
and education by publishing worldwide in

Oxford New York

Auckland Cape Town Dar es Salaam Hong Kong Karachi
Kuala Lumpur Madrid Melbourne Mexico City Nairobi
New Delhi Shanghai Taipei Toronto

With offices in

Argentina Austria Brazil Chile Czech Republic France Greece
Guatemala Hungary Italy Japan Poland Portugal Singapore
South Korea Switzerland Thailand Turkey Ukraine Vietnam

Oxford is a registered trade mark of Oxford University Press
in the UK and in certain other countries

© Oxford University Press 2011

British Library Cataloguing in Publication Data

Data available

ISBN: 978-0-19-847936-9

10 9 8

Printed in Great Britain by Bell & Bain Ltd., Glasgow

Acknowledgements

Illustrations by Tim Archbold

Design by Oxford Designers and Illustrators

Paper used in the production of this book is a natural, recyclable product
made from wood grown in sustainable forests. The manufacturing process
conforms to the environmental regulations of the country of origin.

Written by Ruth Miskin and Charlotte Raby

Read Write Inc. Get Writing! CD acknowledgements

Illustrations © Tim Archbold and Rosie Brooks.

The publisher would like to thank the following for permission
to reproduce photographs:

Green CD: OUP; Henk Bentlage/Shutterstock.com; Iain Garrett/OUP;
Iain Garrett/OUP

Purple CD:Chris King/OUP; Babusi Octavian Florentin/Shutterstock.com.

Pink CD: Suzanne Tucker/Shutterstock.com; Monkey Business Images/
Shutterstock.com; pio3/Shutterstock.com; Chris King/OUP; Oxford
Scientific/Photolibrary; Dr.Merlin Tuttle/Science Photo Library; Michael
Lynch/Shuterstock.com; zolran/Shutterstock.com

Orange CD: Chris King/OUP

Yellow CD: Serhiy Kobyakov/Shutterstock.com; Denis Dryashkin/
Shutterstock.com; Saiko3p/Shutterstock.com; Tatiana Popova/Shutterstock.
com; Gresei/Shutterstock.com; Nikola Bilic/Shutterstock.com; Tatiana
Popova/Shutterstock.com; Viktar Malyshchyts/Shutterstock.com; Frank Jr/
Shutterstock.com; Saiko3p/Shutterstock.com; D7INAMI7S/Shutterstock.
com; Jill Fromer/iStock.com; Andrei Rybachuk/Shutterstock.com;
Excalibur/iStock.com; Chris King/OUP; Emilia Stasiak/Shutterstock.com

Blue CD: Fibrus Ekaterina/Shutterstock.com; Steve Stone/iStock.com;
Photodisc/OUP; Thomas Maher/iStock.com; Icontec/OUP; Kerstin Klaassen/
iStock.com; Rob Eyers/iStock.com; iofoto/Shutterstock.com.; Jane McIlroy/
Shutterstock.com

Grey CD: Teresa Azevedo/Shutterstock.com; Richard Peterson/
Shutterstock.com; Tony Campbell/Shutterstock.com; rusm/iStock.com;
Mountain Light Studios/Shutterstock.com; Kevin Wheatley/Shutterstock.
com; Mountain Light Studios/Shutterstock.com; Richard Baker/In Pictures/
Corbis; Paul Doyle/Photolibrary; NASA Images/Alamy; Lena Grottling/
Shutterstock.com; Media Union/Shutterstock.com

Minimum System Requirements
PC
- Pentium® III 1 GHz processor or equivalent
- Windows® XP SP 3
- DVD drive
- 256 MB RAM
- 700 MB available hard disk space
- 1024 x 768 screen resolution with 16-bit colour depth
- Mouse or equivalent pointing device
- Keyboard or equivalent input device
- Microsoft® Office 2003

Mac
- PowerPC G4 1.1 GHz processor, Mac mini with Intel® Core™ 1.66 GHz processor or equivalent
- Mac OS X 10.4.11
- DVD drive
- 256 MB RAM
- 700 MB available hard disk space
- 1024 x 768 screen resolution with 16-bit colour depth
- Mouse or equivalent pointing device
- Keyboard or equivalent input device
- Microsoft® Office 2003

INSPIRATIONAL SUPPORT FOR TEACHERS
For free professional development
videos from leading experts, plus other
resources and free eBooks, please go to
www.oxfordprimary.co.uk

HELPING YOU ENGAGE PARENTS
We have researched the most common concerns
and worries parents have about their children's
literacy and provide answers and support in
www.oxfordowl.co.uk
This site contains advice on how to share
a book, how to pronounce pure sounds,
how to encourage boys' reading, and much
more. We hope you will find the site
useful and recommend it to your parents.

Contents

Introduction 4

Writing in *Read Write Inc. Phonics* 6

***Read Write Inc.* principles and how they apply to writing** 8

How to grow good writers 10

Oral language comprehension 11

    1. Storytimes 11

    2. Talk through the day 16

    3. Talk and write through play 19

***Get Writing!* lesson plans** 20

    Get Writing! Red Ditty Books 1–10 20

    Get Writing! lesson plans: Books 1–7 22

    Get Writing! coverage chart 28

    Get Writing! lesson plans: Green Storybooks 32

    Get Writing! lesson plans: Purple Storybooks 47

    Get Writing! lesson plans: Pink Storybooks 62

    Get Writing! lesson plans: Orange Storybooks 78

    Get Writing! lesson plans: Yellow Storybooks 96

    Get Writing! lesson plans: Blue Storybooks 121

    Get Writing! lesson plans: Grey Storybooks 146

Assessment 172

Handwriting 181

Installing and using the CD 190

Speed Sounds charts 191

Introduction

This *Get Writing! Handbook* provides clear guidance on how to teach writing within *Read Write Inc. Phonics* and how to grow accomplished, confident writers. It should be used in conjunction with the *Phonics Handbook*, which gives an overview of the whole *Read Write Inc. Phonics* programme and contains lesson plans for the reading activities, and the *Speed Sounds Lesson Plans* which provide support for the teaching of the sounds children need to learn to read the Storybooks and Non-fiction Books.

This *Handbook* includes:

☆ detailed lesson plans for teaching the activities in the *Get Writing!* Books. These are used alongside the Storybooks and Non-fiction Books to develop children's writing skills, from simple sentences to extended writing tasks for fiction and non-fiction

☆ guidance on assessing children's writing

☆ advice on how to develop children's 'oral comprehension'

☆ step-by-step teaching notes on handwriting, from basic letter formation to simple methods to help children learn a straightforward joined style

☆ ideas for storytime activities.

The accompanying CD is for use on an interactive whiteboard. All the files you need when teaching writing using the *Get Writing! Handbook* are included on the CD, and the resources are editable so that you can adapt them to suit the needs of your class.

The resources comprise:

☆ 'Edit' files to check the 'Edit' activity with children

☆ 'Write the sentences' files, to help inspire children, build ideas and model writing. These include images, audio and animations

☆ 'Power word' files to focus on and clarify new vocabulary

☆ 'Word banks' containing lists of Power words

☆ Handwriting checklists and example words for handwriting

☆ Achievement certificates to celebrate children's progress.

For more information about installing and using the CD, see p.190.

Read Write Inc. Phonics Writing Resources

Level	Reading	Teaching resources	Writing	Teaching resources
Red	Red Ditty Books		10 *Get Writing!* Red Ditty Books	
Green	Green Storybooks and Non-fiction Books		*Get Writing!* Green Book	
Purple	Purple Storybooks and Non-fiction Books	*Phonics Handbook*	*Get Writing!* Purple Book	
Pink	Pink Storybooks and Non-fiction Books		*Get Writing!* Pink Book	*Get Writing!* Handbook with CD-ROM
Orange	Orange Storybooks and Non-fiction Books	*Speed Sounds Lesson Plans*	*Get Writing!* Orange Book	
Yellow	Yellow Storybooks and Non-fiction Books		*Get Writing!* Yellow Book	
Blue	Blue Storybooks and Non-fiction Books		*Get Writing!* Blue Book	
Grey	Grey Storybooks and Non-fiction Books		*Get Writing!* Grey Book	

Once children have learned the Set 1 Speed Sounds and are reading the Red Ditty Books, they use the *Get Writing!* Books to develop their writing skills. There are ten *Get Writing!* Books that accompany the Red Ditty Books and then one *Get Writing!* Book for each of the seven Storybook/Non-fiction levels.

Writing in *Read Write Inc. Phonics*

There are three main processes involved in writing: handwriting, encoding (spelling) and language comprehension. Each process is taught discretely, step-by-step, so children are helped both in *what* to write and *how* to write until the *how* to write becomes so effortless that all their energy can go into *what* they write.

Practical day-by-day guidance is given to support new teachers and teaching assistants, but it also provides a strong scaffold so experienced teachers have the energy and time to plan creatively.

Handwriting

Children are taught how to form the letters of the alphabet accurately, quickly and effortlessly. Basic formation is taught using handwriting phrases and checklists so children have a mnemonic support to visualise the shape of each letter.

This formation is practised every day until children can write the alphabet letters quickly and easily. Teachers are then given very simple methods to help children learn a straightforward joined style (see pp. 181–189). *Handwriting is taught for up to ten minutes, four times a week during class time and not as part of the phonics lessons.*

Encoding

The *Speed Sounds Lesson Plans* give detailed support in how to *teach* children both to decode for reading and encode for writing. These lessons teach new phonic knowledge and review previous knowledge. The *Get Writing!* Book lessons give children *further practice* in different contexts.

At first, children learn to read and write just one spelling for each of the 44 sounds – the transparent alphabetic code (see Simple Speed Sounds chart on p. 191). This enables children to write any word using phonically legal spelling, for example, 'ay' is used to write *day, trayn, mayk, strayt,* 'ee' to write *green, dreem, pees, kee, hapee;* 'ow' to write *window, jowk, gowt.* Children are encouraged to be adventurous in the words they write before they master the complex alphabetic code with all its spelling alternatives (see Complex Speed Sounds chart on p. 192). There are also a few 'Red Words' (high frequency words with an uncommon spelling) which children are helped to spell correctly from the beginning of the programme e.g. *the, he, she, go, said, of.*

While children are using the Green, Purple, Pink and Orange *Get Writing!* Books they can use 'phonically legal' spellings in their writing.

Children are then introduced to different spellings for the same sound ('same sound, different appearance'), e.g. *day, train, make; green, dream, piece, key, happy.* Words containing these alternative spellings are practised throughout the Yellow, Blue and Grey *Get Writing!* Books.

Language comprehension

Language comprehension is developed throughout the school day – in storytimes, in discussion about everyday occurrences and during children's play, as well as in the specific *Get Writing!* lessons.

1. Storytimes

Storytimes are key to supporting children's writing. Teachers select their favourite good quality stories for each age group and use engaging activities to help children gain a deep familiarity with each story and develop a wide oral vocabulary and syntax necessary for later writing.

Storytime is planned with the whole class every day for 20 minutes – not always at the end of the day when children are tired. The story of *Cinderella* is used as a template for ways that storytimes can be used to develop sentence building and vocabulary (see p.11).

2. Talk through the day

Some children can go though whole days at school without needing to speak in a whole sentence. Children will find it hard to write in sentences if they do not speak them! The purpose of this section is to give teachers ideas to develop vocabulary and syntax using everyday occurrences. This will deliberately help to 'grow' children's spoken vocabulary for writing, by using words likely to be outside their current store of word meanings, at the same time as reviewing and embedding newly learned words.

High-level talk is used in incidental and planned activities throughout the day (see p.16).

3. Talk and write through play

Planning the vocabulary associated with play activities helps to make the most of adults' time when they work alongside children in water, sand, outdoor play, the home corner, painting and modelling. Talk is planned to accompany most play activities (see p.19).

Get Writing! Book lesson plans

These lessons form the main body of this *Handbook*. The ten *Get Writing!* Red Ditty Books first provide an introduction to writing whole sentences. Then in *Get Writing!* Books 1–7 oral sentence building and vocabulary development are brought together with encoding and handwriting in step-by-step writing activities linked to the *Read Write Inc.* Storybooks. For the first four levels (Green, Purple, Pink and Orange *Get Writing!* Books 1–4), while children are at an early stage of encoding, the lessons are split between oral sentence building and developing short sentences for writing. There are usually two parts to the 'Composition' Activities, a) and b), and teachers may choose to do one or both, depending on the needs of the children.

The later levels (Yellow, Blue and Grey *Get Writing!* Books 5–7) support children's writing by using oral sentence building alongside the modelling of writing. Two composition tasks are usually provided – the first is often based on the characters' 'feeling/saying/thinking/happening' bubbles and the second gives a specific purpose for writing, often based upon a non-fiction text.

The *Get Writing!* lessons are planned as part of the *Read Write Inc. Phonics* lessons (see timetables in the *Phonics Handbook* pp.63–66).

It cannot be stressed enough that children must progress through *Read Write Inc. Phonics* **at the pace of their decoding** and not the pace of their encoding and handwriting.

(See p.32 for the lesson plans for the *Get Writing!* Books.)

Read Write Inc. principles and how they apply to writing

Read Write Inc. has five underlying principles – the five Ps:

1 Pace

Pace is key to *Read Write Inc. Phonics*. Firstly, for children to complete the programme as quickly as possible they need to know the sounds thoroughly, but only read as many books as necessary to learn to decode effortlessly.

This has huge implications for writing as children are grouped according to their decoding/ reading ability and not their writing. Some children may complete their writing speedily and fluently, while others may still write slowly. These children must be assisted with their writing, and not held back because they write slowly.

Reading always takes priority over writing in deciding how quickly children progress through *Read Write Inc. Phonics*. To hold back a child because he cannot write quickly is detrimental to all his future progress at school; there are very few people in the world who can write as well as they can read. (See the Assessment section on p.172.)

To ensure no time is wasted, use 'silent signals' to ensure quick, effective classroom management. They save you from using your voice for low-level class management in shouting, shushing and nagging.

Silent signals

Silent stop signal

☆ Hold a hand in the air (without clapping). Do not talk while your hand is raised. Children raise their hands in response and check their partner and others at the table have seen the signal, gently tapping an arm if necessary. If the signal fails, practise – all children should respond.

My turn, your turn (MT/YT) signal

☆ This is needed for choral work.
   My turn: touch your chest with your palm
   Your turn: open your palm to the children
   Tell the children this is your signal and not theirs.

Perfect partner position signal

☆ Teach children that when you run your hand down your opposite arm, it is a signal for them to sit side-by-side ready to talk to their partner.

2 Praise

Always praise the children while they write, even if you are frustrated when a child does not write down what they have said only a minute before!

Assist children step-by-step, praising constantly and never nagging. If a child can't think of what to say, help him to think of an idea. If a child can't remember his idea, help him to remember. If a child can't write quickly, finish writing the sentence for him. If a child has forgotten to spell a word correctly – again – help him to correct it.

3 Purpose

Set the purpose at the beginning of each activity so the children fully understand what they are learning and why. However do not ask children to write out a learning objective!

The purpose of the teaching is made clear through modelling and thinking out loud (TOL). TOL is a device used to show the thinking that goes into working out *what* to say and then *how* to write it. It is planned chatter to let children 'see' what we think; as if we have a 'thinking bubble' coming out of our heads. It is used to show them how we make decisions about what we are thinking and feeling and how we decide the best word/sentence to write.

Don't make it look too easy! Hesitate as you TOL. Ask yourself questions and answer them yourself.

4 Participation

Participation is key to *Read Write Inc.* All children take part in all of the lesson.
Full participation is gained through choral work My turn/Your turn (MT/YT) and partner work.

My turn/Your turn (MT/YT)

This is used when you need the children to copy. Children should always sit where they can see your mouth and eyes easily, and you theirs – whether they are sitting on the carpet or at tables (sit in a v so you can see; sit in a v so I can see). As you build up sentences, you will ask children to copy so all children say the words, phrases and sentences out loud – this is vital if they are going to write them down.

Partner work

Partner work is deeply embedded in the programme because it is so much easier for children to TOL to a partner than it is to try out their ideas in front of the whole class. In *Read Write Inc.* writing, children always 'turn to your partner' (TTYP) to try out and then practise their ideas before they write.

Feedback

After children have turned to their partners to answer a question, take feedback in four main ways:

a. 'Choose Two': select two children to share their answers. Do not choose hand raisers – they will still try to take over!
b. 'Paraphrase': rephrase and elaborate on a child's answer.
c. 'Choral': ask children to show thumbs up or down, if the answer is short and needs only a yes/ no or a one or two word response.
d. 'Popcorn': ask children to call out their answers – when the answer is short with many different answers, e.g. 'Give me angry words!'

Listen carefully as they respond, build upon the idea, say it back and then get the children to repeat your phrase or sentence.

5 Passion

Be passionate in your teaching. Show the children how much you love teaching the lessons. Exaggerate your modelling of thinking and behaviour. Make your teaching larger than life so that children engage in the learning. The greater the passion, the faster their progress!

How to grow good writers

Children who are good writers have a lot to say. They have parents/carers whose running commentary links current experiences with past events and stories: 'Let's build a castle like the one in King Arthur, with high battlements and a huge moat all around it.' Mum is never just *happy*, she's *ecstatic*, *over the moon*. Things are rarely just *good* – they are *amazing*, *wonderful*; vocabulary is extensive and varied; complex syntax is used on an everyday basis. (Hart and Risley 2005)

Good writers have their own personal storytellers and, by the age of three, will have had at least 1700 hours of intimate storytimes. They understand *Each Peach Pear Plum* because they know nursery rhymes by heart. They recognise the irony and humour in *Revolting Rhymes* because they are so familiar with fairy stories. They expect stories to have beginnings and exciting bits in the middle and happy endings.

Good writers often have parents/carers who really listen to them and build on everything they say: 'Horse! Yes, it's a lovely old shire horse.' They are given options: 'Would you like to wear your pink spotty dress or your fluorescent T-shirt and shorts?' Their parents/carers develop their vocabulary using closed questions to encourage them to use new words and at other times open questions to try out new ideas. Good writers are praised a lot: 'What a clever boy you are!' Their parents/carers explain consequences and give reasons.

Once children with this stimulus can read for themselves, they will not only understand most of what they read, but will also be able to get hold of new words for themselves – asking the same questions they have always asked: 'What does this mean? Why do you think…?'

These are the children who have many ideas to write about and vocabulary to draw upon. They are imaginative because they have imagined other worlds and places. As soon as these children can encode, they become writers because they know what writers do. They connect quickly with their teachers and have lots of experiences and ideas to offer in class discussions.

At another extreme, there are children of parents/carers who don't have the knowledge and understanding to extend their children's thinking or experience. By age three, these children will have had only 25 hours of storytelling, and will have heard limited vocabulary and syntax. It's hard for these children to suddenly *be* imaginative and creative.

The huge challenge facing schools is to do something radical to make up for the many hours of elaborated talk that many have missed; so that *all* children have access into the way of 'school thinking'. Numbers of children and shortage of time necessitate that we plan as much talking time in school as possible, so children's thinking and vocabulary can be developed through a wide range of experiences and stimulating storytimes.

Only if we plan the talk and praise and enthuse very deliberately can we begin to close the gap.

1 Storytimes

The first step in making the best use of storytimes is for the staff group to decide upon a canon of well-known stories. Choose about ten stories per year group, ones that can be read in a sitting. Include fairy stories, traditional tales, myths and fables, as well as stories by famous contemporary authors. This canon and with it, the shared knowledge and vocabulary, will strengthen year-by-year and can be drawn upon to study other stories. You will, of course, read many other favourite stories out loud to children as well.

Make storytime a priority. Once children have gained familiarity with a story, through many readings, the activities below will help them to explore the characters' actions and motives; develop a rich vocabulary; build sentences and descriptions orally; and connect ideas, events and characters from one story to the next. These activities can be applied to any fairy story or legend. The example provided is based on the story of *Cinderella*, retold by Michael Foreman.

Reading aloud to the children

Prepare your reading thoroughly, as though you were going to give a performance, thinking about where you will place the stress and actions. Teach the meanings of unfamiliar words at a different time.

Before you start reading, enthuse about the story. Tell the children how you loved hearing it over and over again as a child. Let the story weave its own magic; don't stop to talk about it on the first few readings. Avoid putting lesson objectives on the board!

Join in

Purpose: to help children remember vocabulary and phrases from the story.

Once the children know the story get them to join in with refrains.

Exaggerate particular words and phrases and use actions and facial expressions to help, for example, '*She had to wash all the windows, scrub the stairs, polish the floors, chop the wood and cook and serve all the meals.*'

'*Cinderella was unnerved by the sudden silence as all eyes turned towards her. Then a murmur of admiration spread through the crowd: "How beautiful she is!"*'

Jump in

Purpose: to help children remember vocabulary and phrases from the story.

Play Jump in. Decide the vocabulary you want the children to enjoy and say it out loud. When you hesitate, ask children to say the missing word or phrase, e.g.

'*Oh, poor little…Cinderbritches.*'

'*A murmur of…admiration spread through the crowd.*'

Read and re-read until children know key parts of the story off by heart, gradually lowering your voice until the children take over.

Call and respond

Purpose: to help children remember vocabulary and phrases from the story.

Decide on questions that will provide descriptive responses. Use the exact response from the text. Act out the responses – exaggerate and pull faces to help the children remember the lines.

Say the responses with the children until they can say them without you. Choose six or so questions for each part of the story – not all on the same day, for example, *before the ball:*

'*So what was Cinderella's stepmother like?*' She was 'the most stuck-up and snooty woman in the world'.

'*And what was Cinderella like?*' She was 'a lovely and sweet-natured girl'.

'*What were her stepsisters like?*' They grew more ugly because their hearts were bitter, which made their faces sour.'

'*What did the stepmother make Cinderella do?*' 'Wash all the windows, scrub the stairs, polish the floors, chop the wood and cook and serve all the meals.'

'*And what did her stepsisters do?*' They 'didn't have to lift a finger. They sat about all day in their fine dresses and went to parties in the evening'.

Phrases to keep forever

Purpose: to help children build up a rich bank of phrases from the story, using the phrases ironically through the day.

Choose phrases that you continue to use during the day so children learn phrases and sayings that make up a bank of shared sayings, for example, when a child has fallen over, everyone can say:

'*Dearie me! Why all the tears, my child?*' or

'*Oh, poor little Cinderbritches!*'

When someone has painted a fantastic picture:

'*Well! You can imagine my amazement!*'

When getting ready for PE, really quickly:

'*Instantly they were transformed into…*'

Grow the story

Use these activities when the children know the story well.

a. Story scenes

Purpose: to develop vocabulary and build sentences, orally.

Draw the chart. TOL as you work out the story scenes with the children.

The beginning: Before the ball	Scene 1 The sisters are cross with Cinderella	Scene 2 The sisters receive an invitation	Scene 3 Fairy Godmother helps Cinderella
The middle: At the ball	Scene 4 Cinderella arrives at the ball	Scene 5 Cinderella forgets the time	
The end: After the ball	Scene 6 No one fits the slipper	Scene 7 Cinderella marries Prince Charming	

☆ Enlarge the chart – add pictures if necessary, in the home corner for children to choose the scene they want to act out.

☆ For each scene, take on the given role, and tell the children who they will be.

☆ In their given role ask the children to TTYP to answer each question (below).

☆ Take feedback using Choose Two (see p.9), then TOL as you build up sentences, orally.

☆ Do not make it look too easy as you think of what to say. Encourage the children to help you so they take ownership of the sentence. Use MT/YT every time you expand the sentence together.

☆ Once you have decided upon the final sentence, use actions and pull faces to help the children remember the sentence. Repeat until they can all say it after you.

Scene 1: The sisters are cross with Cinderella

Teacher role: Stepsister 1   Children's role: Stepsister 2

☆ Stepsister 1: 'I am so cross with Cinders today – she is so lazy, and good for nothing – let's make her work this morning. What shall we get her to do?'
e.g. polish the mirrors: 'Yes, let's make her polish the mirrors until they shimmer. Yes, let's make her polish the mirrors until they shimmer and twinkle.'
Sweep the floor: 'Yes, let's make her sweep the floor until there's no dust. Yes, let's make her sweep the floor until not a spot of dust remains.'
Wash the windows. 'Yes, wash the windows until they sparkle! Yes, wash the windows until they sparkle and gleam!'

Scene 2: The sisters receive an invitation

You will need some samples of fabric suitable for smart dresses.
Teacher role: Stepsister 1   Children's role: Stepsister 2

☆ Stepsister 1: 'I am so excited about going the ball. What shall I wear? I have so many gorgeous fabrics to choose from for my dress. I've got scarlet cloth, golden cloth, violet, lemon cloth.' (Use MT/YT to say the colours of all the fabrics until children can say the colours without you.)

☆ Repeat with the types of fabric – silk, velvet, satin and so on.
Pick up two fabrics and say: 'We must be the most beautiful at the ball.
Shall we choose this crimson silk or this violet silk for our ball gown?'
Stepsister 2s: 'Let us choose…for our ball gown.'
Stepsister 1: 'No, that won't do. Shall we choose lemon velvet or green velvet?'
Stepsister 2s: 'Let us choose… for our beautiful ball gown.'

☆ Repeat a few times, getting more and more impatient as you make a decision.

☆ Make a final decision on what colour and fabric you will have and TOL as you build a sentence, for example:
'Our ball gown shall be golden yellow.
Our ball gown shall be made of golden yellow silk.
Our ball gown shall be made of the most beautiful golden yellow silk in the whole world.'

Scene 3: Fairy Godmother helps Cinderella

Teacher role: Fairy Godmother   Children's role: Cinderella

Fairy Godmother: 'You need to look beautiful for the ball. So what do you want to wear? Let's start with the dress.
What colour would you like your dress to be?'

e.g. white: '**Not just** white, you shall have a lovely creamy white. **Not just** creamy white, you shall have a lovely creamy white, like vanilla ice-cream.
Now what will you wear on your head?'

e.g. A crown: '**Not just** a crown, you shall have a golden crown. **Not just** a golden crown, you shall have a golden crown encrusted with rubies and diamonds.'

b. What if not?

Purpose: for children to talk about how changing one event or character in the story can have a dramatic impact on the story.

☆ Ask children to TTYP to discuss these questions. Use Choose Two to feedback their ideas.
  What if not *patient*…? What if Cinderella had been *impatient*?
  What if not *handsome*…? What if the prince had been *ugly*?
  What if not *forgetful*? What if Cinderella had *remembered* to leave the ball before midnight?
  What if not *ugly*? What if the stepsisters had been *attractive*?

c. Let me tell you my story

Purpose: for children to retell the story in the role of a character, exploring the character's actions and motives; to develop vocabulary; to build sentences and descriptions orally.

Teacher: in role as Prince Charming   Children: Cinderella

☆ Ask questions about each part of Cinderella's story, using different connectives as you build on their ideas, as though confirming everything.
☆ Prince Charming: 'I want to know everything about you. Don't miss out any detail.'
☆ Start at the very beginning. Ask 'Cinderellas' to TTYP to quickly decide on their answers to each of the prince's questions. Take feedback, question and build on what is said, for example:
  'My mother died.'
  '*Many years ago*, your mother died.'
  'You must have been very young. Poor you.'
  '*On top of all that*, your sisters weren't kind to you. What did they do?'
  '*Fortunately*, you were rescued. How did this happen?'
  'What happened *next*?'
  'So *eventually* you met me. What did you think when you came into the ball?'
  '*Finally* the shoe you left behind found its owner! How did this make you feel?'

d. Quiz the character

Purpose: for children to explore the characters' actions and motives; build sentences and descriptions orally.

Teacher: in role as interviewer

Children: Cinderella – at the start of the story, then the stepsisters

☆ Use the set questions below and ask the children to TTYP. Tell the children they are in role as Cinderella, and then repeat with other characters.
☆ In their given role ask the children to TTYP to answer each question.
☆ Take feedback using Choose Two, then TOL as you build up the replies, orally.
☆ Use follow-up questions as though you are an interviewer: 'So what you're saying is… That's interesting…Do you mean that…?'
☆ Use MT/YT every time you expand the sentence together.
☆ Once you have decided upon the final sentence, use actions and pull faces to help the children remember the sentence. Repeat until they can all say it after you, for example:

i. 'When were you the most happy?'
    e.g. When my mother was alive.
    'What did you do together?'
    Cuddle, read stories.
    'You were happiest when your mother was alive. You used to cuddle at night when she read stories.'

ii. 'What do you worry about most?'
    That I can't escape.
    'So what will happen then?'
    Stuck here, working hard.
    'You are worried because you will have to work hard forever and ever.'
    etc.

e. Grow a setting

Purpose: for children to develop vocabulary; for children to build sentences and descriptions orally.

☆ Put the children in role as the stepsisters in Scene 6. Ask them, in role, to TTYP to answer each question: 'What can you see/hear/smell? What are you doing? What are you saying? What are thinking?'

☆ Take feedback and make notes to help you remember their ideas, for example:
'Where are you sitting?' e.g. *In the parlour/drawing room.*
'What can you see?' e.g. *A beautiful room/fancy chairs/sunny window.*
'What are you doing?' e.g. *Nothing/sewing/playing the piano/eating cakes.*
'What are you saying?' e.g. *'I am so excited I can hardly keep still.'*

☆ TOL as you build up sentences, orally. Do not make it look too easy as you think of what to say. Encourage the children to help you so they take ownership of the sentence.

☆ Use MT/YT every time you expand the sentence together.

☆ Once you have decided upon the final sentence, use actions and pull faces to help the children remember the sentence. Repeat until they can all say it after you, for example:
'We are sitting in our parlour, eating cakes.'
'We are sitting in our parlour eating huge cream cakes.'
'Sitting in our bright sunny parlour, we are eating huge cream cakes.'

☆ Repeat with different sentences.

f. Storyworld

Purpose: for children to act out the fairy story and apply the talk developed above, independently; for children to apply their developing Speed Sound knowledge in independent play writing.

☆ When the children are very familiar with the story turn your home corner into the particular play story world.

☆ Provide the props for children to act out each part of the story above.

☆ Provide scenarios for the children to write – using spellings of sounds they have been taught so far, for example:
– shopping lists for Cinderella: *cayks, biscits, orinj joos, apls, banarnus*
– lists of things that the stepsisters want Cinderella to do: *sweep the flor/mayk the beds/stack the logs/ighyun the dressis/polish the windows*
– thank-you letter to the Fairy Godmother
– invitation to the ball
– diary for Cinderella to record her miserable life!

English has a great number of words that have similar meanings – synonyms. Although we know a lot of these, we tend not use many in our everyday talk. If, however, we increase the range of words we use, repeatedly, day-by-day, children's vocabulary will develop more quickly. So, rather than *happy*, be *over the moon, joyful, ecstatic*. Rather than *sad*, be *miserable, forlorn, melancholy*! Become a walking thesaurus – use sticky notes to list these 'power words' (synonyms) that you will use, consciously and deliberately, throughout the day. See a list of words to use on pp.17–18.

You will use many of the power words in the *Get Writing!* lessons too, so combined with the activities below you will immerse the children in a greater range of words throughout the day. The more children say them out loud, the more likely it is that they will use them in their writing. Use them in PE lessons, moving around the school, in lessons and in play. It does take planning. If you are working with a team of people, work out the vocabulary and activity you are all going to use each week. Keep returning to the same vocabulary. Show the children that you love using new words.

Which word?

Purpose: to introduce new vocabulary.

If we ask a child how they feel they can only draw upon the existing word store – sad/happy. Ask the children to choose a word from two options so they have to say the word out loud, and, as children's vocabulary grows, encourage them to offer other options, for example:
'Are you feeling anxious or excited about acting in assembly?'
'Do you think this music sounds miserable or just a bit gloomy?'
'Do you think crunchy or crispy is the best word to describe this apple?'
'Shall we use "over the moon" or "on top of the world" to say how pleased we are that James is back?'
'Do you want the thick creamy yoghurt or lovely spongy pudding?'
'Shall we hobble or shuffle to the hall? Creep or zoom?'
During PE: 'Shall we leap or stroll? Crouch or stretch? Dart or slink?'
'Are you feeling furious or really disappointed about losing your new gloves?'

Not just...

Purpose: for children to hear and say out loud shades of synonyms in a range of contexts through the day.

Comment on everyday happenings. Supply words to begin with but as children's vocabulary increases encourage children to join in. Children copy after the sentence using MT/YT, for example:
'He's not just feeling sad, he's feeling…really miserable.'
'Mrs Booth is not just angry, she's furious because…'
'Sam's not just fast, he's a super speedy runner.'
'Jenny's not just clever, she's fantastically talented.'
'This peach isn't just delicious, it's…mouthwateringly succulent.'
'I'm not just tired, I'm…ready to drop.'
'We're not just happy, we're over the moon.'

Running commentary

Purpose: for children to hear a wide range of vocabulary in the context of everyday situations.

Keep a running commentary going about what children are doing and how you are feeling. Build connections between current events and past events. Use the phrase 'It reminds me of when…'. Get the children to copy some of things you say using MT/YT.

'That painting is trickling everywhere on the floor. It's a very drippy painting. Just like Henry's last week.'

'I love bright and crisp days like today. It reminds me of when we all went for a long stroll by the sea. Do you remember that day? TTYP'

'I'm feeling full of anticipation about our day ahead – I feel on top of the world! We have got so many exciting things to do.'

'What a considerate thing to do to lend Abdul your coat, it reminds me of when Fatima lent her gloves to Sophie last week.'

Stories all about us

Purpose: to build simple stories around everyday events; to help children speak in full and varied sentences, drawing upon their increasing vocabulary.

Build stories with the children about everyday things in their lives: bathtime, bedtime, not sleeping, going to see grandma, a special tea time, birthdays, falling over, getting a new dog, being late for school, arguing with a brother, painting a picture, going to see the doctor/vet, incidents that happen in the home corner. Show them that stories can be built out of the tiniest event. It shows how our everyday lives are made up of hundreds of little stories.

Children love having stories told with them as the main characters. In advance of the activity, choose one child to take on the role of 'expert' on an incident or event that has recently happened. Tell the children that you are all going to find out everything about what has happened, so you can build a story together.

As you build up the sentence get all the children to copy you using MT/YT. TOL as you build the story, asking the children to help you build each sentence. Use connectives as you build the story: *at the beginning, next, then, fortunately, finally, in the end.*

Do not write the story down while the children are with you! This takes too long and is likely to be beyond the children's writing ability at this stage.

Walking thesaurus

Use these words through the day. Do not write them on cards for the children until they are reading the Yellow Storybooks. Then, select a few words at a time to display. Too many words on display become wallpaper, so only display the words you are focusing on that week. Stack the other words in a pocket chart to be retrieved easily, when needed.

size/amount: enormous, vast, like a balloon, bottomless, massive, tiny, minute, minuscule

many: heap of, countless, plenty

move: speedy, dash, rush, race, run, sprint, bolt, dart, gallop, charge, shoot, hurtle, fly, speed, zoom, scurry, scuttle, scamper, scoot, zip

dawdle: linger, dally, dilly-dally, amble, stroll, trail, move at a snail's pace, shuffle, scrape, drag, scuffle, scuff, limp

say: bellow, grumble, sigh, mutter, moan, shout, yell, cry (out), call (out), roar, howl, bawl, call at the top of one's voice, shriek, scream, hiss, yell, whisper, murmur, mumble, whine, sob, snivel, wail, groan

nasty: malicious, spiteful, unpleasant, disagreeable, disgusting, awful, dreadful, horrible, terrible, vile, foul, loathsome, revolting, repulsive, odious, horrendous, appalling, atrocious, offensive, obnoxious, ghastly, horrid, gruesome, spiteful

nice: enjoyable, pleasant, agreeable, delightful, marvellous, charming, fabulous

kind: considerate, thoughtful, unselfish, sympathetic, understanding, big-hearted

smelly: unappetizing, foul-smelling, stinking, rank

texture: shiny, glassy, glossy, silky, polished, creamy, velvety, bright, crisp, thick, fluffy, rough, bumpy, lumpy, knobbly, crunchy, twisty

appearance: smart, stylish, fabulous, ugly, warty, hairy, smelly, scruffy, tatty, untidy, messy, grubby

sad: dejected, depressed, downcast, miserable, down, despairing, wretched, glum, gloomy, doleful, dismal, melancholy, forlorn, heartbroken, down in/at the mouth, down in the dumps

happy: excited, cheerful, cheery, merry, joyful, jolly, delighted, smiling, beaming, grinning, pleased, content, satisfied, sunny, thrilled, exhilarated, ecstatic, overjoyed, walking on air, jumping for joy, chirpy, over the moon, on top of the world, tickled pink

angry: mad, annoyed, cross, irritated, furious, enraged, infuriated, in a temper, raging, fuming, seething, outraged, livid, apoplectic, hot under the collar, steamed up, in a lather, seeing red

shock: astonished, amazed, astounded, startled, stunned, speechless, shaken up, flabbergasted

fear: scared, startled, alarmed, terrified, panicked, disturbed, dismayed, scared stiff, scare someone out of their wits, scared to death, make their hair stand on end, jump out of their skin

take: get hold of, grasp, grip, clasp, clutch, grab, hold, clench, catch, seize, snatch

noise: din, racket, rumpus, cacophony, uproar, commotion, clatter, caterwauling, hullabaloo

quiet: silent, still, hushed, noiseless, soft, muffled, hushed, peaceful, sleepy, tranquil, calm

naughty behaviour: prank, trick, mischief, rascal, rogue, villain, pest

eat: gobble (up/down), bolt (down), wolf (down), swallow, chew, munch, chomp, guzzle, tuck into

time and causal connectives: suddenly, immediately, in a moment, as soon as, fortunately, finally, so, because, so that

Talk through play

Purpose: for children to hear vocabulary associated with each play activity; to use new vocabulary independently.

In the Foundation years ensure children 'choose' all activities so they have full access to the language associated with all areas of learning. Plan the power words, the extended sentences and the way you will build the children's sentences with the staff, so they also use this vocabulary as they move around the room. Say the words with the children before they get to the play activity, so that when they do they are more likely to use the words. Build upon the words and sentences day-by-day, week-by-week. Use texture/colour words/movement words, for example:

Play dough: 'Mmmm don't you love forcing your hands into the play dough: squishy squashy, squish, squash… Let's say *force my hands in – squish, squash, squish, squash.*'
Get children to repeat the words in silly voices – low, high, like a giant, witch or fairy.
Mud: (pretending) 'Let's squeeze mud through our fingers: squelchy, welchy, yucky mmm…
Let's say…*squeeze the mud through my fingers – squelchy, welchy, yucky mmm.*'
Bikes: 'We have a new speedy bike. It whizzes and whirls you like a firework. Let's say…'
While the children are playing pin the words on sticky notes (small, for the teacher, next to each activity, to ensure they are used). When the children can read the words, add them to a 'power word wall'. Plan for all staff to use these words, and to encourage the children to use them during their play. Make up chants that you can say with the children while they play:
'I love mud. We love mud. We all love mud.
Thick and squishy.
Squishy wishy squelchy welchy mud.
I love mud. We love mud.'

Write through play

Purpose: for children to apply their developing Speed Sound knowledge in independent play writing.

Equip every play area with pencils and paper so children can start to write using the sounds you have taught them. Model the sort of writing they could do as you introduce each play activity. Encourage the children to use sounds they have been taught to spell words, e.g. *shopping lists: cofee, milk, joos, orinj, apl, cabij*

jobs to do: colect cleening, pic up Jon, bigh card.

Get children to make labels for things in the home corner, changing them each day – provide cards for children to make their own: *tabl/tbl, chair/chr, spoon, nighf, fork, cubud, flor, rug, window.*

Cut ready-made shapes and bubbles for children to write their own labels for displays of paintings and models e.g: *Big red bowt on the see by John; hapee mum by Khadija; green and bloo picher by Molly; torl tour by Helen.*

Instructions: pleez put yor pensils here, shut the dor, wosh yor hands, flush the loo, wosh up yor brushis.

Things we need for our visit: cowts, hats, scarvs, pens, bords, sandwichis, apls, biscits.

Get Writing! lesson plans

Once children have learned the Set 1 Speed Sounds and are reading the Red Ditty Books, they can use the accompanying *Get Writing!* Books alongside the Red Ditty Books and Storybooks to develop their writing skills. There are ten *Get Writing!* Red Ditty Books that accompany the Red Ditty Books and one *Get Writing!* Book for each of the seven Storybook/Non-fiction levels.

Get Writing! Red Ditty Books 1–10

The Red Ditty Books for reading are an important bridge between the reading of single words and whole stories. The *Get Writing!* Red Ditty Books, in turn, provide an introduction into the writing of whole sentences.

The *Get Writing!* Red Ditty Books contain short Ditties for the children to read and two writing activities for each Ditty: 'Complete a sentence' and 'Hold a sentence'. Brief teaching notes on the reading activities are provided on pages 2 and 3 of each *Get Writing!* Red Ditty Book. (For more detailed notes see the *Phonics Handbook* p.44.) The following teaching notes for the 'Complete a sentence' and 'Hold a sentence' activities are blueprint lesson plans and can be used for these activities in all the *Get Writing!* Red Ditty Books.

Complete a sentence

Purpose: for children to 'hold' the beginning of a sentence while composing and writing the last words.

- ✰ Turn/cover the reading page so the children cannot copy.
- ✰ Tell the children what the pictures represent down the right hand side of the page.
- ✰ Ask the partners to read the starter stem to each other.
- ✰ Use Fred Fingers to sound out the word in the picture before children write the word.
- ✰ Where there is no picture, ask the children to read the stem and decide on a word they would use to complete the sentence.
- ✰ Ask children to write the sounds they can hear.

Hold a sentence

Purpose: for children to remember or 'hold' a whole sentence while focusing on spelling and spaces between each word.

The following example is from Ditty 3 in *Get Writing! Red Ditty Book 2*. N.B. Punctuation is not taught at the Ditty stage.

My turn/Your turn

- ✰ Say the sentence, using MT/YT – in this example – *I got a chip* – and emphasise a word that will help the children remember the sentence, e.g. *I got a chip.*
- ✰ Ask the children to repeat until you know they can all remember the sentence.

First word

☆ Ask the children to tell you the first word – 'I'. As this is a red word, write this for them.

☆ Ask the children to read the word on the board.

Second word

☆ Ask the children to show you three fingers. (See Fred Fingers in the *Phonics Handbook* p.59.)

☆ Say 'got'.

☆ Tell them to press one sound onto each finger as they say g-o-t. (Do not join in with them or show your fingers.)

☆ Write the word on to the board. (Do not let a child write the word.) Say: 'I must leave a finger space before I write "got" – otherwise the word will say Igot!'

☆ Ask the children to read the two words on the board.

Third word

☆ Ask the children to tell you the next word – 'a'.

☆ Say: 'I must leave a finger space before I write "a"!'

☆ Ask the children to read the three words on the board.

Fourth word

☆ Ask the children to tell you the next word – 'chip'.

☆ Ask the children to show you three fingers.

☆ Say 'chip' again.

☆ Tell them to press one sound on to each finger as they say ch-i-p.

☆ Say: 'I must leave a finger space before I write "chip".'

☆ Write the word on to the board.

☆ Ask the children to read the four words on the board.

Ask the children to re-read the whole sentence.

Cover up or rub out the sentence.

Ask the children to pick up their pencils ready to write. Say the sentence again. Ask the children to write.

Support them as they write – help them to write all the sounds.

If one child finishes before another, ask the quick child to write 'can I have a can of pop'.

Write the first sentence on the board one word at a time and get the children to add in any letter they have missed out. Praise the children for writing each word.
Ask the children to read their own sentence again. Praise!

Assessment

☆ Do all the children know the sounds when they put the sounds on their fingers? If not, reinforce Fred Fingers in your Speed Sounds lessons.

Key teaching points

☆ The children are grouped for reading progress so some children will write the sentence quickly and easily, while others will write slowly.

☆ Support the slower writers by asking them to dictate the sounds to you.

☆ Give extra support to these children – often boys – later each day.

Get Writing! lesson plans: Books 1–7

The seven *Get Writing!* Books have been written to be used alongside the Storybooks at each of the seven levels: I Green, 2 Purple, 3 Pink, 4 Orange, 5 Yellow, 6 Blue and 7 Grey.

The characters and topics from the Storybooks and Non-fiction Books also appear in the *Get Writing!* Books. As well as providing written practice in the phonic knowledge the children have acquired through reading the Storybooks and Non-fiction Books, the *Get Writing!* Books also provide practice in developing writing step-by-step – from simple to more complex sentences, paragraphs and ultimately extended compositions.

Children write a wide range of text types and in a variety of different styles including letters, poems, instructions, adverts, speech bubbles, thought bubbles, recounts, newspaper reports, diary entries, non-chronological reports, posters, labels, postcards, menus, shopping lists and invitations. See the chart on pp.28–31 which details the range of writing across the seven *Get Writing!* Books.

'Check' boxes are included in the *Get Writing!* Books to encourage children to check for finger spaces, capital letters, full stops, spelling errors, question marks, exclamation marks and speech marks in their writing. The continual reminders provided by the check boxes will help such checking to become automatic for the children.

The later *Get Writing!* Books include pages for children to plan their writing, for example, through mind maps or note-taking, before embarking on an extended writing task.

The *Get Writing!* activities

There are nine *Get Writing!* activities:

1. Play 'Fred Rhythms' to learn to spell the words – encoding
2. Play 'Fred Fingers' to memorise the spelling – encoding
3. Carry out a spelling check – encoding
4. Take a spelling test – encoding
5. Hold a sentence – encoding
6. Build a sentence – language comprehension and encoding
7. Edit for spelling and punctuation – language comprehension and encoding
8. Composition: picture prompts – language comprehension and encoding
9. Composition – language comprehension and encoding

N.B. *Get Writing!* Books I–4 only use activities 5, 7 and 8.

Activities I–5 are encoding activities using words from the Storybooks or Non-fiction Books. Then there are four language comprehension activities to develop children's composition, all developed through oral drafting.

Pages 23–27 contain blueprint lesson plans for activities I–5 and 7. However, detailed specific teaching notes are provided for activities 6 and 8 and 9. These are provided for each Storybook at each level. Two of the five Non-fiction Books at each level also have related activities in the *Get Writing!* Books. It is not necessary to do writing activities for all the Non-fiction Books as this could slow children down and children write a range of non-fiction texts in the composition activities linked to the Storybooks.

Activity 1: Play 'Fred Rhythms' to learn to spell the words

The purpose of this activity is for children to identify any potential problem grapheme in the word.

☆ Copy the Green and Red Words onto your flipchart from the spelling section in the *Get Writing!* Book.

☆ Add any common words that children have had difficulty spelling from their last piece of writing in the children's 'Your Words' box.

☆ For each Green and Red Word listed in the section:
Think out loud as you look at the word and consider if there is a problem grapheme.
Example word – horse.
TOL: 'I think the "se" in horse may cause us a problem – let's say this spelling – with feeling!' (Use letter names.)
Look at the Speed Sounds chart and point to 'se' in the sound box.
Say 'se' (same sound, different appearance) – the alternative grapheme for 's' with feeling.
(If there is no problem – don't invent one.)

☆ For each Green and Red Word listed in the section:
My turn
Read the word: horse.
Read the sounds in Fred Talk: 'h- or- se'.
Now say the spelling (letter names) in a rhythm – se – with extra feeling: 'h – or – se'
Say the word again.
Your turn
Get the children to repeat as you point to the graphemes – do not join in.
Repeat with all the Green and Red Words.
Use a range of voices for the difficult grapheme in the Red Word, as that is the part of the word that is the hardest.

☆ There is often a direct correlation between children's success in spelling the words and the teacher's energy and enthusiasm. The greater the feeling, the greater the success.

☆ Observe the children as they say the sounds and graphemes (do not join in) – make sure your vulnerable children are joining in.

Activity 2: Play 'Fred Fingers' to memorise the spelling

The purpose of this activity is for children to practise saying the sounds and spelling – remembering the problem grapheme with extra feeling (without looking at the word).

☆ Make sure that children cannot see the words you are about to spell.

☆ Before you start, make sure your children know how to hold and touch their Fred Fingers (see *Phonics Handbook* p.59).

Example word: horse

My Turn

For each Green and Red Word listed in the section:

Say: (example) 'I need three fingers.'

Say 'horse'.

Say the sounds as you press each sound onto three fingers – h-or-se.

Say the spelling (letter names) as you trace the graphemes onto three fingers – putting feeling onto 'se'

Say 'horse'.

Your Turn: children repeat your actions.

Speed up when you are sure the children can put the rhythm onto their fingers.

☆ This is the same as the Fred Fingers activity in the Word Time! lesson in the *Speed Sounds Lesson Plans*.

☆ Show the children how you want them to look at their fingers, before you start spelling.

☆ Children use their non-dominant hand for fingers and the teacher must check they point in the correct reading direction.

☆ Talk is the key. By being able to articulate the possible errors they will make, the children will be less likely to make them.

☆ Check all children exaggerate the problem grapheme. If not, re-model.

Activity 3: Carry out a spelling check

The purpose of this activity is for children to practise spelling words with the tricky grapheme.

☆ *Model partner teaching. Exaggerate the way you:*
Help your partner identify the tricky grapheme – say the problem grapheme out loud with feeling.
Spell every word correctly – saying the sounds and spelling if he gets stuck.

☆ Set the purpose: tell Partner 1s that they are the teacher. Say: 'Teach your partner to spell the Red Words first and then the trickier Green Words. For example, make sure your partner spells "could" with "oul".'

☆ Move around, praising Partner 1s.

☆ Use the stop signal, and then praise the teaching partners again for helping their partner spell the words.

☆ Ask Partner 1s to praise Partner 2s: 'Great spelling!'

☆ Repeat with Partner 2s as the teacher.

☆ Praise the teaching partners who help their partners practise the tricky part of the word.

☆ Observe the children as they support their partner. Does the teaching partner help their partner learn the trickier part of the word? Can the children spell the trickier words? If yes, move onto activity 4. If not, keep playing 'Fred Rhythms' and 'Fred Fingers'.

Activity 4: Take a spelling test

The purpose of this activity is for children to check they can spell the words.

☆ You will need a pen and board; children will need their spelling jotters, a pencil and a coloured pen.

☆ Say the words from the spelling list. Ask the children to write them down.

☆ Ask children to mark their own spellings with a coloured pen:
   Write the word on the board, e.g. 'horse'.
   Say: 'If you wrote "se" in "horse", give it a tick. If not – change it.'
   Repeat with the other words.
   Praise the children for correcting the words.

☆ Be generous with ticks.

☆ Build an atmosphere where children feel safe and happy to share their errors with the class.

☆ Continue to display the harder words.

☆ Check the children are using the correct spelling in their own writing. If not, repeat the teaching of the harder words the following week.

Activity 5: Hold a sentence

The purpose of this activity is for children to develop the ability to 'hold' a total sentence before writing it down and for children to practise encoding and secretarial skills.

☆ Use My turn/ Your turn (MT/YT) to say the sentence and ask the children to repeat.

☆ Repeat using different voices, emphasising the same words each time until the children can say the sentence clearly.

☆ Mime writing the capital letters and punching the full stop.

☆ Ask the children to open their books, pick up their pencil and repeat the sentence again.

☆ Support the children as they write. Go through the 'Check' box with the children, encouraging them to check if they have the punctuation and graphemes listed.

☆ Write the sentence word by word on the board.

☆ Ask the children to mark their own sentence with a coloured pen.

☆ Reinforce learning by giving the children lots of ticks for remembering punctuation and the trickier graphemes.

☆ Make a note of common problems so you can practise these through the day.

☆ Do not underestimate the number of times you need to repeat the sentence. Children often need to hear it five or six times before they can 'hold' it.

Activity 6: Build a sentence

The purpose of this activity is for children to build a picture that includes and shows the meaning of a given word.

Specific notes for the *Build a sentence* activity for each Storybook are provided on p.96 onwards (notes for Yellow, Blue and Grey). The notes below provide general guidance for this activity.

- ☆ The children will have had plenty of practice in building sentences out loud since the beginning of the programme. They will now start to write the sentences that they have built with you.
- ☆ However, some children encode quickly and so remember their sentences, while others encode slowly and need support in remembering the sentence.
- ☆ In a few instances, you will need to ask the child to write the first few words and dictate the rest to you.
- ☆ The more we help the children become quick encoders the sooner they will be able to remember to 'hold' the thought while they write. Handwriting lessons, at a different time of the day, will help children to speed up their writing. See Handwriting p.181.
- ☆ We must know, before the children pick up their pencils, that they know what they will write – and that they can hold their sentence out loud.
- ☆ The Build a sentence words should feed into the children's creative writing, so display the sentences and work and make links explicit for the children.

Activity 7: Edit

The purpose of this activity is for children to develop their own editing skills.

- ☆ Display the 'Edit' sentence on the CD. This will be the first file for each book i.e. 1.1, 2.1, 3.1. Ask partners to read the sentence and work out the errors together.
- ☆ Go through the 'Check' box with the children, encouraging them to check if they have the punctuation and graphemes listed.
- ☆ Select children to feed back the errors. Click 'Edit' to highlight the errors one by one. Then click 'Reveal' to show the correct sentence.
- ☆ Ask the children to correct the errors in their *Get Writing!* Books.

- ☆ Use 'Edit' for partners to correct one sentence in each other's writing.
- ☆ Give a lot of support to children at the beginning. If it is too hard, work out the errors together as a group, first.
- ☆ Make strong links for the children between these editing activities and children editing their own work.

Activities 8 and 9: Composition: picture prompts and Composition

Specific notes for Activities 8 and 9 for each Storybook are provided on p.32 onwards. The notes below provide general guidance for these activities.

The purpose of this activity is for children to write a composition using the pictures/frames/charts and to apply vocabulary, sentence structures and ideas developed throughout the week.

- ☆ While children are using the Green to Orange *Get Writing!* Books the composition activities are split into two parts: 'Saying the sentence' and 'Writing the sentence'. At this stage children can say a lot more than they can write.
- ☆ Saying the sentence does not limit the length or complexity of the sentence by the words or amount that children can physically write for themselves. It is therefore not modelled on the board. In the Yellow to Grey Books there is no 'Say the sentence' section in the notes; however teachers will still TOL and children will say sentences out loud before they write.

Say the sentence

☆ Saying the sentence focuses on developing power words within a sentence.

☆ Guidance is provided for the teacher to think out loud (TOL) building up the sentences, orally, about the picture prompt in the *Get Writing!* Book and on the CD.

Write the sentence

☆ The written sentence is shorter and simpler and focuses on what children can physically write. It is long enough to challenge the faster writer in the group. Slower writers must be supported – see Assessment section on p.172.

☆ Note that if a child can write a lot more than the sentence provided, it is likely that the child should be at a higher level of reading and writing.

☆ Teachers practise saying the simple sentences with the word/phrase provided, using children's ideas e.g. *Ned is fed up.*

☆ A sentence is then modelled, focusing on spelling, spaces and punctuation. Children practise saying their own sentence out loud so they have the inner resources to focus upon encoding.

☆ The model sentence is then covered up/rubbed out.

Role-play

☆ Role-play is often used for both Activities 8 and 9 to develop children's talk from the perspective of a particular character. The teacher takes on her role whole-heartedly throughout this activity so children adopt their role easily and enthusiastically.

Get Writing! coverage chart – Composition activities	
Get Writing! Red Ditty Books.	
The Ditties provide two simple writing activities, 'Complete a sentence' and 'Hold a sentence' which provide an important bridge between the writing of single words and whole sentences.	
Get Writing! Book 1 Green	
On the bus	8 a) Write simple sentences: complete speech bubbles 8 b) Write simple sentences: complete speech bubbles
My dog Ned	8 a) Write simple sentences: describe how Ned feels 8 b) Write simple sentences: describe how Ned walks
Six fish	8 a) Write simple sentences: complete speech bubbles 8 b) Write descriptive sentences
The spell	8 a) Write imperative sentences 8 b) Write labels: describe noises from the pot
Black Hat Bob	8 a) Write sentences: write in role, complete speech bubbles 8 b) Complete a Wanted poster: describe Red Hat Rob
Tug, tug	8 a) Write sentences: write in role, infer how characters might feel, complete speech bubbles 8 b) Write sentences: complete speech bubbles
Chips	8 a) Write descriptive sentences: complete speech bubbles 8 b) Write dialogue: complete speech bubbles
The web	8 a) Write sentences: complete speech bubbles 8 b) Write sentences: complete speech bubbles
Pip's pizza	8 Write descriptive sentences, using adjectives
Stitch the witch	8 a) Write descriptive sentences: complete thought bubbles 8 b) Write a magic spell
We can all swim!	8 Write sentences describing how creatures move
What am I?	8 a) Write descriptive sentences about what a cat can do 8 b) Write descriptive sentences about what an owl can do
Get Writing! Book 2 Purple	
Ken's cap	8 a) Write sentences in role 8 b) Write sentences describing Ken's cap
A bad fox	8 a) Write sentences with synonyms for run 8 b) Write descriptive sentences with synonyms for said
Big Blob and Baby Blob	8 a) Write descriptive sentences: complete speech bubbles 8 b) Write descriptive sentences
Tim and Tom	8 a) Write descriptive sentences from a character's point of view 8 b) Write labels for a beach stall
Tag	8 a) Describe action; describe how a character feels 8 b) Write labels: describe noises that a rocket makes
Elvis	8 Write an advert for Elvis the elf
Flip Frog and the bug	8 a) Write descriptive sentences with synonyms for eat 8 b) Write commands: give advice to the bug to escape the frog
Red Ken	8 a) Write descriptive sentences: complete speech bubbles 8 b) Write sentences describing action
Billy the Kid	8 a) Write sentences to describe the troll: complete thought bubbles 8 b) Write sentences describing feelings
In the bath	8 a) Write imperative sentences 8 b) Write a splashy poem

Hens	8 a) Write simple sentences about hens
Puppets	8 a) Write captions 8 b) Write instructions
Get Writing! Book 3 Pink	
Scruffy Ted	8 a) Write labels 8 b) Write imperative sentences
Tab the cat	8 a) Write sentences with synonyms for happy 8 b) Write descriptive sentences
In the sun	8 a) Write sentences using adjectives 8 b) Write words describing noises the sea makes
The dressing up box	8 a) Write sequence of getting into fancy dress using connectives *First, Next, Then, Last* 8 b) Write descriptive sentences about feelings, writing from own experience; design a fancy dress outfit
Tab's kitten	8 a) Writing in role 8 b) Writing in role
Sanjay stays in bed	8 a) Write dialogue with synonyms for said 8 b) Write explanatory sentences
The greedy green gremlin	8 a) Write dialogue 8 b) Write sentences describing actions
In the night	8 a) Write in role conveying feelings 8 b) Write in role conveying feelings
Snow	8 Write a poem about what they want to do in the snow
So cool	8 a) Write from their own experience about what sort of cool flat they would like to live in 8 b) Write sentences showing excitement
Jay's clay pot	8 Write instructions using the connectives *First, Then, Next, In the end*
Bats	8 a) Write a non-chronological report about bats with sentences that contrast what the bat does at night and in the day 8 b) Write a poster about bats
Get Writing! Book 4 Orange	
Playday	8 a) Write from their own experience about how they would feel if they had a play day 8 b) Write sentences about what they would do if they had a play day
I think I want to be a bee	8 Write descriptive sentences about what animal they would like to be and what the animal does
A bad fright	8 a) Write sentences about how they would get dressed up using *First, Next, Then, Last* 8 b) Write descriptive sentences in role
Follow me!	8 a) Write sentences comparing feelings in the past and the present 8 b) Write a description of the crow
Too much!	8 Write a letter giving advice
A good cook?	8 Write a menu, use descriptive language
Come on, Margo!	8 a) Write questions that convey excitement 8 b) Write descriptive sentences

My sort of horse	8 a) Write descriptive sentences 8 b) Write labels, use descriptive language
Haircuts	8 a) Write about choices and give reasons 8 b) Write descriptive sentences
My best shirt	8 a) Recount events 8 b) Write in role, describe thoughts and feelings
Look out!	8 a) Write sentences describing actions 8 b) Write labels, use descriptive language
Hunt the tortoise	8 a) Write descriptive sentences with 'but' 8 b) Recount events
Jam tarts	8 Write a shopping list for a picnic, use descriptive language
Jim's house in 1874	8 Compare the past and the present; complete a table
Get Writing! Book 5 Yellow	
The duckchick	8 Make comparisons: write about differences, complete a table 9 Recount events, describe action
Off sick	8 Design a door sign: use imperative sentences 9 Infer and write from a character's point of view
Tom Thumb	8 Write a 'Lost' poster, use descriptive sentences 9 Write sentences using deductive skills, understand and write about how a character might feel
The gingerbread man	8 Write a report about the gingerbread man running away, describing actions, using connective language 9 Write sentences using deductive skills, understand and write about what a character might think, write a story ending
Robin Hood	8 Write a detailed description of Little John 9 Infer and write from a character's point of view (Robin Hood and Little John), write dialogue
Lost	8 Write a postcard, recount events 9 Infer and write from a character's point of view, describe feelings
Do we have to keep it?	8 Write instructions 9 Write about choices and give reasons
Danny and the Bump-a-lump	8 Make notes, develop the notes into a description, write labels 9 Write a letter, use ambitious verbs and connective language
Grow your own radishes	8 Write notes using descriptive language, complete a chart 9 Write a fruit and vegetables poem
The foolish witch	8 Write a new beginning for a story, infer and write from a character's point of view 9 Write a menu, describe food
In the park	8 Describe how you move in the park, use verbs 9 Design and describe a park; write about choices and give reasons
A mouse in the house	8 Write labels, use descriptive language 9 Write a non-chronological report about a mouse
Get Writing! Book 6 Blue	
Barker	8 Write dialogue, use connectives (because) and description 9 Write a recount, convey sense of drama and excitement
The poor goose	8 Write advice; empathise with someone else's feelings 9 Retell a story from a character's point of view

Hairy fairy	8 Write a newspaper report, write 'factual' sentences 9 Write descriptive comparisons; compare Crow and the other birds
King of the birds	8 Present an argument, use connectives (because) 9 Write descriptive sentences
Our house	8 Write a letter, pose questions 9 Write descriptive sentences, use a variety of sentence starts
The jar of oil	8 Write an advert, use descriptive language 9 Write in role, write about thoughts and feelings
Jade's party	8 Plan a party 9 Write a party invitation
Jellybean	8 Write a letter; give advice and explanations 9 Write a poem about pets
A box full of light	8 Write a descriptive poem 9 Retell the end of a story from a character's point of view
The hole in the hill	8 Write a persuasive song/poem 9 Write a persuasive letter
On your bike	8 Write a personal recount, use connectives 9 Write about how to take care of your bike
At the seaside	8 Write a detailed list 9 Write descriptive sentences
Get Writing! Book 7 Grey	
Rex to the rescue	9 Plan and write an information booklet
The lion's paw	9 Make notes and develop them to write from a character's point of view, building atmosphere
I dare you	9 Write in the first person, writing from experience, about thoughts, feelings and actions
Looking after a hamster	9 Write a poem
How silly!	9 Write from experience about thoughts and feelings
Wailing Winny's car boot sale	9 Write a poem, use descriptive language
Toad	9 Make notes and develop them, draw conclusions from events
Andrew	9 Make notes and use them to write a diary entry, write a recount
Dear Vampire	9 Write a letter in role, give advice
Vulture culture	9 Write a non-chronological report using comparisons
A celebration on planet Zox	9 Make notes and plan and write dialogue in role
A very dangerous dinosaur	9 Make notes about a dinosaur and use them to write a descriptive poem
The invisible clothes	9 Write in role to explore feelings (letter)
A job for Jordan	9 Design and write a persuasive poster
A place in space: the Moon	9 Plan and write a poem about walking on the Moon

Get Writing! lesson plans: Green Storybooks

Green Storybook 1   *On the bus*

Introducing the story

> racket   din   hullabaloo   ear-splitting

☆ Use these 'power words' when introducing the story during reading Activity 3. Write them on sticky notes so you remember to use them through the lesson/day.

*See Blueprint lesson plans for **Activity 5 Hold a sentence** and **Activity 7 Edit** on pp.25–26. (NB: Activities 1–4 Spelling, Activity 6 Build a sentence and Activity 9 Composition only appear in the Yellow, Blue and Grey books.)*

Activity 8 Composition: picture prompts

Power words

☆ TOL (Think out loud) to relate back to the story: *Just imagine – what a funny bus with so many animals. It must have been really loud on the bus.*

☆ Use MT/YT (My turn/Your turn) to repeat these 'power words' and to extend the language: *What a tremendous **racket**/**din**/a huge **hullabaloo**/a terrible **ear-splitting** noise.*

Say the sentences

☆ TOL as you build up the sentences, orally, about the bus.

☆ Ask the children to help you remember some of the 'power words'.

☆ Use MT/YT every time you expand the sentence together.

☆ Do not make it look too easy as you think of what to say. Encourage the children to help you so they take ownership of the sentence.

☆ Once you have decided upon the final sentence, use actions and facial expressions to help the children remember the sentence. Repeat until they can all say it after you.

☆ Make sure that every time you model a sentence orally you include 'power words', use MT/YT to expand the sentence and actions, facial expressions and repetition to help children remember it, as described above.

☆ ***The noise was** deafening. **The noise was** so deafening, I had to cover my ears. **The noise was** so deafening, I had to cover my ears and bury my head in my hands.*

☆ Repeat with other sentence stems, e.g. ***I can't stand** the noisy hen. **I can't stand** the noisy hen squawking. **I can't stand** the noisy hen squawking and screeching.*

☆ Use the 'power words' and stems from the sentences you have built in this activity throughout the day, e.g. ***I can't stand** the **racket**/**din** in the classroom when everyone is changing for games. What a **hullabaloo** in here.*

Write the sentences

a) *What a din! What are they saying?*

☆ Show the image of the bus with all the noisy passengers on **CD** (file 1.2). See p.3 of the *Get Writing!* book for this activity.

☆ Tell the children that you are all on the noisy bus. Say: *What a racket! What a din. What a hullabaloo! All this yelping and squawking.* Ask them to TTYP (Turn to your partner) and think of more words to describe the noise. Ask them to Popcorn their feedback: *purr, yap, miaow, scream…*

☆ Ask the children to choose one of the passengers and take their role. As you raise your hand in the air, tell them to start off quietly and gradually build up the noise until there is a tremendous din. Ask the children to think of the noise the hen might make: *yap, sing, scratch, squawk, cluck…*

☆ Practise saying sentences with these words, e.g., *I can cluck/I can squawk/I can scratch.*

☆ Click on the next screen (hen). Model writing a sentence with one of the words, e.g., *cluck*. TOL and ask children to help as you sound out each word using Set 1 and 2 sounds. Model how you re-read the sentence after writing each word to check it makes sense, leave spaces between words, and how you start with a capital letter and finish with a full stop. Ensure that you do this every time you model writing sentences with the children.

☆ Rub out/cover up *cluck* and repeat the process with the next screen (long thin dog).

☆ Rub out/cover up your writing and tell the children to write some sentences in the hen's speech bubbles in their *Get Writing!* Books, using either their own ideas or yours, if they need the support. Then ask them to write sentences for the dog's speech bubbles.

b) What is the girl saying?

☆ Show the image of the new passenger on **CD** (file 1.3). See p.4 of the *Get Writing!* Book for this activity.

☆ Ask the children to repeat the very loud noise on the bus. Take the role of a new passenger getting onto the noisy bus. Start complaining, saying *Stop the clucking! Stop the yapping! Stop the yelling! Stop the squawking!*

☆ Tell the children to take the role of the new passenger. Use MT/YT to say the same sentences.

☆ Practise saying the sentences in an angry voice. *Stop the clucking! Stop the yapping!* etc.

☆ Model writing the sentence with one of the words, e.g. *c-l-u-ck-i-ng.* TOL and ask children to help as you sound out each word, and then write it. Copy *the* from the Red Word cards. Model how you re-read the sentence after writing each word to check it makes sense. Rub out/cover up *clucking* and repeat the process with the other choices.

☆ Rub out/cover up your writing and tell the children to write some sentences in the speech bubbles in their *Get Writing!* Books. Repeat with *yapping/yelling*, etc.

Green Storybook 2   *My dog Ned*

Introducing the story

> *limp   shuffle   hobble   glum   miserable*

☆ Use these 'power words' when introducing the story during reading Activity 3. Write them on sticky notes so you remember to use them through the lesson/day.

*See Blueprint lesson plans for **Activity 5 Hold a sentence** and **Activity 7 Edit** on pp.25 – 26.*

Activity 8 Composition: picture prompts

Power words

☆ TOL to relate back to the story: *Poor Ned was unwell with his bad leg. He must have felt so* **glum**/**miserable**. Tell the children this means very sad. Ask them to show you glum, miserable faces!

☆ Use MT/YT to repeat the 'power words'. *Poor Ned feels* **glum**/**miserable**.

☆ TOL: *I wonder how Ned walked. With a* **limp**/**shuffle**/**hobble**? Offer your own ideas and take children's feedback.

☆ Ask the children to mime how Ned might move, and describe this walk to their partner, e.g. *Poor Ned has a terrible* **limp**/*an awful* **shuffle**.

Say the sentences

☆ TOL as you build up the sentences, orally, about how Ned felt at the beginning of the story.

☆ Use MT/YT each time you expand on the sentence stem until they can all say it after you. ***At first poor Ned felt*** *miserable.* ***At first poor Ned felt*** *really miserable.* ***At first poor Ned felt*** *so* *glum that all he could do was hobble. **At first poor Ned felt** so glum that all he could do was shuffle and hobble.*

☆ Repeat the above about how Ned's feelings change at the end of the story. **At the end Ned** *leapt up.* **At the end Ned** *was bouncy.* **At the end Ned** *leapt up, full of bounce, and licked the vet.*

☆ Use the 'power words' and stems from the sentences you have built in this activity throughout the session and day, e.g. contrast how you or the children are feeling using the sentence stems. **At first** *I felt a bit* **glum/miserable**. **At the end** *of the morning I felt full of joy!*

Write the sentences

a) How is Ned feeling?

☆ Show the image of Ned on **CD** (file 2.2). See p.6 of the *Get Writing!* Book for this activity.

☆ Act out being a very sad and poorly Ned at the beginning of the story. Tell the children they are Ned and to look as poorly as Ned. Ask them to TTYP and explain how they are feeling. Ask them to Popcorn ideas, e.g. *miserable, fed up, glum.*

☆ Practise saying the sentence with each word/phrase, e.g. *Ned is fed up.*

☆ Model writing the sentence with one of the choices, e.g. *fed up,* using Set 1 and 2 sounds. Remember to model rereading for sense, and checking word spaces and punctuation. Rub out/ cover up the words *fed up* and repeat the process with the other choices.

☆ Rub out/cover up your writing and tell the children to write some sentences below the picture of Ned in their *Get Writing!* Books, using either their own ideas or yours, if they need the support.

b) How is Ned walking?

☆ Click on the next screen (Ned limping). Ask the children to TTYP and remember how Ned moved. Ask the children to Popcorn feedback, e.g. *limp, shuffle, hobble.*

☆ Practise saying the sentence with the words, e.g. *Ned shuffles. Ned limps.*

☆ Model writing the sentence with one of the words, using Set 1 and 2 sounds. Rub out/cover up the word *shuffles* and repeat the process with the other choices.

☆ Rub out/cover up your writing and tell the children to write some sentences below the second picture of Ned in their *Get Writing!* Book.

Green Storybook 3   *Six fish*

Introducing the story

> huge   enormous   vast   explode

☆ Use these 'power words' when introducing the story during reading Activity 3. Write them on sticky notes so you remember to use them through the lesson/day.

See Blueprint lesson plans for **Activity 5 Hold a sentence** *and* **Activity 7 Edit** *on pp.25–26.*

Activity 8 Composition: picture prompts

Power words

☆ TOL to relate back to the story. *Fat Cat kept on eating. He ate six fish. He was* **enormous**! *I think he was going to* **explode**!

☆ Remind the children how Pug Dog gave Fat Cat a scare. Use MT/YT to extend the language. *Pug Dog burst the balloon. It went pop/bang/boom! It* **exploded**.

☆ Ask the children to TTYP and choose their favourite word to describe the noise the balloon made. Popcorn feedback.

Say the sentences

☆ TOL as you build up sentences about Fat Cat.

☆ Use MT/YT each time you expand on the sentence stem until they can all say it after you. *That cat is like* a huge balloon. *That cat is like* a vast balloon. *That cat eats so much he is like* an enormous orange balloon.

☆ Remind the children what happened when the balloon went pop. *When the balloon went pop Fat Cat* got a shock. *When the balloon went pop Fat Cat* got a terrible shock. *When the balloon went pop Fat Cat* got a terrible shock and thought he had exploded!

☆ Use the 'power words' and stems from the sentences you have built in this activity throughout the session and day, e.g. *I've eaten so much lunch that I feel like an* **enormous** *pumpkin! When you came in the class so quietly* **I got a shock**.

Write the sentences

a) What is Pug Dog saying?

☆ Show the image of Pug Dog and Fat Cat on **CD** (file 3.2). See p.8 of the *Get Writing!* Book for this activity.

☆ Act out the role of Pug Dog. Say: *You are such a greedy cat. I can't believe you can eat six whole fish. I am shocked.*

☆ Ask the children to TTYP to help you think of what to say to Fat Cat as he eats the six fish. Ask the children to Popcorn feedback: *Stop. You will pop/burst/explode.*

☆ Practise saying the sentences, e.g. *Stop. You will pop. Stop. You will burst.*

☆ Model writing the sentences with one of the words, e.g. *pop* using Set 1 and 2 sounds. Remember to model rereading for sense, and checking word spaces and punctuation. Show how you copy *you* from the Red Word card.

☆ Rub out/cover up your writing and tell the children to write some sentences into one of the speech bubbles in their *Get Writing!* Book, using either their own ideas or yours, if they need the support.

☆ Repeat with *burst/explode*.

b) What does Fat Cat look like?

☆ Click on the next screen (Fat Cat looking enormous). Ask the children to TTYP to think about which words would describe Fat Cat when he has been so greedy and eaten the six fish. Ask the children to Popcorn feedback: *huge, enormous, gigantic, like a balloon, as big as a house.*

☆ Model writing the words. TOL and ask children to help as you sound out each word and then write it. Use current phonic knowledge to write the words.

☆ Rub out/cover up your writing and tell the children to write some words below the picture of Fat Cat in their *Get Writing!* Book.

Green Storybook 4 *The spell*

Introducing the story

furious   glee   up to mischief

☆ Use these 'power words' when introducing the story during reading Activity 3. Write them on sticky notes so you remember to use them through the lesson/day.

*See Blueprint lesson plans for **Activity 5 Hold a sentence** and **Activity 7 Edit** on pp.25–26.*

Activity 8 Composition: picture prompts

Power words

☆ TOL to relate back to the story: *Stitch the Witch was **furious** with her cat. She cast a spell to turn it into a frog as she cackled with terrible **glee**!* Ask the children to show you how they would look if they were furious.

☆ Use MT/YT to repeat the 'power words': *She was **furious**. She cackled with **glee**. She was **up to mischief**.*

Say the sentences

☆ TOL as you build up the sentences 'orally' about Stitch the witch and her bubbling cauldron.

☆ Use MT/YT each time you expand on the sentence stem until they can all say it after you. ***Stitch the witch*** *cackled with glee.* ***Stitch the witch*** *cackled with terrible glee.* ***Stitch the witch*** *cackled with terrible glee as she stirred and mixed the pot.*

☆ Ask the children: *What noises does the bubbling pot make?* Use TTYP and Popcorn feedback. Add more ideas of your own, e.g. *bubble, plop, fizz, hiss, crack, pop.* ***Listen! I can hear the pot*** *bubble and plop.* ***Listen! I can hear the pot*** *fizz and hiss.* ***Listen! I can hear the pot*** *bubble, plop, fizz and hiss.*

☆ Relate back to the story and ask: *What shall we put in the pot?* ***Pop in a*** *fat juicy slug.* ***Pop in*** *six dusty cobwebs.* ***Pop in a*** *wing of a moth.*

☆ Use the 'power words' and stems from the sentences you have built in this activity throughout the session and day, e.g. *Is Jack **up to mischief**?*

Write the sentences

a) *What goes in the pot?*

☆ Show the image of the cauldron on **CD** (file 4.2). See p.10 of the *Get Writing!* Book for this activity.

☆ Listen to the bubbling cauldron audio.

☆ Act out being Stitch the witch. Say in a witchy voice: *Bubble, trouble, bubble, trouble. What shall we pop in the pot today? Ha ha ha ha ha (cackle)!* Ask children (still as the witch) to TTYP for suggestions. Choose children to feed back, e.g. *wing of a moth, leg of a rat, a fat slug.*

☆ Tell the children that they are Stitch the witch and use MT/YT to chant, in witchy voices, what they will put in the pot. *Pop in a wing of a moth.* Repeat with *six cobwebs, leg of rat, a fat slug.*

☆ *Practise saying the sentences, e.g. Pop in a wing of a moth. Pop in six cobwebs, etc.*

☆ Model writing the sentence with one of the phrases, e.g. *wing of a moth,* using Set 1 and 2 sounds. Remember to model rereading for sense, and checking word spaces and punctuation. Show how you copy *of* from the Red Word card.

☆ Rub out/cover up the phrase *wing of a moth* and repeat the process with the other choices.

☆ Rub out/cover up your writing and tell the children to write some sentences into the cauldron in their *Get Writing!* Books, using either their own ideas or yours, if they need the support.

b) *What can you hear from the pot?*

☆ Drag and drop the items into the pot on **CD** (file 4.3). See p.11 of the *Get Writing!* Book for this activity.

☆ Ask children to TTYP to think of noises that each item would make as it drops into the pot. Choose children to feed back, e.g. *hiss, bubble, pop, fizz, spit.*

☆ Use MT/YT to make the noises. Exaggerate the *hiss, bubble, pop, spit.*

☆ Model writing each word using Set 1 and 2 sounds.

☆ Rub out/cover up your writing and tell the children to write some words into the bubbles in their *Get Writing!* Books.

Green Storybook 5   *Black Hat Bob*

Introducing the story

snatch   grasp   rascal   rogue

☆ Use these 'power words' when introducing the story during reading Activity 3. Write them on sticky notes so you remember to use them through the lesson/day.

*See Blueprint lesson plans for **Activity 5 Hold a sentence** and **Activity 7 Edit** on pp.25 – 26.*

Activity 8 Composition: picture prompts

Power words

☆ TOL to relate back to the story: *Black Hat Bob was not going to let go of his cash box when Red Hat Rob tried to **snatch** it.*

☆ Use MT/YT to repeat these 'power words'. *When he got on the ship Red Hat Rob tried to seize/ **grasp**/**snatch**/steal the cash box.* Take children's ideas once you have offered yours.

☆ Use MT/YT to extend the language: *That Red Hat Rob was a **rascal**. He was a thieving **rogue**.*

☆ Ask the children to TTYP and describe Red Hat Rob. Popcorn feedback.

Say the sentences

☆ TOL as you build up sentences, orally, about the terrible thief Red Hat Rob.

☆ Use MT/YT each time you expand on the sentence stem until they can all say it after you. ***Red Hat Rob tried to** snatch the cash box. **Red Hat Rob tried to** sneak up and snatch the cash box. **Red Hat Rob tried to** sneak up and snatch the cash box from Black Hat Bob.*

☆ Repeat with other sentence stems, e.g. ***Red Hat Rob is a** rascal. **Red Hat Rob is a** grasping rascal. **Red Hat Rob is a** grasping rascal who stole all the cash.*

☆ Use the 'power words' and stems from the sentences you have built in this activity throughout the session and day, e.g. *Can you sneak up and try to **snatch** the ball?*

Write the sentences

a) *What is Black Hat Bob saying?*

☆ Show the image of Red Hat Rob and Black Hat Bob on **CD** (file 5.2). See p.13 of the *Get Writing! Book* for this activity.

☆ Act out being in role as the pirates as Red Hat Rob grabs Black Hat Bob's cash box. Ask the children to TTYP and think what Black Hat Bob says, e.g. *Let go of my cash box./You must not take my cash box./How dare you take my cash box.*

☆ Practise saying the sentences, e.g. *Let go of my cash box. Let go of my…*

☆ Model writing one of the sentences using Set 1 and 2 sounds. Remember to model rereading for sense, and checking word spaces and punctuation. Show how to copy *go, of* and *my* from the Red Word cards.

☆ Rub out/cover up your writing and tell the children to write a sentence into one of the speech bubbles in their *Get Writing! Book*, using either their own ideas or yours, if they need the support.

☆ Repeat the process with another sentence.

b) *Help us find Red Hat Rob.*

☆ Click on the next screen (Red Hat Rob *Wanted* poster). See p.14 of the *Get Writing! Book* for this activity.

☆ Act out being in role as a police officer. Say: *Do you know a pirate called Red Hat Rob? It has come to my attention that he has tried to steal a huge amount of cash from Black Hat Bob. Will you help me find him? Tell me everything you know about him.* Ask the children to TTYP and to Popcorn feedback, e.g. *tall, ugly, mean, red hat.*

- ☆ Use MT/YT to say the description, e.g. *He is tall. He has a red hat. He is horrible.*
- ☆ Model writing one of the sentences using Set 1 and 2 sounds. Show how you copy *he* from the Red Word card. Repeat the process with another sentence.
- ☆ Rub out/cover up your writing and tell the children to write a description of Red Hat Rob into the *Wanted* poster in their *Get Writing!* Books.

Green Storybook 6   *Tug, tug*

Introducing the story

annoyed   haul

- ☆ Use these 'power words' when introducing the story during reading Activity 3. Write them on sticky notes so you remember to use them through the lesson/day.

*See Blueprint lesson plans for **Activity 5 Hold a sentence** and **Activity 7 Edit** on pp.25 – 26.*

Activity 8 Composition: picture prompts

Power words

- ☆ TOL to relate back to the story: *Poor old Black Hat Bob. He wasn't very lucky with his fishing. He must have felt very bored waiting for a fish to pull on his fishing line.*
- ☆ Use MT/YT to repeat these 'power words'. *As Black Hat Bob sat there all day he got **annoyed**.* Ask the children to show you annoyed expressions.
- ☆ Ask the children to mime pulling up a fish from the sea. TOL: *How did you pull up your fish? I **hauled** up/yanked up/pulled up my fish.* Take children's ideas once you have offered yours.
- ☆ Use MT/YT to extend the language. As the children mime pulling in their fish, get them to say *Wow! That's a big one. **Haul** it in!*

Say the sentences

- ☆ TOL as you build up sentences, orally, about Black Hat Bob's fishing trip.
- ☆ Use MT/YT each time you expand on the sentence stem until they can all say it after you. ***Black Hat Bob was sitting** in the boat. How was he feeling?* TTYP and feed back. Say the new sentence using a couple of the children's ideas. ***Black Hat Bob was sitting** in the boat feeling tired and bored.*
- ☆ Ask: *Why was he feeling that way?* TTYP and feed back. Say the new sentence using a couple of the children's ideas. ***Black Hat Bob was sitting** in the boat feeling tired and bored because there weren't any fish.*
- ☆ Use the 'power words' and stems from the sentences you have built in this activity throughout the day, e.g. *You look **annoyed** – what's the problem?*

Write the sentences

a) *What does Black Hat Bob want to eat?*

- ☆ Show the image of Bob on **CD** (file 6.2). See p.16 of the *Get Writing!* Book for this activity.
- ☆ Tell the children they are Bob and they are talking out loud, thinking about what he will eat with his fish. TOL as you think dreamily of all the lovely things you will eat tonight. *At the end of today I will have the most wonderful tea/dinner.* Ask the children to TTYP. Popcorn their suggestions. Model the response sentences and use MT/YT to practise them. *I will have chips with my fish. I will have tomato ketchup/vinegar/peas/bread with my fish.*
- ☆ Practise saying the sentences, e.g. *I will have chips with my fish. I will have…with my fish.*
- ☆ Model writing the sentence with one of the words, e.g. *chips* using Set 1 and 2 sounds Remember to model rereading for sense, and checking word spaces and punctuation. Rub out/ cover up *chips* and repeat the process with the other choices.

☆ Rub out/cover up your writing and tell the children to write some sentences into the speech bubbles in their *Get Writing!* Book, using either their own ideas or yours, if they need the support.

b) *What is Black Hat Bob saying?*

☆ Click on the next screen (Bob sitting in his boat looking bored). This activity is also on p.16 of the *Get Writing!* Book.

☆ Act out being Bob being fed up. Say (in a bored voice): *I have been sitting here all day in my little boat. When will I ever catch a fish?* In role, ask the children: *Do you have any idea how I'm feeling?* Ask them to TTYP and then Popcorn their ideas, e.g. *bored, annoyed, fed up.*

☆ Say: *Yes! That is exactly how I'm feeling. I am bored/fed up/miserable/tired/annoyed.*

☆ Practise saying the sentences. *I am fed up. I am…*

☆ Model writing the sentence with one of the words, e.g. *miserable,* using Set 1 and 2 sounds. Rub out/cover up *miserable* and repeat the process with the other choices.

☆ Rub out/cover up your writing and tell the children to write some sentences into the speech bubbles in their *Get Writing!* Book.

Green Storybook 7   *Chips*

Introducing the story

> disappear   annoyed   grumpy

☆ Use these 'power words' when introducing the story during reading Activity 3. Write them on sticky notes so you remember to use them through the lesson/day.

*See Blueprint lesson plans for **Activity 5 Hold a sentence** and **Activity 7 Edit** on pp.25–26.*

Activity 8 Composition: picture prompts

Power words

☆ TOL to relate back to the story: *At first Kim had a huge pile of hot crispy chips but as her friends came by they began to **disappear**.*

☆ Use MT/YT to repeat these 'power words'. Ask the children to TTYP and think how Kim might feel. TOL: *She might feel hungry/**annoyed**/**grumpy**/let down.* Take children's ideas once you have offered yours.

☆ Use MT/YT to extend the language: *Poor Kim – she looked at the empty bag and was **annoyed**. Poor Kim – she felt **grumpy** because her friends had let her down.*

Say the sentences

☆ TOL as you build up sentences, orally, about Kim and her disappearing chips.

☆ Use MT/YT each time you expand on the sentence stem until they can all say it after you. ***At first Kim had a*** *bag of crisp chips.* ***At first Kim had a*** *steaming bag of thick, crisp chips.* ***At first Kim had a*** *steaming hot bag of thick, crisp chips.*

☆ Repeat with other sentence stems, e.g. ***As her friends came by*** *Kim had fewer and fewer chips.* ***As her friends came by*** *Kim had fewer and fewer chips until they disappeared.*

☆ Remind the children how cross Kim looked when she saw all her delicious chips had gone! TOL: *She stared at the empty bag. She was glum, annoyed and left with a rumbling tum!*

☆ Use MT/YT to expand on the sentence stem. ***In the end Kim felt*** *annoyed with her friends.* ***In the end Kim felt*** *annoyed with her greedy friends.*

☆ Use the 'power words' and stems from the sentences you have built in this activity throughout the session and day, e.g. contrast how you or the children are feeling using the sentence stems. ***At first*** *I was so excited about reading the book.* ***At the end*** *of the story I was in a magical dream.*

Write the sentences

a) *What is Kim saying about chips?*

☆ Show the image of Kim on **CD** (file 7.2). See p.18 of the *Get Writing!* Book for this activity.

☆ Act out being in role as Kim before the children took her chips. Model holding your chips saying enthusiastically: *I love my chips, don't you? I love my huge bag of steamy yummy chips.*

☆ Tell the children they are Kim and to smell their chips wrapped in paper, *mmmmm*, and to TTYP for words to describe their chips. Take feedback, e.g. *hot, yummy, crisp, thick, crunchy.*

☆ Practise saying the sentences, with feeling, e.g. *My chips are crunchy. My chips are…*

☆ Model writing the sentence with one of the words, e.g. *crunchy* using Set 1 and 2 sounds. Remember to model rereading for sense, and checking word spaces and punctuation. Show how you copy *my* and *are* from the Red Word cards.

☆ Rub out/cover up *crunchy* and repeat the process with the other choices.

☆ Rub out/cover up your writing and tell the children to write some sentences into the speech bubbles in their *Get Writing!* Book, using either their own ideas or yours, if they need the support.

b) *What is Kim saying to her friends?*

☆ Act out being in role as Kim after the children took her chips. See p.19 of the *Get Writing!* Book for this activity. Model holding your empty bag, saying miserably: *All my chips have gone. All my lovely huge bag of steamy yummy chips.*

☆ Ask the children to look sadly at their empty paper wrappings and to TTYP for words they wish they had said to their friends. Take feedback, e.g. *You can only have one chip. No, I am hungry. They are all for me! Go away. No, I want the chips!*

☆ Practise saying a sentence, with feeling, e.g. *No. I want the chips.*

☆ Click on the next screen (Kim and Sam). Model writing your sentence using Set 1 and 2 sounds. Copy *No, I* and *want* from the Red Word cards.

☆ Rub out/cover up your writing and tell the children to write a sentence into one of the speech bubbles in their *Get Writing!* Book.

☆ Click onto the next screen (Kim and Tim) and repeat with another sentence.

Green Storybook 8   *The web*

Introducing the story

> crunch   chomp   crush   in a fix

☆ Use these 'power words' when introducing the story during reading Activity 3. Write them on sticky notes so you remember to use them through the lesson/day.

See Blueprint lesson plans for **Activity 5 Hold a sentence** *and* **Activity 7 Edit** *on pp.25 – 26.*

Activity 8 Composition: picture prompts

Power words

☆ TOL to relate back to the story: *Spin was keen to munch and* **crunch** *up those bugs but the bugs were in luck because Spin had got himself* **in a fix**!

☆ Use MT/YT to repeat these 'power words'. TOL: *Spin was keen to* **chomp** *the bugs in his web.* Take children's ideas once you have offered yours.

☆ Ask the children to mime Spin caught on his own web. TOL: *I wonder what he might call out. Help, I'm* **in a fix**/in a jam/in a trap!

☆ Use MT/YT to extend the language. As the children mime being stuck in the web, get them to say: *Help, I'm* **in a terrible fix**.

Say the sentences

☆ TOL as you build up sentences, orally, about Spin the spider.

☆ Use MT/YT each time you expand on the sentence stem until they can all say it after you. *I will munch up the six fat bugs. **I will** munch and crunch up the six fat bugs. **I will** munch and crunch up the six delicious juicy bugs.*

☆ Relate back to the story and ask what Spin would call out when he found he was stuck, e.g. ***Help**, **I am** in a fix! **Help**, **I am** in a fix and stuck fast! **Help**, **I am** in a fix and stuck fast in my web!*

☆ Use the 'power words' and stems from the sentences you have built in this activity throughout the session and day, e.g. *Oh no! I'm **in a fix**. Can you help me?*

Write the sentences

a) *What is Spin saying about the bugs?*

☆ Show the image of Spin in his web on **CD** (file 8.2). See p.21 of the *Get Writing!* Book for this activity.

☆ Act out being Spin. Say: *I am one hungry spider today. I want to eat and eat bugs all day. I am going to munch and crunch and chomp and crunch!*

☆ Use MT/YT to say *munch munch*, then *crunch crunch*, then *chomp chomp*.

☆ Practise saying the sentences, e.g. *I will chomp the six bugs. I will munch…*

☆ Model writing the sentence with one of the words, e.g. *chomp*. TOL and ask children to help as you sound out each word using Set 1 and 2 sounds. Remember to model rereading for sense, and checking word spaces and punctuation. Rub out/cover up the word *chomp* and repeat the process with the other choices.

☆ Rub out/cover up your writing and tell the children to write what Spin says into the speech bubbles in their *Get Writing!* Book, using either their own ideas or yours, if they need the support.

b) *What is Spin saying now?*

☆ Click on the next screen (Spin stuck in his web). Act out being Spin stuck on his web. Say desperately: *Help. I am stuck. Help. I am in a fix. Help. I am in a jam.*

☆ Tell the children that they are Spin and use MT/YT to practise saying the sentences *Help. I am stuck.*

☆ Model writing the sentences with one of the words, e.g. *stuck* using Set 1 and 2 sounds. Rub out/cover up the word *stuck* and repeat the process with the other choices.

☆ Rub out/cover up your writing and tell the children to write what Spin says into the speech bubbles in their *Get Writing!* Books.

Green Storybook 9   *Pip's pizza*

Introducing the story

> *reek   whiff   delicious*

☆ Use these 'power words' when introducing the story during reading Activity 3. Write them on sticky notes so you remember to use them through the lesson/day.

*See Blueprint lesson plans for **Activity 5 Hold a sentence** and **Activity 7 Edit** on pp.25 – 26.*

Activity 8 Composition: picture prompts

Power words

☆ TOL to relate back to the story: *The delicious smell of the pizza made Zip's tum rumble.*
☆ Use MT/YT to repeat the 'power words'. *He could smell a **whiff** of cheesy pizza. Zip smelled the awful **reek** of fish and egg.*
☆ Ask the children to TTYP to describe what Zip thought the pizza smelled like. Did he like the sweet aroma or did the terrible reek put him off eating?
☆ Use MT/YT to extend the language: *Pip's pizza had a **terrible reek**! Yuk!*

Say the sentences

☆ TOL as you build up sentences about Pip's pizza.
☆ Use MT/YT each time you expand on the sentence stem until they can all say it after you. ***Can you smell the** terrible smell of Pip's pizza? **Can you smell the** terrible reek of Pip's pizza? **Can you smell the** terrible reek of Pip's pizza disaster?*
☆ Repeat with other sentence stems, e.g. ***Zip could not wait to** eat the delicious pizza. **Zip could not wait to** crunch the delicious pizza crust.*
☆ Relate back to the story and ask: *What shall we put on the pizza? **Pop on** crunchy nuts. **Pop on** smeary sticky red jam. **Pop on** egg and fish.*
☆ Use the 'power words' and stems from the sentences you have built in this activity throughout the session and day, e.g. ***I cannot wait to** crunch on this **delicious** apple.*

Write the sentences

What goes on the pizza?
☆ Show the image of Pip on **CD** (file 9.2). See p.23 of the *Get Writing!* Book for this activity.
☆ Act out being Pip: *I just love making pizzas. I love putting all sorts of things on a pizza. I love pineapple, cheese, tomato, beans and crunchy nuts.*
☆ Ask the children to TTYP and discuss what they would like to put on their pizza. Ask them to Popcorn their answers, e.g. *chocolate, ice-cream!*
☆ Click on the next screen and drag and drop different toppings onto the pizza as you discuss this.
☆ Use MT/YT to chant: *Pop crunchy nuts on the pizza. Pop chocolate on the pizza.* Repeat with other toppings.
☆ Practise saying the sentence: *Pop crunchy nuts on the pizza.*
☆ Display **CD** (file 9.3), showing the pizza base and ingredients. Model writing the sentence with one of the choices, e.g. *chocolate,* using Set 1 and 2 sounds. Remember to model rereading for sense, and checking word spaces and punctuation. Show how you copy *the* from the Red Word card. Rub out/cover up the word *chocolate* and repeat the process with other choices.
☆ Rub out/cover up your writing and tell the children to write into the pizza in their *Get Writing!* Books.

Introducing the story

bliss   delight   gladness

☆ Use these 'power words' when introducing the story during reading Activity 3. Write them on sticky notes so you remember to use them through the lesson/day.

*See Blueprint lesson plans for **Activity 5 Hold a sentence** and **Activity 7 Edit** on pp.25–26.*

Activity 8 Composition: picture prompts

Power words

☆ TOL to relate back to the story: *What a wonderful day for the cat. I bet he purred with **bliss** when he got his wishes.*

☆ Ask: *How do you think the cat felt when his wishes were granted?* Use MT/YT to repeat these 'power words'. *He is full of **delight**/full of joy. He purrs with **bliss**/**gladness**.* Take children's ideas once you have offered yours.

☆ Use MT/YT to extend the language: *I think the cat felt utter joy. He purred with **blissful gladness**.*

Say the sentences

☆ TOL as you build up sentences about the cat's wishes.

☆ Use MT/YT each time you expand on the sentence stem until they can all say it after you. ***When the wish came true*** *the cat purred.* ***When the wish came true*** *the cat purred with delight.* ***When the wish came true*** *the cat purred with delight and bliss.*

☆ Repeat with other sentence stems, e.g. ***I wish I had*** *a delicious fresh fish.* ***I wish I had*** *a dish of cold sweet milk.* ***I wish I had*** *a mouse to chase.*

☆ Use the 'power words' and stems from the sentences you have built in this activity throughout the session and day, e.g. ***I wish I had*** *a delicious mug of creamy hot chocolate. When I saw your work I was **delighted**.*

Write the sentences

a) What is the cat thinking?

☆ Show the image of the cat on **CD** (file 10.2). See p.25 of the *Get Writing!* Book for this activity.

☆ Act out being the cat. Say: *There are some things that every cat loves, you know. We like warm comfy places, delicious food and playing games – just like you children.*

☆ Ask the children to TTYP to think what you would wish for as a cat. Choose children to feed back.

☆ After each suggestion, use MT/YT to chant the phrase *I wish I had a soft comfy bed. I wish I had a mouse to chase.* Use a different tone of voice each time, e.g. moany/wistful/excited.

☆ Practise saying the sentence with the words *soft comfy bed*, i.e. *I wish I had a soft comfy bed.*

☆ Model writing the sentence using one of the phrases, e.g. *soft comfy bed* using Set 1 and 2 sounds. Remember to model rereading for sense, and checking word spaces and punctuation. Rub out/ cover up *soft comfy bed* and repeat the process with different wishes.

☆ Rub out/cover up your writing and tell the children to write into the thought bubbles in their *Get Writing!* Books, using either their own ideas or yours, if they need the support.

b) What is the spell?

☆ Display **CD** (file 10.3). This activity is also on p.25 of the *Get Writing!* Book.

☆ Act out being the witch. Say: *There are some things that every witch gets cross about, you know. We get angry when spells don't work, when we don't get our own way and when we don't get what we want.*

☆ Tell the children they are the witch and to TTYP to think about the sorts of things they get cross about as a witch. Choose children to feed back. Tell them you want them to help you invent a new spell phrase that will always work. Give suggestions, e.g. *bobbo bobbo bibble, stompy pompy, flimp flomp.* Ask the children to TTYP to make up silly words.

☆ Model writing a silly phrase using Set 1 and 2 sounds. Repeat the process with different phrases.

☆ Rub out/cover up your writing and tell the children to write into the magic spell boxes in their *Get Writing!* Book.

Green Non-fiction Book 2 *We can all swim!*

Introducing the book

glide   paddle   graceful/ly

☆ Use these 'power words' when introducing the book during reading Activity 3. Write them on sticky notes so you remember to use them through the lesson/day.

*See Blueprint lesson plans for **Activity 5 Hold a sentence** and **Activity 7 Edit** on pp.25–26.*

Activity 8 Composition: picture prompts

Power words

☆ TOL to relate back to the story: *Fish are so **graceful**, the way they **glide** around the fish tank. The duck isn't so **graceful**. It **paddles**.*

☆ Use MT/YT to repeat these 'power words'. *The fish **glides gracefully** but the duck **paddles**.*

☆ Ask the children to TTYP and discuss where they might find the fish or duck swimming. Take children's ideas once you have offered yours. *The fish might swim in its tank and the duck might swim on a pond.*

☆ Use MT/YT to extend the language: *The fish swims around the colourful coral in its tank. The duck swims on the dirty, reedy pond.*

Say the sentences

☆ TOL as you build up sentences, orally, about the duck and the fish. Ask the children to help you remember some of the 'power words'.

☆ Use MT/YT every time you expand the sentence stem as you build it up together. Do not make it look too easy as you think of what to say. Encourage the children to help you so they take ownership of the sentence.

☆ Expand a simple sentence by asking questions. Use MT/YT each time you expand the sentence: **The duck** *swims on a pond. How was it swimming?*

☆ Ask children to TTYP and feed back. Say the new sentence using a couple of the children's ideas. **The duck** *paddles on a pond. What was the pond like? Let's describe it in more detail.*

☆ TTYP and feed back. Say the new sentence using a couple of the children's ideas, e.g. **The duck** *paddles on a huge reedy pond.*

☆ Repeat with other animals from the book, e.g. **The fish** *swims in the tank.* (How?) **The fish** *glides as it swims around the tank.* (What was the tank like?) **The fish** *glides as it swims around the colourful coral and waving weeds.*

☆ Once you have decided upon the final sentence, use actions and facial expressions to help the children remember the sentence. Use MT/YT to repeat the sentence until they can all say it after you.

☆ Use the 'power words' and stems from the sentences you have built in this activity throughout the session and day, e.g. *The dancers are so **graceful** that they seem to **glide**.*

Write the sentences

Write about the animals.

☆ Show the image of the fish on **CD** (file NF2.2). See p.27 of the *Get Writing!* Book for this activity.

☆ Model writing the stem *The fish*. TOL and ask children to help as you sound out each word and then write it.

☆ Ask the children to TTYP and discuss how and where the fish might swim. Use 'Choose Two' to take feedback.

☆ Write *glides in the weeds in the tank*. Use current phonic knowledge to write the words.

☆ Rub out/cover up your writing and tell the children to write how the fish moves and describe its tank in their *Get Writing!* Book.

☆ Click on the next screen (duck). Repeat the activity, modelling the stem *The duck…*

Green Non-fiction Book 4   *What am I?*

Introducing the book

> *jet-black   pounce   leap   spring*

☆ Use these 'power words' when introducing the book during reading Activity 3. Write them on sticky notes so you remember to use them through the lesson/day.

*See Blueprint lesson plans for **Activity 5 Hold a sentence** and **Activity 7 Edit** on pp.25–26.*

Activity 8 Composition: picture prompts

Power words

☆ TOL to relate back to the story: *That cat was a beautiful **jet-black** colour. It could dash and **pounce**.*

☆ Ask: *How would you describe the cat?* Use MT/YT to repeat these 'power words'. *The cat was **jet-black**. It was as black as night.*

☆ Ask: *Do you remember how the cat moved?* Take children's ideas once you have offered yours. TOL: *The cat could **pounce**. It could **leap**. It could **spring**. The cat could run. It could dash. It could sprint.*

☆ Use MT/YT to extend the language: *That **jet-black** cat could **spring** high into the air and dash across the garden.*

Say the sentences

☆ TOL as you build up sentences, orally, about the cat.

☆ Use MT/YT each time you expand on the sentence stem until they can all say it after you. ***I am** a black cat. **I am a** jet-black cat. **I am** a jet-black cat as dark as the night.*

☆ Repeat with other sentence stems, e.g. ***I can** spring into the air. **I can** spring into the air to pounce on mice. **I can** spring into the air to pounce soundlessly on mice.*

☆ Use the 'power words' and stems from the sentences you have built in this activity throughout the session and day, e.g. *You have **jet-black** hair. Can you **spring** into the air and **pounce** like a cat?*

Write the sentences

a) *Write about the cat.*

☆ Show the image of the cat on **CD** (file NF4.2). See p.29 of the *Get Writing!* Book for this activity.

☆ Model writing the stem *I am a*. TOL and ask children to help as you sound out each word and then write it.

☆ Ask the children to TTYP and discuss how to describe the cat. Use 'Choose Two' to take feedback.

☆ Write *jet-black cat*. Use current phonic knowledge to write the words.

☆ Rub out/cover up your writing and tell the children to write their description of the cat in their *Get Writing!* Book.

☆ Click on the next screen (cat running).

☆ Ask the children to TTYP and discuss what the cat is doing. Use 'Choose Two' for feedback.

☆ Model writing the stem *I can*. TOL and ask children to help as you sound out each word and then write it.

☆ Write *dash*. Use current phonic knowledge to write the words.

☆ Rub out/cover up your writing and tell the children to write their description of the cat running in their *Get Writing!* Book, using either their own ideas or yours, if they need the support.

☆ Click on the next screen (cat jumping). Repeat for the stem *I can* (*spring from up high*).

b) *Write about this animal.*

☆ Ask the children to TTYP and discuss what the other animal in their *Get Writing!* Book p.29 could be. (It is an owl.)

☆ Tell the children to write an *I can* sentence about the owl in their *Get Writing!* Book.

Purple Storybook 1   *Ken's cap*

Introducing the story

enormous   vast   massive   stylish

☆ Use these 'power words' when introducing the story during reading Activity 3. Write them on sticky notes so you remember to use them through the lesson/day.

See Blueprint lesson plans for Activity 5 Hold a sentence and Activity 7 Edit on pp.25 – 26. (NB: Activities 1 – 4 Spelling, Activity 6 Build a sentence and Activity 9 Composition only appear in the Yellow, Blue and Grey books.)

Activity 8 Composition: picture prompts

Power words

☆ TOL (Think out loud) to relate back to the story: *Dan and Ken dug a deep hole but then Ken lost his favourite cap. At last they realised the cap was buried in the pit!*
☆ Use MT/YT (My turn/Your turn) to repeat the 'power words'. *Poor Ken lost his smart/**stylish**/fabulous cap.*
☆ How else might the children describe the cap? Take children's ideas once you have offered yours.
☆ Use MT/YT to extend the language: *Poor Ken. His **stylish** cap was buried in the **enormous**/**vast**/**massive** pit.*

Say the sentences

☆ TOL as you build up the sentences together, orally, about Ken's missing cap.
☆ Use MT/YT every time you expand the sentence together. Do not make it look too easy as you think of what to say. Encourage the children to help you so they take ownership of the sentence.
☆ Once you have decided upon the final sentence, use actions and facial expressions to help the children remember it. Use MT/YT each time you expand on the sentence stem until they can all say it after you. **Ken has lost his** *smart cap.* **Ken has lost his** *stylish blue cap.* **Ken has lost his** *favourite fabulous blue cap!*
☆ Make sure that every time you model a sentence orally you include 'power words', use MT/YT to expand the sentence and actions, facial expressions and repetition to help children remember it, as described above.
☆ Repeat with other sentence stems, e.g. **Dan said** *"Let's dig up the pit and find your cap".* **Dan said** *"Let's dig up the massive pit and find your cap".* **Dan said** *"Let's dig up the enormous pit and find your cap".*
☆ Use the 'power words' and stems from the sentences you have built in this activity throughout the session and day, e.g. *You look very **stylish** with your new hair cut. That is a **massive** amount of food!*

Write the sentences

a) *What is Dan saying?*
☆ Show the image of Ken and Dan on **CD** (file 1.2). See also p.3 of the *Get Writing!* Book.
☆ Act out being Ken saying to Dan *I've lost my hat.* Tell the children they are Dan and to TTYP (Turn to your partner) to think what they can do to help Ken. Ask the children to Popcorn ideas, e.g. *I can dig it out./I can get my digger.*
☆ Practise saying the sentence with each word/phrase, e.g. *I can help you dig. I can get my digger.*

Purple

☆ Model writing the sentence with one of the choices, e.g. *I can help you dig.* TOL and ask children to help as you sound out each word using Set 1 and 2 sounds. Show how to copy *I* and *you* from the Red Word cards. Model how you re-read the sentence after writing each word to check it makes sense, leave spaces between words, and how you start with a capital letter and finish with a full stop. Ensure that you do this every time you model writing sentences with the children. Rub out/cover up the words *help you dig* and repeat the process with the other choices.

☆ Rub out/cover up your writing and tell the children to write some sentences in the speech bubbles in their *Get Writing!* Book, using either their own ideas or yours, if they need the support.

b) *Write about Ken's cap.*

☆ Click on the next screen (Ken's cap). This activity is also on p.3 of the *Get Writing!* Book.

☆ Ask the children to TTYP to describe Ken's cap. Ask the children to Popcorn feedback, e.g. *It was smart/blue/fab/the best.*

☆ Practise saying the sentence with the choices, e.g. *Ken lost his fab cap.*

☆ Model writing the sentence with one of the choices. TOL and ask children to help as you sound out each word and then write it. Use current phonic knowledge to write the words. Model how you re-read the sentence after writing each word to check it makes sense. Rub out/cover up the word *fab* and repeat the process with the other choices.

☆ Rub out/cover up your writing and tell the children to write some sentences in Ken's cap in their *Get Writing!* Book.

Purple Storybook 2   *A bad fox*

Introducing the story

slink off   sneak away   soaking   drenched

☆ Use these 'power words' when introducing the story during reading Activity 3. Write them on sticky notes so you remember to use them through the lesson/day.

See Blueprint lesson plans for **Activity 5 Hold a sentence** and **Activity 7 Edit** on pp.25–26.

Activity 8 Composition: picture prompts

Power words

☆ TOL to relate back to the story: *Fox caught Red Hen and ran off but the man caught him and dropped him in the pond!*

☆ Use MT/YT to repeat the 'power words'. *When he caught Red Hen, Fox tried to* **slink off**/*dash off*/*dart off*/**sneak away**.

☆ Use MT/YT to extend the language. *But Fox got caught and ended up in the pond* **soaking** *wet*/**drenched** *through!*

Say the sentences

☆ TOL as you build up the sentences together, orally, about how Fox felt at the beginning of the story.

☆ Use MT/YT each time you expand on the sentence stem until they can all say it after you. ***At first Fox tried to*** *run off with Red Hen.* ***At first Fox tried to*** *sneak away.* ***At first Fox tried to*** *sneak away with Red Hen.*

☆ Repeat the process showing how Fox's situation has changed by the end of the story. Ask the children to help you remember some of the 'power words'. ***At the end Fox was*** *wet.* ***At the end Fox was*** *soaking wet.* ***At the end Fox was*** *soaking wet and sorry!*

✿ Use the 'power words' and stems from the sentences you have built in this activity throughout the session and day, e.g. **At first** I tried to slink out of the room and hide! **At the end** of play I was **soaking wet!**

Write the sentences

a) *What is Fox saying?*

✿ Show the image of Fox on **CD** (file 2.2). See p.5 of the *Get Writing!* Book for this activity.

✿ Act out being in role as Fox. Model sneakily peeping round and looking at Red Hen and say: *I will get Red Hen and run off!* Tell the children they are Fox and to TTYP to discuss how they might move when they catch Red Hen. Ask the children to Popcorn ideas, e.g. *sprint, dash, sneak.*

✿ Practise saying the sentence with each word/phrase, e.g. *I will get Red Hen and dash away/sprint off/slink off.*

✿ Model writing the sentence with one of the choices, e.g. *I will get Red Hen and dash away* using Set 1 and 2 sounds. Remember to model rereading for sense, and checking word spaces and punctuation. Rub out/cover up the words *dash away* and repeat the process with the other choices.

✿ Rub out/cover up your writing and tell the children to write some sentences in the speech bubbles in their *Get Writing!* Book, using either their own ideas or yours, if they need the support.

b) *What is Red Hen saying?*

✿ Click on the next screen (Fox with Red Hen in his mouth). Ask the children to TTYP to remember how Red Hen cried for help. Ask the children to act out being Red Hen saying, *Let me go.* Encourage them to say the words in different ways, e.g. *pleading, shouting, whispering, crying.*

✿ Ask the children to TTYP and discuss how Red Hen might ask for help. Popcorn feedback, e.g. *shout, yell, sob, call.*

✿ Practise saying the sentences with the words, e.g. *"Let me go," Red Hen yells.*

✿ Model writing the sentences with one of the words using Set 1 and 2 sounds. Rub out/cover up the word *yells* and repeat the process with the other choices.

✿ Rub out/cover up your writing and tell the children to write some sentences below the picture of Red Hen in their *Get Writing!* Books.

Purple Storybook 3   *Big Blob and Baby Blob*

Introducing the story

> embarrassed   furious   hot and bothered   full of mischief   a pest

✿ Use these 'power words' when introducing the story during reading Activity 3. Write them on sticky notes so you remember to use them through the lesson/day.

*See Blueprint lesson plans for **Activity 5 Hold a sentence** and **Activity 7 Edit** on pp.25–26.*

Activity 8 Composition: picture prompts

Power words

✿ Use MT/YT to repeat the 'power words'. *Poor Big Blob felt **embarrassed/furious/hot and bothered** because Baby Blob was so naughty!*

✿ Ask the children to TTYP and think about how Baby Blob behaved, e.g., *I think Baby Blob was **full of mischief/a pest**!* Take the children's ideas once you have offered yours.

✿ Use MT/YT to extend the language. *Poor Big Blob felt **embarrassed** because Baby Blob was being **a pest!** Big Blob was annoyed because Baby Blob was **full of mischief.***

Say the sentences

☆ TOL as you build up the sentences together, orally, about how Big Blob felt about Baby Blob's antics.

☆ Use MT/YT each time you expand on the sentence stem until they can all say it after you. *At first Big Blob was embarrassed. At first Big Blob was embarrassed, and then annoyed. At first Big Blob was embarrassed, then annoyed and finally furious!*

☆ Use the 'power words' and stems from the sentences you have built in this activity throughout the session and day, e.g. comment on your feelings and encourage the children to do so too. *At first I was embarrassed to read aloud. I was full of mischief at break time.*

Write the sentences

a) *What is Big Blob saying?*

☆ Show the image of Big Blob and Baby Blob on **CD** (file 3.2). See p.7 of the *Get Writing!* Book for this activity.

☆ Act out being in role as Big Blob. Model being exasperated by Baby Blob. Tell Baby Blob off: *Baby Blob! Stop! I am so cross, I will go pop!*

☆ Now tell the children that they are Big Blob and to TTYP to think about what they can say to Baby Blob to tell him off! Ask the children to Popcorn ideas, e.g. *You are a pest. This is not fun. I am cross.*

☆ Practise saying the sentences with each word/phrase, e.g. *Stop. You are a pest. Stop. This is not fun. Stop. I am cross.*

☆ Model writing the sentences with one of the choices, e.g. *Stop. You are a pest.* using Set 1 and 2 sounds. Remember to model rereading for sense, and checking word spaces and punctuation. Show how to copy *you* and *are* from the Red Word cards. Rub out/cover up *You are a pest* and repeat the process with the other choices.

☆ Rub out/cover up your writing and tell the children to write some sentences in the speech bubbles in their *Get Writing!* Book, using either their own ideas or yours, if they need the support.

b) *What does Baby Blob grab?*

☆ Click on the next screen (Baby Blob in pushchair, grabbing things). This activity is also on p.7 of the *Get Writing!* Book.

☆ Ask the children to TTYP to remember what antics Baby Blob got up to. Popcorn feedback, e.g. *grabs a big bun, grabs a bag of chips, grabs a red hat.*

☆ Practise saying the sentence with one of the choices, e.g. *Baby Blob grabs a red hat.*

☆ Model writing the sentence with one of the choices using Set 1 and 2 sounds. Rub out/cover up the words *a red hat* and repeat the process with the other choices.

☆ Rub out/cover up your writing and tell the children to write some sentences around the picture of Baby Blob in their *Get Writing!* Book.

Purple Storybook 4   *Tim and Tom*

Introducing the story

plunge   leap   rush   dart   dash

☆ Use these 'power words' when introducing the story during reading Activity 3. Write them on sticky notes so you remember to use them through the lesson/day.

*See Blueprint lesson plans for **Activity 5 Hold a sentence** and **Activity 7 Edit** on pp.25–26.*

Activity 8 Composition: picture prompts

Power words

☆ TOL to relate back to the story: *The twins Tim and Tom went with their dad to the beach. They loved to **leap** and splash in the sea and run and **dash** about on the sand!*

☆ Use MT/YT to repeat the 'power words'. *First Tim and Tom went for a swim. They liked to dive/**plunge**/**leap** into the sea. What else might they do in the waves?* Take children's ideas once you have offered yours.

Say the sentences

☆ TOL as you build up the sentences together, orally, about how the boys played on the beach.

☆ Use MT/YT each time you expand on the sentence stem until they can all say it after you. ***At first Tom and Tim*** *liked to dive into the sea.* ***At first Tom and Tim*** *liked to dive and plunge into the sea.* ***At first Tom and Tim*** *liked to splash, dive and plunge into the sea.*

☆ Repeat the process describing what the boys did next. Ask the children to help you remember some of the 'power words'. ***Next they began*** *to rush and run on the sand.* ***Next they began to*** *rush and dash around.* ***Next they began to*** *dart and flash like fish in the sea.*

☆ Use the 'power words' and stems from the sentences you have built in this activity throughout the session and day, e.g. to show the order action: ***At first I dived*** *into the pool.* ***Next I plunged*** *under the water.*

Write the sentences

a) *What are Tim and Tom saying about the beach?*

☆ Show the image of Tim and Tom on the beach on **CD** (file 4.2). See p.9 in the *Get Writing!* Book for this activity.

☆ Act out being Tim or Tom and enthusiastically talk about what a great outing you have had. *I love it at the beach. I can run and swim. I can dash and splash. It is such fun!*

☆ Tell the children that they are Tim and Tom and to TTYP to think of words to describe how they play when they are at the beach. Ask the children to Popcorn ideas, e.g. *swim, run, dash, rush, splash.*

☆ Say that you want to put two ideas together and link them with the word 'and'. Practise saying the sentence with each word/phrase, e.g. *I can run and swim. I can splash and dash.*

☆ Model writing the sentence with one of the choices, e.g. *I can run and swim.* using Set 1 and 2 sounds. Remember to model rereading for sense, and checking word spaces and punctuation. Rub out/cover up the words *run and swim* and repeat the process with the other choices/the next screen (Tim and Tom running on the beach).

☆ Rub out/cover up your writing and tell the children to write some sentences in the speech bubbles in their *Get Writing!* Book, using either their own ideas or yours, if they need the support.

b) *What is on the stall?*

☆ Show the image of the beach stall on **CD** (file 4.3). See p.10 of the *Get Writing!* Book for this activity.

☆ As you drag and drop each item onto the stall (sticks of rock, nets, flags, caps, windmills, duck rings, arm bands), get the children to TTYP and think of words to describe the items for sale. Popcorn feedback, e.g. *a red cap, jolly flags.*

☆ Practise saying the phrases with the words, e.g. *a red cap/rock pool nets.*

☆ Model writing one of the captions using Set 1 and 2 sounds. Rub out/cover up the caption and repeat the process with the other choices.

☆ Rub out/cover up your writing and tell the children to write captions for the beach stall in their *Get Writing!* Book.

Purple Storybook 5   *Tag*

Introducing the story

blasted off   zoomed off   horrified   shook like a leaf

✿ Use these 'power words' when introducing the story during reading Activity 3. Write them on sticky notes so you remember to use them through the lesson/day.

*See Blueprint lesson plans for **Activity 5 Hold a sentence** and **Activity 7 Edit** on pp.25–26.*

Activity 8 Composition: picture prompts

Power words

✿ TOL to relate back to the story: *Pip, Zip and Tip played Tag but Tip chose a rocket to hide in and the rocket **blasted off** into space!*

✿ Remind the children of how the rocket blasted off and how Tip felt. Use MT/YT to extend the language. *The rocket **blasted off** into space and Tip was **horrified**. The rocket **zoomed off** into space with Tip stuck inside. The rocket shot off into space and Tip **shook like a leaf**.*

Say the sentences

✿ TOL as you build up the sentences together, orally, about how Tip felt when he realised he was stuck in a rocket as it blasted off into space.

✿ Use MT/YT each time you expand on the sentence stem until they can all say it after you. **When the rocket blasted off** *Tip was shocked.* **When the rocket blasted off** *Tip's shocked face stared out the window.* **When the rocket blasted off** *Tip's whole body shook like a leaf!*

✿ Repeat the process describing the rocket blasting off. Ask the children to help you remember some of the 'power words'. **The rocket** *blasted off with terrific speed.* **The rocket** *zoomed off with terrific speed.* **The rocket** *exploded up into space with terrific speed.*

✿ Use the 'power words' and stems from the sentences you have built in this activity throughout the session and day, e.g. to describe fast movements and shocked reactions. *I know it is silly but when I saw the spider **I shook like a leaf**! Tim **exploded** like a rocket when they jumped out on him from their hiding places!*

Write the sentences

a) *What is Tip feeling and saying?*

✿ Show the image of Tip in the rocket on **CD** (file 5.2). See p.12 in the *Get Writing!* Book for this activity.

✿ Act out being in role as Tip as he talks aloud. *The rocket ship is moving and juddering! What are these terrible sounds? Arrggh! This is awful! This is terrible!*

✿ Tell the children that they are Tip and to TTYP to describe how they feel or what they will do as the rocket blasts off. Ask the children to Popcorn ideas, e.g. *sad, scared, afraid/cry, yell, shout for help.*

✿ Practise saying the feeling sentence with each word/phrase, e.g. *Oh no. I am scared.*

✿ Model writing the sentences with one of the choices, e.g. *Oh no. I am scared.* using Set 1 and 2 sounds. Remember to model rereading for sense, and checking word spaces and punctuation. Show how to copy *I* and *no* from the Red Word cards. Rub out/cover up the word *sad* and repeat the process with the other choices.

✿ Rub out/cover up your writing and tell the children to write some sentences in the feeling bubble in their *Get Writing!* Book, using either their own ideas or yours, if they need the support.

✿ Repeat the process for the happening sentence.

b) *What noises does the rocket make?*

☆ Ask the children to TTYP to remember how the rocket took off with Tip inside it. Act out being one of Tip's friends describing the rocket shooting off. *The rocket went whoosh! It roared and went bang! It was a tremendous din!*

☆ Show the image of the rocket blasting off on **CD** (file 5.3). See p.12 of the *Get Writing!* Book for this activity.

☆ Ask the children to TTYP and discuss what noises the rocket blasting off might make. Choose children to feed back. Tell them you want to write down the noises of the rocket. Give suggestions: *grrrr, whir, whoosh, bang, brrr, zip, zam, bim, bam.* Ask the children to TTYP and make up words to describe the rocket.

☆ Model writing the noises using Set 1 and 2 sounds.

☆ Rub out/cover up your writing and tell the children to write the sounds around the rocket in their *Get Writing!* Book.

Purple Storybook 6   *Elvis*

Introducing the story

repair   patch up   speedy   nimble

☆ Use these 'power words' when introducing the story during reading Activity 3. Write them on sticky notes so you remember to use them through the lesson/day.

*See Blueprint lesson plans for **Activity 5 Hold a sentence** and **Activity 7 Edit** on pp.25–26.*

Activity 8 Composition: picture prompts

Power words

☆ TOL to relate back to the story: *Elvis the elf is so helpful and likes to sing as he **repairs** things. He really is wonderfully **speedy!***

☆ Use MT/YT to repeat the 'power words'. *Elvis can fix a witch's wand/**repair** an imp's hat/**patch up** a doll's dress. Elvis is **nimble** and **speedy** when he **repairs** things.*

Say the sentences

☆ TOL as you build up the sentences together, orally, about how Elvis can mend anything.

☆ Use MT/YT each time you expand on the sentence stem until they can all say it after you. ***Elvis is** quick and nimble. **Elvis is** quick and nimble as he mends. **Elvis is** quick and nimble as he mends and fixes.*

☆ Repeat with other sentence stems, e.g. ***Watch him** fix a witch's wand. **Watch him** repair an imp's hat. **Watch him** patch up a doll's dress.*

☆ Use the 'power words' and stems from the sentences you have built in this activity throughout the session and day, e.g. *What **nimble** fingers you have when you thread the beads. Shall we **repair** this?*

Write the sentences

Write about what Elvis the elf can do.

☆ Show the image of the blank advert on **CD** (file 6.2). See p.14 of the *Get Writing!* Book for this activity.

☆ Read the title *Elvis the elf.* Act out being in role as Elvis and ask the children to help you write an advert for your mending service. *I need to tell people all the things I can do and say that I'm really quick and helpful. Can you help me?* Ask the children to TTYP to think of what Elvis can do. Ask the children to Popcorn ideas, e.g. *fix an imp's red hat, mend a witch's wand, patch up a big sock.*

☆ Practise saying the sentence with each word/phrase, e.g. *He can mend a doll's pink dress.*

☆ Model writing the sentence with one of the choices, e.g. *He can mend a doll's pink dress.* using Set 1 and 2 sounds. Remember to model rereading for sense, and checking word spaces and punctuation. Show how to copy *he* from the Red Word card. Rub out/cover up the words *mend a doll's pink dress* and repeat the process with the other choices.

☆ Rub out/cover up your writing and tell the children to write some sentences in the advert in their *Get Writing!* Book, using either their own ideas or yours, if they need the support.

☆ Children can work together to add other words/phrases to the advert e.g. *Elvis is quick. He can help.* Continue until you are happy with the advert.

Purple Storybook 7   *Flip Frog and the bug*

Introducing the story

> juicy   delicious   mouth-watering   crunchy   gobble

☆ Use these 'power words' when introducing the story during reading Activity 3. Write them on sticky notes so you remember to use them through the lesson/day.

*See Blueprint lesson plans for **Activity 5 Hold a sentence** and **Activity 7 Edit** on pp.25–26.*

Activity 8 Composition: picture prompts

Power words

☆ Use MT/YT to repeat the 'power words'. *Flip thought the bug looked **delicious/juicy/mouth-watering**. He wanted to **gobble** it up!*

☆ Use MT/YT to extend the language. *Flip watched as his **mouth-watering** meal buzzed off. Flip danced with excitement at the thought of munching the **delicious, crunchy** bug. Flip was sure he would **gobble** up the **juicy** bug he was chasing.*

Say the sentences

☆ TOL as you build up the sentences together, orally, about Flip and the bug.

☆ Use MT/YT each time you expand on the sentence stem until they can all say it after you. ***Can you see the*** *juicy bug?* ***Can you see the*** *juicy bug as it buzzes about?* ***Can you see the*** *mouth-watering bug as it buzzes about?*

☆ Repeat with other sentence stems, e.g. ***Flip could not wait to*** *crunch up the delicious bug.* ***Flip could not wait to*** *gobble up the delicious bug.*

☆ Use the 'power words' and stems from the sentences you have built in this activity throughout the session and day, e.g. *I cannot wait to eat my **crunchy, delicious** apple. Your drink looks cool and **mouth-watering**.*

Write the sentences

a) *What is Flip Frog saying?*

☆ Show the image of Flip on **CD** (file 7.2). See p.16 of the *Get Writing!* Book for this activity.

☆ Act out being in role as Flip. Model rubbing your tummy and saying *I will leap at that delicious bug and munch it up.*

☆ Tell the children that they are Flip and to TTYP to describe how they will eat up the bug. Ask the children to Popcorn ideas, e.g. *gobble, crunch, munch.*

☆ Practise saying the sentence with each word/phrase, e.g. *I will get the big hairy bug and munch it up! I will get the green bug and crunch it up!*

☆ Model writing the sentence with one of the choices, e.g. *I will get the big hairy bug and munch it up.* using Set 1 and 2 sounds. Remember to model rereading for sense, and checking word spaces and punctuation. Show how to copy *I* and *the* from the Red Word cards. Rub out/cover up the words *big hairy bug* and *munch it up* and repeat the process with the other choices.

☆ Rub out/cover up your writing and tell the children to write some sentences in the speech bubbles in their *Get Writing!* Books, using either their own ideas or yours, if they need the support.

b) *Tell the bug how to get away from Flip Frog.*

☆ Show the image of the bug and listen to it buzz about on **CD** (file 7.3). This activity is also on p.16 of the *Get Writing!* Book.

☆ Ask the children to TTYP to remember how the bug escaped from Flip. Ask the children to act being the bug as it buzzes to the twig/rock/log and past the mud. Ask the children to TTYP to remember all the places the bug hid. Popcorn feedback, e.g. *twig, log, rock, mud.*

☆ Say you are going to give advice to the bug so it can escape from Flip. Practise saying the sentences with the words, e.g. *Quick. Buzz to the log.*

☆ Model writing the sentences with one of the words using Set 1 and 2 sounds. Rub out/cover up the words *to the log* and repeat the process with the other choices.

☆ Rub out/cover up your writing and tell the children to write some sentences next to the picture of the bug in their *Get Writing!* Books.

Purple Storybook 8   *Red Ken*

Introducing the story

sticky   slimy   slippery   leaps   soars

☆ Use these 'power words' when introducing the story during reading Activity 3. Write them on sticky notes so you remember to use them through the lesson/day.

*See Blueprint lesson plans for **Activity 5 Hold a sentence** and **Activity 7 Edit** on pp.25–26.*

Activity 8 Composition: picture prompts

Power words

☆ TOL to relate back to the story: *Poor Ken! When Dan came back with the sand he tipped the sand down and it landed on the plank where the paint was. The paint **soared** through the air and – splat – landed on Ken's head.*

☆ Use MT/YT to repeat the 'power words'. *The paint **soars** through the air onto Ken's head! The paint **leaps** up and onto Ken's head!*

☆ Ask the children to think what Ken might feel running down his head. TOL: *He might feel **sticky**/ **slimy**/cold wet paint dripping down.*

☆ Use MT/YT to extend the language. *Poor Ken. **Sticky, slippery** paint dripped down his neck. Poor Ken. Cold, **slimy** paint dripped down his neck.*

Say the sentences

☆ TOL as you build up the sentences together, orally, about Ken.

☆ Use MT/YT each time you expand on the sentence stem until they can all say it after you.

- ✩ Use questions to add detail to a simple stem, e.g. *How did the paint move through the air?* **The paint** *soared through the air.* How did it land? **The paint** *landed with a splat!* **The paint** *landed with a huge splosh!* **The paint** *landed on Ken's head and flopped on his face!*
- ✩ Use the 'power words' and stems from the sentences you have built in this activity throughout the session and day, e.g. *That glue is* **sticky** *and* **slimy.** *That bird* **soared** *overhead.*

Write the sentences

a) What is Ken saying?

- ✩ Show the image of Ken covered in paint on **CD** (file 8.2). See p.18 of the *Get Writing!* Book for this activity.
- ✩ Act out being in role as Ken. Model being Ken covered in dripping paint. *Yuk! This sticky, wet paint landed – splat – on my head.*
- ✩ Tell the children that they are Ken and they have the paint dripping down their necks. Ask them to TTYP to describe what it feels like. Ask the children to Popcorn ideas, e.g. *wet, sticky, cold, yucky.*
- ✩ Practise saying the sentence with feeling, e.g. *The cold paint drips down my neck. The wet paint drips down my neck. The sticky paint drips down my neck.*
- ✩ Model writing the sentence with one of the choices, e.g. *The wet paint drips down my neck.* using Set 1 and 2 sounds. Remember to model rereading for sense, and checking word spaces and punctuation. Show how to copy *the* from the Red Word cards. Rub out/cover up the word *wet* and repeat the process with the other choices.
- ✩ Rub out/cover up your writing and tell the children to write some sentences in the speech bubbles in their *Get Writing!* Book, using either their own ideas or yours, if they need the support.

b) What happened to the paint?

- ✩ Click on the next screen (Ken being covered in paint). See p.19 of the *Get Writing!* Book for this activity.
- ✩ Ask the children to TTYP to remember how the paint flew through the air and landed on Ken. *What noise might it have made as it landed?*
- ✩ Ask the children to TTYP and discuss the noise of the paint as it landed on poor old Ken. Popcorn feedback, e.g. *splat, crash, splosh, flop.*
- ✩ Practise saying the sentence with the words, e.g. *The paint went up and then splosh/flop/splat/crash, it hit Ken.*
- ✩ Model writing the sentence with one of the words using Set 1 and 2 sounds. Rub out/cover up the word *splosh* and repeat the process with the other choices.
- ✩ Rub out/cover up your writing and tell the children to write some sentences below the picture of Ken in their *Get Writing!* Book.

Purple Storybook 9 *Billy the Kid*

Introducing the story

grumpy crouch squat

- ✩ Use these 'power words' when introducing the story during reading Activity 3. Write them on sticky notes so you remember to use them through the lesson/day.

See Blueprint lesson plans for **Activity 5 Hold a sentence** *and* **Activity 7 Edit** *on pp.25–26.*

Activity 8 Composition: picture prompts

Power words

☆ TOL to relate back to the story: *The troll sat all day waiting to be mean to people who crossed his bridge. He was in a very bad mood!*

☆ Use MT/YT to repeat the 'power words'. *As the troll sat there all day he felt cross/**grumpy**.*

☆ Say: *You are all the troll. Show me how you squat. Show me how you **crouch**. Show me how you guard the bridge, looking mean and nasty!*

Say the sentences

☆ TOL as you build up sentences together, orally, about the troll.

☆ Use MT/YT each time you expand on the sentence stem until they can all say it after you. **The troll was** *sitting on the bridge.*
Ask: *How was he sitting?* TTYP and feed back. Say the new sentence using a couple of the children's ideas. **The troll was** *crouching on the bridge.*
Ask: *What did he look like?* TTYP and feed back. Say the new sentence using a couple of the children's ideas. **The** *green, warty* **troll was** *crouching on the bridge.*
Ask: *How was he feeling?* TTYP and feed back. Say the new sentence using a couple of the children's ideas. **The** *green, warty, angry* **troll was** *crouching on the bridge.*

☆ Use the 'power words' and stems from the sentences you have built in this activity throughout the day. *I felt really **grumpy** this morning when I realised we had run out of biscuits.*

Write the sentences

a) What is Billy the Kid thinking?

☆ Show the image of the troll and Billy the Kid on **CD** (file 9.2). See p.21 of the *Get Writing!* Book for this activity.

☆ Ask the children to act out being Billy the Kid thinking about the hideous troll guarding the bridge. Ask them to TTYP and describe the troll, then Popcorn feedback, e.g. *It is a cross, smelly troll. It is a glum, fat troll.*

☆ Model writing the sentence with one of the words, e.g. *grumpy* using Set 1 and 2 sounds. Remember to model rereading for sense, and checking word spaces and punctuation. Rub out/ cover up *glum* and repeat the process with the other choices.

☆ Rub out/cover up your writing and tell the children to write some sentences into the thought bubbles in their *Get Writing!* Book, using either their own ideas or yours, if they need the support.

b) How does the troll feel?

☆ Click on the next screen (troll sitting on his bridge). This activity is also on p.21 of the *Get Writing!* Book.

☆ Act out being the cross troll. Say in a cross voice: *I sit here all day. No one asks me politely if they can cross my bridge. It makes me feel angry and mean – grrrrr!* In role, ask the children: *Do you have any idea how I'm feeling?* Ask children to TTYP and then Popcorn their ideas, e.g. *angry, fed up.*

☆ Say: *Yes! That is exactly how I'm feeling. I am fed up/grumpy/cross/glum.*

☆ Practise saying the sentences. *I am fed up. I am…*

☆ Model writing the sentence with one of the words, e.g. *cross* using Set 1 and 2 sounds. Rub out/ cover up *cross* and repeat the process with the other choices.

☆ Rub out/cover up your writing and tell the children to write some sentences into the speech bubbles in their *Get Writing!* Book.

Introducing the story

in a rage   exasperated   splatter

☆ Use these 'power words' when introducing the story during reading Activity 3. Write them on sticky notes so you remember to use them through the lesson/day.

*See Blueprint lesson plans for **Activity 5 Hold a sentence** and **Activity 7 Edit** on pp.25 – 26.*

Activity 8 Composition: picture prompts

Power words

☆ TOL to relate back to the story: *Mum was **exasperated** that Ben did not listen to her! At last he got in the bath but put Mum **in a rage** when she saw the mess he made!*

☆ Use MT/YT to repeat these 'power words'. *She was **exasperated**/**in a rage**. Ben made the water go splash, splish, splosh, and **splatter**.*

Say the sentences

☆ TOL as you build up the sentences together, orally, about Ben in the bath.

☆ Use MT/YT each time you expand on the sentence stem until they can all say it after you. ***Mum was** in a rage. **Mum was** red with rage. **Mum was** red with rage because Ben did not listen.*

☆ Ask: *What noises does the water in the bath make?* TTYP and Popcorn feedback, adding more ideas of your own, e.g. *plip, plop, patter, splat, splash, splish, splosh, drip, drop, splatter.*

☆ Say: *Let me try saying it.* MT/YT: ***Listen, I can hear the water** drip, drop. **Listen, I can hear the water** splish, splash, splosh. **Listen, I can hear the water** patter, splatter, splosh.*

☆ Relate back to the story and ask: *What shall we put in the bath?* ***Pop a** duck in the bath. **Pop a** big jug in the bath. **Pop a** red ship in the bath.*

☆ Use the 'power words' and stems from the sentences you have built in this activity throughout the session and day, e.g. ***Listen, I can hear** the children splashing in the water. When I found the broken toy I was **in a rage**!*

Write the sentences

a) *What will Ben put in the bath?*

☆ Show the image of Ben in the bath on **CD** (file 10.2). See p.23 in the *Get Writing!* Book for this activity. Listen to the water noises audio.

☆ Act out being Ben. Say (in a cheeky voice): *Splish, splash, splosh! What shall we put in the bath today? Hmmm…* Ask children, still as Ben, to TTYP for suggestions. Choose children to feed back, e.g. *a red play ship that toots, Danny the Duck, a big spotty jug.*

☆ Click on the next screen and drag and drop different objects into the bath describing them as you do so. *Jug, ship that toots, duck, squirty toy.* You may want to use some of the examples that the children offered earlier as well.

☆ Practise saying the sentences, e.g. *Put in a big red ship. Put in a…*

☆ Show the image of the bath on **CD** (file 10.3). Model writing the sentence with one of the suggestions e.g. *big red ship* using Set 1 and 2 sounds. Remember to model rereading for sense, and checking word spaces and punctuation. Show how you copy *put* and *the* from the Red Word cards.

☆ Rub out/cover up the words *big red ship* and repeat the process with the other choices.

☆ Rub out/cover up your writing and tell the children to write some sentences in the bath in their *Get Writing!* Book, using either their own ideas or yours, if they need the support.

b) *Write a splashy poem.*

☆ Show the image of Ben in the bath on **CD** (file 10.4). See p.24 in their *Get Writing!* Book for this activity. Listen to the splashy audio.

☆ Ask children to TTYP to remember the noises that they can hear as Ben plays in the bath. Choose children to feed back, e.g. *plip, plop, patter, splat, splash, splish, splosh, drip, drop, splatter.*

☆ Tell the children that they are going to write a watery poem. Use MT/YT to make the noises. Exaggerate the *sssplat, ssplash, ssplosh*, etc. Ask the children which words they think go together well to make a rhythm or a splashy water sound.

☆ Click on the next screen and show the watery poem writing frame. Model writing each word using Set 1 and 2 sounds.

☆ Rub out/cover up your writing and tell the children to write words into the water drops in their *Get Writing!* Books.

Purple Non-fiction Book 1   *Hens*

Introducing the book

> *without stopping   ceaselessly   search   hunt*

☆ Use these 'power words' when introducing the book during reading Activity 3. Write them on sticky notes so you remember to use them through the lesson/day.

*See Blueprint lesson plans for **Activity 5 Hold a sentence** and **Activity 7 Edit** on pp.25 – 26.*

Activity 8 Composition: picture prompts

Power words

☆ TOL to relate back to the book: *What were the hens **searching** for? They were **hunting** for insects and slugs.*

☆ Use MT/YT to repeat the 'power words'. *They **search** for insects. They peck and **hunt** for bugs.*

☆ Use MT/YT to extend the language. *The hens **search** for insects **ceaselessly** in the shady pen. The hens peck and **hunt** in the straw-covered ground.*

Say the sentences

☆ TOL as you build up the sentences together, orally, about the hens.

☆ Use MT/YT every time you expand the sentence together. Do not make it look too easy as you think of what to say. Encourage the children to help you so they take ownership of the sentence.

☆ Once you have decided upon the final sentence, use actions and facial expressions to help the children remember the sentence. Use MT/YT each time you expand on the sentence stem until they can all say it after you.

☆ Expand a simple sentence by asking questions. Use MT/YT each time you expand the sentence: ***The hens** look for slugs.* Ask: *How are they looking for the slugs?* TTYP and feed back.

☆ Say the new sentence using a couple of the children's ideas: ***The hens** scratch and search for slugs.* Ask: *How do they move? Let's describe that in more detail.* TTYP and feed back. Say the new sentence using a couple of the children's ideas, e.g. ***The hens** scratch and search for slugs without stopping.*

☆ Repeat with other activities the hens might do, e.g. ***The hens** run in the pen. (How?) **The hens** dart about in the pen. (What was the pen like?) **The hens** dart about in the shady pen.*

☆ Use the 'power words' and stems from the sentences you have built in this activity throughout the session and day, e.g. *Let's **hunt** for the 'ck' sound in this word.*

Write the sentences

Write about hens.

☆ Show the images of the hens on **CD** (file NF1.2). See p.26 of the *Get Writing!* Book for this activity.

☆ Say that you are going to write an information page about keeping hens. Ask the children to TTYP to remember what hens can do. Ask the children to Popcorn ideas, e.g. *scratch for slugs, peck at bugs, run in the pen, nest in the shed, sit on eggs.*

☆ Practise saying the sentence with each phrase, e.g. *Hens can scratch for slugs/peck at bugs/run in the pen/nest in the shed/sit on eggs.*

☆ Model writing the sentence with one of the choices, e.g. *Hens can scratch for slugs.* TOL and ask children to help as you sound out each word using Set 1 and 2 sounds. Model how you re-read the sentence after writing each word to check it makes sense, leave spaces between words, and how you start with a capital letter and finish with a full stop. Rub out/cover up the words *scratch for slugs* and repeat the process with the other choices.

☆ Rub out/cover up your writing and tell the children to write some sentences in the information sheet in their *Get Writing!* Book, using either their own ideas or yours, if they need the support.

Purple Non-fiction Book 5   *Puppets*

Introducing the book

fasten   join   brilliant

☆ Use these 'power words' when introducing the book during reading Activity 3. Write them on sticky notes so you remember to use them through the lesson/day.

*See Blueprint lesson plans for **Activity 5 Hold a sentence** and **Activity 7 Edit** on pp.25–26.*

Activity 8 Composition: picture prompts

Power words

☆ TOL to relate back to the story: *In the book it shows you what you need to make a hand puppet. I think you would stick on the felt and fasten the buttons to make a funny puppet snake.*

☆ Use MT/YT to repeat the 'power words'. *You need to glue on the felt and **join** the eyes to the sock. It is a **brilliant** snake puppet.*

Say the sentences

☆ TOL as you build up the sentences together, orally, about how you make a puppet.

☆ Use MT/YT each time you expand on the sentence stem until they can all say it after you. *Fasten on the felt **to make the snake's tongue.** Glue on the felt **to make the snake's tongue.** Paste on the felt **to make the snake's tongue.***

☆ Repeat with other sentence stems, e.g. **Make a** *fabulous string puppet.* **Make a** *brilliant dancing girl puppet.*

☆ Use the 'power words' and stems from the sentences you have built in this activity throughout the session and day, e.g. using verbs in the imperative form. *Stick on the picture. Glue down the edges. **Fasten** up your buttons.* Remind the children that these verbs tell them *exactly* what to do.

Write the sentences

a) *Write the labels for the things you need for the puppet.*

☆ Show the image of the string, felt, ball and a made puppet in a dress on **CD** (file NF5.2). See p.28 of the *Get Writing!* Book for this activity.

- ☆ Explain that the children are going to write the captions for the pictures.
- ☆ Ask the children to TTYP to describe what they can see. Popcorn feedback, e.g. *string, felt, small puppet.*
- ☆ Ask the children to TTYP to decide what they would write for each caption.
- ☆ Practise saying the caption with the words, e.g. *felt for the dress.*
- ☆ Model writing the sentence with one choice of words using Set 1 and 2 sounds. Remember to model rereading for sense, and checking word spaces and punctuation. Show how to copy *for* and *the* from the Red Word cards.
- ☆ Rub out/cover up your writing and tell the children to write captions for each picture of the puppet and its parts in their *Get Writing!* Book, using either their own ideas or yours, if they need the support.

b) *Write about how to make a puppet.*
- ☆ Click on the next screen (images showing the steps for making a puppet). See p.29 of the *Get Writing!* Book for this activity.
- ☆ Say that you are going to write instructions for making a string puppet together. Act out making a puppet. *First I put on the head. Then I put on the arms. Then I put on the legs. Next I put on the string. Last I do up the string.*
- ☆ Ask the children to TTYP to tell their partner how to make a string puppet. Ask the children to Popcorn ideas, e.g. *put on the head, stick on the arms and legs, push the string, do up the string.*
- ☆ Practise saying the sentences with the connectives *first, then, next, last* to order each phrase, e.g. *First put on the head. Then stick on the arms. Next stick on the legs. Then push the string. Last do up the string.*
- ☆ Tell the children that instructions do not have the word *I* or *you* in them because the verbs/doing words tell the reader what to do.
- ☆ Model writing the sentence with one of the choices, e.g. *First put on the head.* using Set 1 and 2 sounds. Show how to copy *put* and *the* from the Red Word cards. Rub out/cover up the words *First put on the head.* Repeat the process with the other choices.
- ☆ Rub out/cover up your writing and tell the children to write some sentences in the instruction sheet in their *Get Writing!* Book.

Get Writing! lesson plans: Pink Storybooks

Pink Storybook 1   *Scruffy Ted*

Introducing the story

| tatty   grubby   heaps of   plenty |

☆ Use these 'power words' when introducing the story during reading Activity 3. Write them on sticky notes so you remember to use them through the lesson/day.

*See Blueprint lesson plans for **Activity 5 Hold a sentence** and **Activity 7 Edit** on pp.25 – 26. (NB: Activities 1 – 4 Spelling, Activity 6 Build a sentence and Activity 9 Composition only appear in the Yellow, Blue and Grey books.)*

Activity 8 Composition: picture prompts

Power words

☆ TOL (Think out loud) to relate back to the story: *The little girl has **plenty** of toys in her bed, but she loves her Scruffy Ted best!*

☆ Use MT/YT (My turn/Your turn) to repeat the 'power words'. *She loves her **tatty** ted. She loves to snuggle her **tatty** ted!*

☆ Use MT/YT to extend the language. *She is fond of the others but she loves her **grubby** ted. She has a **heap of** toys but her **tatty** ted is best! She has countless other toys but her untidy, **tatty** ted is the best!*

Say the sentences

☆ TOL as you build up the sentences together, orally, about all the toys in the bed.

☆ Use MT/YT every time you expand the sentence together. Do not make it look too easy as you think of what to say. Encourage the children to help you so they take ownership of the sentence.

☆ Once you have decided upon the final sentence, use actions and facial expressions to help the children remember the sentence. Use MT/YT each time you expand on the sentence stem until they can all say it after you. ***I have plenty of toys but** my ted is best. **I have plenty of toys but** my tatty ted is the best. **I have plenty of toys but** my scruffy, tatty ted is better than the rest!*

☆ Repeat with other sentence stems, e.g. ***I like** my rag doll **but I** love Scruffy Ted. **I like** my puppy dog Spot **but I** love Scruffy Ted.*

☆ Make sure that every time you model a sentence orally you include 'power words', use MT/YT to expand the sentence and actions, facial expressions and repetition to help children remember it, as described above.

☆ Use the 'power words' and stems from the sentences you have built in this activity throughout the session and day, e.g. ***I like** your picture **but I** love your writing even more! I have **plenty** of books but I love The Hungry Caterpillar the most!*

Write the sentences

a) *Label Scruffy Ted.*

☆ Show the image of Scruffy Ted on **CD** (file 1.2). See p.3 of the *Get Writing!* Book for this activity.

☆ Say that you are going to describe the ted. TOL: *He is a scruff. He has long legs. He has a soft patch.*

☆ Ask the children to TTYP (Turn to your partner) to recall as many details about Ted as they can and tell them to their partner.

☆ Practise saying the sentence with each phrase, e.g. *He has long legs. He has a soft patch. He has…*

☆ Model writing the sentence with one of the choices, e.g. *He has long legs.* TOL and ask children to help as you sound out each word. Model how you re-read the sentence after writing each word to check it makes sense, leave spaces between words, and how you start with a capital letter and finish with a full stop. Ensure that you do this every time you model writing sentences with the children. Page references to this set of notes are given as a reminder. Rub out/cover up the words *long legs* and repeat the process with the other choices.

☆ Rub out/cover up your writing and tell the children to write some sentences around the picture of Ted in their *Get Writing!* Book, using either their own ideas or yours, if they need the support.

b) *Write about tucking the toys in the bed.*

☆ Show the image of the bed on **CD** (file 1.3). See p.4 of the *Get Writing!* Book for this activity.

☆ Drag a toy into the bed and ask the children to TTYP to describe what they can see. Popcorn feedback, e.g. *a happy rag doll.*

☆ Drag the toys (*Jack-in-the-box, fluffy cat, puppy dog Spot*) in one by one and ask the children to TTYP to describe what they can see.

☆ Practise saying the sentence with the words, e.g. *Tuck in a happy rag doll. Tuck in puppy dog Spot. Tuck in a fluffy cat. Tuck in Jack-in-the-box.*

☆ Display **CD** (file 1.4). Model writing the sentence with one of the choices. TOL and ask children to help as you sound out each word and then write it. Use current phonic knowledge to write the words. Model how you re-read the sentence after writing each word to check it makes sense. Rub out/cover up the sentence and repeat the process with the other choices.

☆ Rub out/cover up your writing and tell the children to write sentences in the bed in their *Get Writing!* Book.

Pink

Pink Storybook 2   *Tab the cat*

Introducing the story

nip   peck   alarming   interest

☆ Use these 'power words' when introducing the story during reading Activity 3. Write them on sticky notes so you remember to use them through the lesson/day.

*See Blueprint lesson plans for **Activity 5 Hold a sentence** and **Activity 7 Edit** on pp.25 – 26.*

Activity 8 Composition: picture prompts

Power words

☆ Use MT/YT to repeat the 'power words'. *The parrot could scratch, **peck** and **nip**. The stick insect didn't **interest** Meg. The rat was **alarming**!*

☆ Use the word *but* to contrast the cat with the other animals. Use MT/YT to extend the language. *The cat liked to curl up **but** the parrot liked to scratch and nip. The cat was fun but the stick insect didn't **interest** Meg. The cat was soft **but** Meg found the rat's sharp teeth **alarming**!*

Say the sentences

☆ TOL as you build up the sentences together, orally, about the cat and Meg.

☆ Use MT/YT each time you expand on the sentence stem until they can all say it after you: ***This cat wants** Meg.* Ask: *How do you know the cat wants Meg?* TTYP and feed back. Say the new sentence using a couple of the children's ideas. *We know **this cat wants** Meg because she purrs at her.*

☆ Use the 'power words' and stems from the sentences you have built in this activity throughout the day, e.g. *That's a very **interesting** story you have shared with us, thank you! Don't be **alarmed** by the thunder – the storm is far away.*

Write the sentences

a) *How did Meg feel when she got her cat?*

☆ Show the image of the Meg and her cat on **CD** (file 2.2). See p.6 of the *Get Writing!* Book for this activity.

☆ Ask the children to act in role as Meg and mime seeing and stroking the cat for the first time. *Meg's mum said, "This cat wants you." How do you think Meg felt when her mum said that?* Ask the children to Popcorn ideas, e.g. *happy, excited, lucky, good.*

☆ Practise saying the sentence with the words: *Meg felt happy/excited/felt lucky when she got her cat.*

☆ Model writing the sentence with one of the choices, e.g. *Meg felt happy when she got her cat.* using Set 1 and 2 sounds. Remember to model rereading for sense, and checking word spaces and punctuation. Show how to copy *she* and *her* from the Red Word cards. Rub out/cover up the words *was happy* and repeat the process with the other choices.

☆ Rub out/cover up your writing and tell the children to write some sentences under the picture of the cat in their *Get Writing!* Book, using either their own ideas or yours, if they need the support.

b) *What can the bad parrot do?*

☆ Click on the next screen (bad parrot). See p.7 of the *Get Writing!* Book for this activity.

☆ Tell the children that this parrot is really grumpy and cross. *It does terrible things. It nips and pecks, it can scratch and shout, it can say bad words! It really is a terrible parrot!*

☆ Ask the children to TTYP to describe what else the terrible parrot can do. Popcorn feedback, e.g. *bite, hit, flap, snap at you.*

☆ Practise saying the sentence with the words, e.g. *A bad parrot can peck and nip you. A bad parrot can scratch and snap at you.*

☆ Model writing the sentence with one of the phrases, e.g. *A bad parrot can peck and nip you.* using Set 1 and 2 sounds. Show how to copy *you* from the Red Word cards.

☆ Rub out/cover up your writing and tell the children to write about the parrot in their *Get Writing!* Book.

Pink Storybook 3   *In the sun*

Introducing the story

> *blasts   bellows   crashes   twisty   salty*

☆ Use these 'power words' when introducing the story during reading Activity 3. Write them on sticky notes so you remember to use them through the lesson/day.

*See Blueprint lesson plans for **Activity 5 Hold a sentence** and **Activity 7 Edit** on pp.25–26.*

Activity 8 Composition: picture prompts

Power words

☆ TOL to relate back to the story: *What fun to spend a day by the seaside! My favourite place is the rock pools. You can find all sorts of creatures and interesting things in them.*

☆ Use MT/YT to repeat the 'power words'. Display **CD** (file 3.2) and drag each word into the focus box and TOL to explain its meaning, e.g. *bellow. When I have to shout loud I **bellow**. A **bellow** is a booming sort of sound. Sometimes the waves in the sea make a huge booming **bellow**.*

☆ Use MT/YT to extend the language. *I found **twisty, salty** shells on the beach. The pebbles look like bright, shiny stars in the rock pool. The wild sea **crashes** and bashes.*

Say the sentences

☆ TOL as you build up the description together, orally, about the beautiful objects and animals you can find in a rock pool.

☆ Use MT/YT each time you expand on the stem until they can all say it after you. **You can find** a red crab. **You can find** a bright red crab. **You can find** a bright red crab scuttling on the sand. **You can see** a shell. **You can see** a twisty shell. **You can see** a twisty shell with a sea snail hidden inside.

☆ Use the 'power words' and stems from the sentences you have built in this activity throughout the session and day, e.g. I can hear the children **bellowing** in the playground! What a strong **salty** smell – is it chips today?

Write the sentences

a) *What can you find in this rock pool?*

☆ Show the image of a rock pool on **CD** (file 3.3). See p.9 of the *Get Writing!* Book for this activity.

☆ TOL as you drag and drop different objects and animals into the rock pool. *A shiny red crab/salty smelly shells/a ship with a flag/a bright red star fish.*

☆ Practise saying each sentence, e.g. *I find a twisty, smelly shell. I find a shiny red crab,* etc.

☆ Display **CD** (file 3.4) and model writing the sentence with one of the choices, e.g. *I find a ship with a flag.* using Set 1 and 2 sounds. Remember to model rereading for sense, and checking word spaces and punctuation. Rub out/cover up the words *a ship with a flag* and repeat the process with the next choice.

☆ Rub out/cover up your writing and tell the children to write some sentences under the rock pool in their *Get Writing!* Book, using either their own ideas or yours, if they need the support.

b) *What noise does the sea make?*

☆ Show the image of the sea and listen to the audio of waves bashing and crashing on **CD** (file 3.5). See p.10 of the *Get Writing!* Book for this activity.

☆ Ask children to TTYP to describe the noises that they can hear. Choose children to feed back, e.g. *crash, whoosh, crunch, hiss, bellow.*

☆ Use MT/YT to make the noises. Exaggerate the sounds as you say them.

☆ Model writing each word using Set 1 and 2 sounds.

☆ Rub out/cover up your writing and tell the children to write words into the writing frame in their *Get Writing!* Books.

Pink Storybook 4   *The dressing up box*

Introducing the story

mysterious   exciting   disguise

☆ Use these 'power words' when introducing the story during reading Activity 3. Write them on sticky notes so you remember to use them through the lesson/day.

*See Blueprint lesson plans for **Activity 5 Hold a sentence** and **Activity 7 Edit** on pp.25 – 26.*

Activity 8 Composition: picture prompts

Power words

☆ TOL to relate back to the story: *It is such fun dressing up. It can really change how you look. You can imagine you are all sorts of characters when you dress up.*

☆ Use MT/YT to repeat the 'power words'. *Meg is **mysterious** in her hat and mask! Kim looks so **exciting** in her Batman top!*

☆ Use MT/YT to extend the language. *Kim is a **mysterious** superhero looking for **excitement**. Meg is a cool **mystery** girl in a disguise.*

Say the sentences

☆ TOL as you build up the sentences together, orally, about dressing up.

☆ Use MT/YT each time you expand on the sentence stem until they can all say it after you. ***It is me in my** black hat. **It is me in my** cool black hat. **It is me in my** cool mysterious black hat and mask.*
***I have** spotty socks on. **I have** long spotty socks on. **I have** long spotty silly socks on!*

☆ Use the 'power words' and stems from the sentences you have built in this activity throughout the session and day, e.g. *You look different. Are you in **disguise**?* Describe a character in the book you are reading in role, e.g. *It is me with my bushy tail and **mysterious** smile following Rosie the Hen!*

Write the sentences

a) *What do you put on?*

☆ Show the image of the child on **CD** (file 4.2). See p.12 of the *Get Writing!* Book for this activity.

☆ Drag different clothes onto the child. TOL as you do so, describing the clothes, e.g. *a pink wig, a cool mask, spotty socks, a black hat.*

☆ Ask the children to TTYP to think of other words to describe the dressing up clothes. Ask the children to Popcorn ideas, e.g. *big black top hat, long spotty socks.*

☆ Click on the next screen and show the connectives box. As you drag them into the focus box, practise saying sentences about dressing up using the connectives *first, then, next, last* to order each phrase, e.g. *First I put on a pink wig. Next I put on long spotty socks.*

☆ Model writing the sentence with one of the choices, e.g. *First I put on a pink wig.* using Set 1 and 2 sounds. Remember to model rereading for sense, and checking word spaces and punctuation. Show how to copy *I* and *put* from the Red Word cards. Rub out/cover up the words *a pink wig* and repeat the process with the other choices.

☆ Rub out/cover up your writing and tell the children to write some sentences in their *Get Writing!* Book, using either their own ideas or yours, if they need the support.

b) *How do you feel when you dress up?*

☆ Show the image of the dressing up box on **CD** (file 4.3). See p.13 of the *Get Writing!* Book for this activity.

☆ Ask the children to TTYP to say what they like to dress up as. Popcorn feedback, e.g. *princess, pirate, super heroes.*

☆ Ask the children to TTYP to describe what clothes they put on when they dress up as that character. Popcorn feedback and help the children use describing words to enrich their sentences, e.g. *long dress, black cape, cool red mask.*

☆ Get the children to TTYP to talk about how they feel when they are dressed up, e.g. *mysterious, funny, different, pretty, magic.*

☆ Practise saying the sentence with the words, e.g. *I feel magic/funny/pretty/cool/different when I dress up.* Model writing the sentence with one of the words, e.g. *I feel magic when I dress up.* using Set 1 and 2 sounds. Rub out/cover up *magic* and repeat the process with the other choices. The sentence could be extended to include a list of what the child dresses up in.

☆ Rub out/cover up your writing and tell the children to write next to the dressing up box in their *Get Writing!* Book. If they have time they can draw their outfit on the child (part c of the activity on p.13 of the *Get Writing!* Book).

Pink

Introducing the story

search   anxious   frantic   over the moon   overjoyed

☆ Use these 'power words' when introducing the story during reading Activity 3. Write them on sticky notes so you remember to use them through the lesson/day.

See Blueprint lesson plans for **Activity 5 Hold a sentence** *and* **Activity 7 Edit** *on pp.25–26.*

Activity 8 Composition: picture prompts

Power words

☆ Remind the children that when Tab woke up and saw her kitten was gone she was very worried. *She was **frantic** with worry.*

☆ Use MT/YT to repeat the 'power words'. *Tab went on a **frantic search**. Tab was full of worry as she searched. Tab began an **anxious** search.*

☆ Use MT/YT to extend the language. *Tab hunted **anxiously** for the kitten. Tab rushed **frantically** to find the kitten. She was **over the moon** when she found him! She was **overjoyed** when she found him!*

Say the sentences

☆ TOL as you build up the sentences together, orally, about the lost kitten.

☆ Ask the children if they have ever got lost. What did their parent/carer say when they found them? *Imagine you were Tab. Perhaps you might say…I am **not just upset**, I am **full of worry**. I am **not just upset**, I am **anxious and scared**. I am **not just upset**, I am **frantic with worry**. I am **not just pleased** to find you, I am **overjoyed**! I am **not just pleased** to find you, I am **over the moon**!*

☆ Use the 'power words' and stems from the sentences you have built in this activity throughout the session and day, e.g. *I am **not just busy**, I am **frantic** today. I am **not just pleased** with your reading progress, I am **overjoyed**!*

Write the sentences

a) *Tab has lost her kitten. What is she saying/thinking?*

☆ Show the image of the Tab on **CD** (file 5.2). See p.15 of the *Get Writing!* Book for this activity.

☆ Ask the children to act in role as Tab looking for her kitten. Give them verbal prompts to focus their role-play. For example, *Quick! Check! Perhaps he has got stuck. Rush to the kitchen. Perhaps the kitten has got lost in a cupboard.*

☆ Ask the children how they felt when they were searching for the kitten. Ask them to TTYP to describe how they felt and to Popcorn ideas, e.g. *upset, full of worry, frantic.*

☆ Practise saying the sentences with each phrase, e.g. *My kitten is lost. I am full of worry. My kitten is lost. I am frantic. My kitten is lost. I am upset.*

☆ Model writing the sentence with one of the choices, e.g. *My kitten is lost. I am upset.* using Set 1 and 2 sounds. Remember to model rereading for sense, and checking word spaces and punctuation. Show how to copy *my* and *I* from the Red Word cards. Rub out/cover up the word *upset* and repeat the process with the other choices.

☆ Rub out/cover up your writing and tell the children to write some sentences into the speech bubbles in their *Get Writing!* Book, using either their own ideas or yours, if they need the support.

Pink

b) *Tab has found her kitten. What is she saying/thinking now?*

☆ Click on the next screen (Tab looking at her kitten). See p.16 of the *Get Writing!* Book for this activity.

☆ Ask the children to TTYP to describe what they can see. Popcorn feedback, e.g. *the kitten having a nap/asleep/on top of Finn.*

☆ Say: *Tab must be so pleased to see her kitten.* Practise saying with enthusiasm the sentences with the words, e.g. *My kitten is on top of Finn. My kitten is asleep. My kitten is found!*

☆ Model writing the sentence with one of the choices, e.g. *My kitten is asleep.* using Set 1 and 2 sounds. Show how to copy *my* from the Red Word cards. Rub out/cover up *is asleep* and repeat the process with the other choices.

☆ Rub out/cover up your writing and tell the children to write in the speech bubbles in their *Get Writing!* Book.

Pink Storybook 6   *Sanjay stays in bed*

Introducing the story

grumble   sigh   mutter   dreary   bored stiff

☆ Use these 'power words' when introducing the story during reading Activity 3. Write them on sticky notes so you remember to use them through the lesson/day.

*See Blueprint lesson plans for **Activity 5 Hold a sentence** and **Activity 7 Edit** on pp.25–26.*

Activity 8 Composition: picture prompts

Power words

☆ TOL about how Sanjay felt in the story.

☆ Use MT/YT to repeat the 'power words'. *It was dull in bed. It was **dreary**.*

☆ Use MT/YT to extend the language. Drag out the synonyms for *moan* and *boring* so they sound really tedious. *Sanjay **grumbled**, "It is dull in bed!" Sanjay **muttered**, "It is **dreary** in bed!" Sanjay **sighed** wearily, "I am **bored stiff**!"*

Say the sentences

☆ TOL as you build up the sentences together, orally, about Sanjay.

☆ Use MT/YT each time you expand on the sentence stem until they can all say it after you.
***Sanjay sighed**, "I am bored." **Sanjay sighed** wearily, "I am bored." **Sanjay sighed** wearily, "I am bored stiff."*
***As he sat in bed** he muttered. **As he sat in bed** he muttered and grumbled. **As he sat in bed** he muttered and grumbled, "This is dull!"*

☆ Use the 'power words' and stems from the sentences you have built in this activity throughout the session and day, e.g. *The troll **grumbled** and **muttered** as he sat under the bridge.*

Write the sentences

a) *Write what Mum is saying to Sanjay and his reply. Use the power words.*

☆ Show the image of Sanjay trying to avoid having a bath, and saying "No way!" on **CD** (file 6.2). See p.18 of the *Get Writing!* books for this activity.

☆ Ask the children to TTYP and think of things they do not like doing. Popcorn their feedback e.g. *pack up the toys, turn off the light, wash your hair, have a bath.*

- ☆ Partner 1 is Mum and Partner 2 is the child. Partner 1 tells the child to do something. Partner 2 replies "No way!"
- ☆ Ask the children to TTYP to tell their partner *how* they replied to Mum. Did they *mutter/sigh/groan*? Ask the children to Popcorn their answers using intonation to show how they are feeling.
- ☆ Practise saying the dialogue, e.g. *Have a bath. "No way," mutters Sanjay.*
- ☆ Model writing the sentence with one of the choices, e.g. *Have a bath. "No way," mutters Sanjay.* using Set 1 and 2 sounds. Remember to model rereading for sense, and checking word spaces and punctuation. Show how to copy *no* from the Red Word cards. Repeat the process with the other choices/screens, e.g. *Wash your hair. "No way," shouts Sanjay. Pack up the toys. "No way," sighs Sanjay.*
- ☆ Rub out/cover up your writing and tell the children to write some sentences in the speech bubbles and Sanjay's reply in their *Get Writing!* Book, using either their own ideas or yours, if they need the support.

b) *What is Sanjay saying?*
- ☆ Show the image of Sanjay in bed on **CD** (file 6.3). See p.19 of the *Get Writing!* Books.
- ☆ Remind the children that Sanjay said he was ill and he was very bored because he could not do anything that is fun.
- ☆ Ask the children to TTYP to think of things Sanjay would like to do. Popcorn feedback, e.g. *play with his toys, watch TV, muck around.*
- ☆ Practise saying the sentences with the words, e.g. *I am in bed. I cannot watch TV. I am in bed. I cannot muck around. I am in bed. I cannot play with my toys.*
- ☆ Model writing the sentences with one of the words using Set 1 and 2 sounds, e.g. *I am in bed. I cannot play with my toys.* Show how to copy *I* and *my* from the Red Word cards. Rub out/cover up *play with my toys* and repeat the process with the other choices.
- ☆ Rub out/cover up your writing and tell the children to write sentences in their *Get Writing!* Book.

Pink Storybook 7 — *The greedy green gremlin*

Introducing the story

> *hoot with laughter   creep   full of mischief   sneaky*

- ☆ Use these 'power words' when introducing the story during reading Activity 3. Write them on sticky notes so you remember to use them through the lesson/day.

*See Blueprint lesson plans for **Activity 5 Hold a sentence** and **Activity 7 Edit** on pp.25–26.*

Activity 8 Composition: picture prompts

Power words

- ☆ TOL to relate back to the story: *Sam has a greedy green gremlin that lives in the sink. It **creeps** around. I do not like it at all.*
- ☆ Use MT/YT to repeat the 'power words'. *If I saw the gremlin I would **creep** away. I would jump up in shock if I found a gremlin in my sink! It would **hoot with laughter**.*

Say the sentences

- ☆ TOL as you build up the sentences together, orally, about the gremlin.
- ☆ Use MT/YT each time you expand on the sentence stem until they can all say it after you, e.g. ***The greedy green gremlin sat*** *by the sink.* Ask: *How was he feeling?* TTYP and feed back.

☆ Say the new sentence using a couple of the children's ideas, e.g. **The greedy green gremlin sat** *by the sink feeling full of mischief.*

☆ Ask: *Why was he feeling that way?* TTYP and feed back. Say the new sentence using a couple of the children's ideas, e.g. **The greedy green gremlin sat** *by the sink feeling full of mischief because he had a sneaky plan.*

☆ Use the 'power words' and stems from the sentences you have built in this activity throughout the day, e.g. *Let's* **creep** *into assembly so quietly we are like mice! I think the Princess in the story was really* **sneaky** *– she never meant to keep her promise.*

Write the sentences

a) Where is the gremlin?

☆ Show the image of the gremlin on **CD** (file 7.2). See p.21 of the *Get Writing!* Book.

☆ Ask: *Where is the gremlin?* Tell the children to TTYP to describe what they can see. Ask the children to Popcorn ideas, e.g. *next to the dirty taps.*

☆ Click on the next screens (gremlin in mug, gremlin in pan) and repeat the process (feedback could be e.g. *in a green cracked mug, in a crusty pan*).

☆ Go through the screens again and practise saying a sentence using each phrase, e.g. *I can see you next to the dirty taps. I can see you in a green cracked mug. I can see you in the crusty pan.*

☆ Model writing the sentence with one of the choices, e.g. *I can see you in a green cracked mug.* using Set 1 and 2 sounds. Remember to model rereading for sense, and checking word spaces and punctuation. Show how to copy *I* and *you* from the Red Word cards. Rub out/cover up the words *in a green cracked mug* and repeat the process with the other choices.

☆ Rub out/cover up your writing and tell the children to write some sentences in the speech bubbles in their *Get Writing!* Book, using either their own ideas or yours, if they need the support.

b) Write what you do when you see the gremlin.

☆ Click on the next screen to show the image of the gremlin behind the taps again. See p. 22 of the *Get Writing!* Book for this activity.

☆ Ask the children to mime being in the kitchen sorting out the dishes. Describe what is happening. Tell them to reach forward and… *Arrghhh! A green flash! A scurrying three-legged creature! A gremlin! Help! Help!*

☆ Ask the children to TTYP to describe what they do when they see the gremlin. Popcorn feedback, e.g. *It makes me jump. I shout out loud. I drop the mug. I creep away.*

☆ Practise saying a sentence that describes their reaction to seeing the gremlin with the words, e.g. *When I see the gremlin I shout out loud. When I see the gremlin I drop the mug. When I see the gremlin I jump up in shock.*

☆ Model writing the sentence with one of the choices, e.g. *When I see the gremlin I shout out loud.* using Set 1 and 2 sounds. Show how to copy *the* from the Red Word cards. Rub out/cover up *shout out loud* and repeat the process with the other choices.

☆ Rub out/cover up your writing and tell the children to write into the happening bubbles in their *Get Writing!* Book.

Introducing the story

> *shook with fright   cold with horror   clammy with fear   safe and sound   relieved*

✫ Use these 'power words' when introducing the story during reading Activity 3. Write them on sticky notes so you remember to use them through the lesson/day.

*See Blueprint lesson plans for **Activity 5 Hold a sentence** and **Activity 7 Edit** on pp.25 – 26.*

Activity 8 Composition: picture prompts

Power words

✫ TOL to relate back to the story: *The little boy in the story could hear all sorts of strange noises. They made him hide under the covers. He was relieved when his mum came in and turned on the light. I think he had let his imagination run wild!*

✫ Use MT/YT to repeat the 'power words'. *He was scared. He **shook with fright**. He went **cold with horror**. He felt **clammy with fear**.*

✫ Use MT/YT to extend the language. *But when his mum came in the room he was **relieved**. He was not scared now – he felt **safe and sound**.*

Say the sentences

✫ TOL as you build up the sentences together, orally, about the scary night.

✫ Use MT/YT each time you expand on the sentence stem until they can all say it after you. ***When Mum came in** I felt safe. **When Mum came in** I felt **safe and sound**. **When Mum came in** I felt **safe and sound** and beamed with delight!*

✫ Use the 'power words' and stems from the sentences you have built in this activity throughout the session and day, e.g. *I am not just worried about what happens next in the story, I am **clammy with fear**!*

Write the sentences

a) *The boy had a lot of frights. What did he say about the frights?*

✫ Show the image of the child in the bed on **CD** (file 8.2). See p.24 of the *Get Writing!* Book for this activity.

✫ Click 'Play' to activate the animation of the bats, rats and goblins. TOL as they move and describe them, e.g. *a creepy rat, a bat that flaps, a smelly goblin.*

✫ Ask the children to TTYP to think of other words to describe the creatures under the bed. Ask the children to Popcorn ideas, e.g. *snappy, mean rat, black bat, green goblin.*

✫ Practise saying the sentence with *I had a fright*, e.g. *I had a fright. It was a black bat in the night. I had a fright. It was a smelly goblin in the night. I had a fright. It was a creepy rat in the night.*

✫ Click on the next screen and model writing the sentences with one of the choices, e.g. *I had a fright. It was a black bat in the night.* using Set 1 and 2 sounds. Remember to model rereading for sense, and checking word spaces and punctuation. Show how to copy *I* and *the* from the Red Word cards. Rub out/cover up the words *black bat* and repeat the process with the other choices.

✫ Rub out/cover up your writing and tell the children to write some sentences under the bed in their *Get Writing!* Book, using either their own ideas or yours, if they need the support.

b) *What is the boy saying now?*

✫ Click on the next screen (boy looking fearful again). See p.25 of the *Get Writing!* Book for this activity.

☆ Tell the children to mime being in their bed late at night listening to creepy sounds. Describe the scary noises as they mime their reactions, e.g. *creepy bumps, a sudden creak, a bat flaps,* etc. Then tell them to imagine they see the door handle turning and build up your description, e.g. *the door handle turns, the door is flung open and…it is MUM!* Ask the children to TTYP to describe how they feel when it is Mum at the door. Popcorn feedback, e.g. *all right now, relieved, safe.*

☆ Click on the next screen to show the picture of Mum with a hot drink, smiling. TOL to describe how it might feel to be scared and then feel safe again. *I shook with fright but then I felt happy and warm. I was cold with horror but then I felt all right.*

☆ Practise saying the sentence using each phrase, e.g. *I shook with fright but then I felt all right. I shook with fright but then I was happy and warm. I shook with fright but then I was safe and sound.*

☆ Model writing the sentence with one of the phrases, e.g. *I shook with fright but then I felt all right.* using Set 1 and 2 sounds. Show how to copy *I* and *all* from the Red Word cards. Rub out/cover up *I felt all right* and repeat the process with the other choices.

☆ Rub out/cover up your writing and tell the children to write in the speech bubbles in their *Get Writing!* Book.

Pink Storybook 9   *Snow*

Introducing the story

> crunches   fluffy   skid   slip   creep   pad

☆ Use these 'power words' when introducing the story during reading Activity 3. Write them on sticky notes so you remember to use them through the lesson/day.

*See Blueprint lesson plans for **Activity 5 Hold a sentence** and **Activity 7 Edit** on pp.25–26.*

Activity 8 Composition: picture prompts

Power words

☆ Remind the children of all the ways you can move through snow. Use MT/YT to extend the language. *The snow **crunches** under my feet. I **skid** and **slip** through the wet snow. I **creep** and **pad** in the deep snow. I zoom and **crunch** in the **fluffy**, cold snow.*

☆ Ask the children to TTYP and choose their favourite word to describe moving in the snow. Popcorn feedback.

Say the sentence

☆ TOL as you build up the sentences together, orally, to describe the snow.

☆ Use MT/YT each time you expand on the sentence stem until they can all say it after you. ***The snow is like** a vast bright sheet. **The snow is like** a cold white blanket. **The snow is like** a world of cotton wool.*

☆ Remind the children how you can move in the snow. ***When you play in the snow** you skid. **When you play in the snow** you skid and slip. **When you play in the snow** you skid and slip wildly about!*

☆ Use the 'power words' and stems from the sentences you have built in this activity throughout the session and day, e.g. *I **slipped** on the wet leaves. I **skidded** wildly about on the ice rink! The autumn leaves **crunch** as I play in them.*

Write the sentences

Write a snow poem.

☆ Show the images of snowy scenes on **CD** (file 9.2). See p.27 of the *Get Writing!* Book for this activity.

☆ Say that you are going to write a poem about the snow together.

☆ Remind the children of the ways they described the snow, e.g. *like crunchy cotton wool, a cold white blanket.*

☆ Ask the children to TTYP to tell them a description of snow that they remember. Ask the children to Popcorn feedback, e.g. *a woollen world, a soft bright sheet.*

☆ Click on the audio icon and listen to the audio of feet crunching in snow. TOL as you describe what you like to do in the snow, e.g. *I like to skid. I like to zip and zoom*, etc.

☆ Click through the next two screens and ask the children to TTYP to talk about what they like to do in snow, e.g. *make a snow man, sledge, have snowball fights.*

☆ Practise saying each line of the poem using the format *I want to slip in the crunchy snow, I want to zip and zoom in the fluffy snow, I want to roll up snowballs in the cold bright snow.*

☆ Click on the next screen (snow poem writing frame) and model writing each of the lines of the poem with one of the choices, e.g. *I want to zip and zoom in the fluffy snow.* using Set 1 and 2 sounds. Remember to model rereading for sense, and checking word spaces and punctuation. Show how to copy the Red Words from the Red Word card. Rub out/cover up the words *zip and zoom in the fluffy snow* and repeat the process with the next line of the poem.

☆ Rub out/cover up your writing and tell the children to write a poem in the snowy scene in their *Get Writing!* Book, using either their own ideas or yours, if they need the support.

Pink Storybook 10   *So cool!*

Introducing the story

> fabulous   amazing   leap with joy   shriek with delight

☆ Use these 'power words' when introducing the story during reading Activity 3. Write them on sticky notes so you remember to use them through the lesson/day.

*See Blueprint lesson plans for **Activity 5 Hold a sentence** and **Activity 7 Edit** on pp.25–26.*

Activity 8 Composition: picture prompts

Power words

☆ TOL to relate back to the story: *Where would you like to live when you grow up? Can you imagine getting a really cool flat for yourself? I would jump for joy!*

☆ Use MT/YT to repeat the 'power words'. *If I got a cool flat I'd **leap with joy**! I'd shout and **shriek with delight**!*

☆ Use MT/YT to extend the language. *It would be **fabulous** to have a fantastic flat. It would be **amazing** and make me **shriek with delight**!*

Say the sentences

☆ TOL as you build up the sentences together, orally, about the cool flat.

☆ Use the words *not just* to include the 'power words'. *My flat is **not just cool**, it is so **fantastic** that it makes me **leap with joy**! My flat is **not just cool**, it is **fabulously** huge. My flat is **not just cool**, it is **amazing**!*

☆ Use the 'power words' and stems from the sentences you have built in this activity throughout the session and day, e.g. *What a **fabulous** word choice! That is an **amazing** idea. When the boys score a goal they all **shriek with delight**!*

Write the sentences

a) *What will you have in your flat?*

☆ Show the image of the girl from the storybook on **CD** (file 10.2). See p.29 of the *Get Writing!* Book for this activity.

☆ Drag different objects into the speech bubble next to the child. TOL as you describe them: *smart bunk beds, lots of pets, cool food,* etc.

☆ Ask the children to TTYP to think of other things that would be cool to have in the flat. Ask the children to Popcorn ideas, e.g. *swimming pool, big TV, ice cream machine.*

☆ Practise saying the sentence using each phrase, e.g. *I will have smart bunk beds in my flat. I will have cool, tasty food in my flat. I will have a big group of pets in my flat.*

☆ Display **CD** (file 10.3) and model writing the sentence with one of the choices, e.g. *I will have a big group of pets in my flat.* using Set 1 and 2 sounds. Remember to model rereading for sense, and checking word spaces and punctuation. Show how to copy *I, of* and *my* from the Red Word cards. Rub out/cover up the words *big gang of pets* and repeat the process with the other choices.

☆ Rub out/cover up your writing and tell the children to write some sentences in their *Get Writing!* Books, using either their own ideas or yours, if they need the support.

b) *What do you do when you see your cool flat?*

☆ Click on the next screen and show the image of a cool flat. See p.30 in the *Get Writing!* Book for this activity.

☆ Ask the children to imagine that they have been given the keys to the flat. Get them to mime turning the key, opening the door and looking around at the wonderful flat full of cool things! Ask the children to TTYP to describe what they can see. Popcorn feedback, e.g. *a fabulous flat, a fantastic flat, loads of cool stuff.*

☆ Ask the children to TTYP and say how they felt when they stood in the fabulous flat. Popcorn feedback, e.g. *I wanted to jump for joy/shout with delight/jump up and down with glee.*

☆ Practise saying the sentence using each phrase, e.g. *When I see my flat I jump for joy. When I see my flat I jump up and down with glee/shout with delight.*

☆ Model writing the sentence with one of the phrases, e.g. *When I see my flat I jump for joy.* using Set 1 and 2 sounds. Show how to copy *I* and *my* from the Red Word cards. Rub out/cover up *jump for joy* and repeat the process with the other choices.

☆ Rub out/cover up your writing and tell the children to write their sentences under the picture their *Get Writing!* Book.

Pink Non-fiction Book 1   *Jay's clay pot*

Introducing the book

beautiful   wonderful   colourful

☆ Use these 'power words' when introducing the book during reading Activity 3. Write them on sticky notes so you remember to use them through the lesson/day.

*See Blueprint lesson plans for **Activity 5 Hold a sentence** and **Activity 7 Edit** on pp.25–26.*

Pink

Activity 8 Composition: picture prompts

Power words

☆ TOL to relate back to the book: *This book is an instruction book. It tells you how to do something. It shows you how to make a **beautiful** pot.*

☆ Use MT/YT to repeat the 'power words'. *It shows you how to make a **wonderful** pot. In the end you will have a **colourful**, spotty pot.*

Say the sentences

☆ TOL as you build up the sentences, orally, about the pot.

☆ Use MT/YT every time you expand the sentence together. Do not make it look too easy as you think of what to say. Encourage the children to help you so they take ownership of the sentence.

☆ Once you have decided upon the final sentence, use actions and facial expressions to help the children remember the sentence. Use MT/YT each time you expand on the sentence stem until they can all say it after you. ***Make a** wonderful spotty pot. **Make a** tall beautiful pot. **Make a** colourful spotty pot.*
*Roll up the clay **to make the pot.** Lay the rings on top of each other **to make the pot.** Press down the rings **to make the pot.***

☆ Use the 'power words' and stems from the sentences you have built in this activity throughout the session and day using the verb in the imperative form, e.g. **roll** *up your sleeves,* **press down** *on the handle.* Remind the children that these verbs tell them *exactly* what to do.

Write the sentences

Write about how to make a clay pot.

☆ Show the images of making the pot on **CD** (file NF1.2). See pp.32–33 in the *Get Writing!* Book for this activity.

☆ Say that you are going to write instructions for making a clay pot together. TOL as you drag and drop images of making a pot into the right order. *First I make the bottom. Then I roll out the rest of the clay. Next I make the rings. Then I lay the rings on top. In the end I have a tall pot.*

☆ Then repeat the process, acting out making the pot as a class.

☆ Ask the children to TTYP to tell their partner how to make a clay pot. Ask the children to Popcorn ideas so you get the instructions retold to you, e.g. *make the bottom, roll out the clay, make the rings, lay the rings, to make a tall pot.*

☆ Practise saying the sentences using the connectives *first, then, next, in the end* to order each phrase, e.g. *First make the bottom of the pot. Then roll out the clay to make the rings. Next press the rings down. Then lay the rings to make a tall pot. In the end you will have a colourful pot.*

☆ Tell the children that instructions do not have the word *I* or *you* in them because the verbs/doing words tell the reader what to do.

☆ Display **CD** (file NF1.3) and model writing the sentence with one of the choices, e.g. *First make the bottom of the pot.* using Set 1 and 2 sounds. Remember to model rereading for sense, and checking word spaces and punctuation. Show how to copy *make* and *the* from the Red Word cards. Model how you re-read the sentence after writing each word to check it makes sense, leave spaces between words, and how you start with a capital letter and finish with a full stop. Rub out/cover up the sentence and repeat the process with the other sentences/screens.

☆ Rub out/cover up your writing and tell the children to write the sentences in the instruction sheet next to the pictures in their *Get Writing!* Book, using either their own ideas or yours, if they need the support.

Introducing the book

timid   shy   frightening   alarming

☆ Use these 'power words' when introducing the book during reading Activity 3. Write them on sticky notes so you remember to use them through the lesson/day.

*See Blueprint lesson plans for **Activity 5 Hold a sentence** and **Activity 7 Edit** on pp.25 – 26.*

Activity 8 Composition: picture prompts

Power words

☆ TOL about the book and use MT/YT to repeat the 'power words'. *Bats can be **frightening** but they are really **timid**. Bats can be **alarming** when they flap about. Some people find bats scary.*

☆ Use MT/YT to extend the language. *Some people find bats **frightening** but actually they like to stay hidden.*

Say the sentences

☆ TOL as you build up the sentences together, orally, about bats.

☆ Use MT/YT each time you expand on the sentence stem until they can all say it after you.

☆ Use a variety of sentence stems, e.g. ***When bats** flap about it is **alarming**. **When bats** hunt for insects at night it can be scary. **When bats** fly about it can be **frightening**.*

☆ Use the 'power words' and stems from the sentences you have built in this activity throughout the session and day, e.g. *The birds in the wildlife area are very **timid** – they like to stay hidden. When the door banged suddenly, that was **frightening**!*

Write the sentences

a) *Write about bats in the day and at night.*

☆ Show the images of the bats on **CD** (file NF3.2). See p.35 of the *Get Writing!* Book for this activity.

☆ Say that you are going to write some sentences that contrast what the bat does in the day and in the night.

☆ Ask the children to TTYP to tell their partner what the bats do in the day and the night. Ask the children to Popcorn ideas, e.g. *sleep, rest, hunt for insects, fly about, feed.*

☆ Practise saying the sentence with the phrases. *In the day the bats sleep but at night they fly about. In the day the bats hang from a tree but at night they hunt.*

☆ Click on the next screen and model writing the sentence with one of the choices, e.g. *In the day the bats sleep, but at night they fly about.* using Set 1 and 2 sounds. Remember to model rereading for sense, and checking word spaces and punctuation. Show how to copy *the* and *they* from the Red Word cards. Rub out/cover up the words *sleep* and *fly about* and repeat the process with the other choices.

☆ Rub out/cover up your writing and tell the children to write some sentences in the information sheet in their *Get Writing!* Book, using either their own ideas or yours, if they need the support.

b) *Write some facts about bats.*

☆ Show the image of bat flying at night and listen to the bat audio on **CD** (file NF3.3). See p.36 in the *Get Writing!* Book for this activity.

☆ Say: *We have been reading about bats. Some of us were scared of bats. Are you still scared? Let's write a poster to persuade people that bats are not scary.*

☆ Ask the children to TTYP to describe how they used to feel about bats. Popcorn feedback, e.g. *scared, frightened, unhappy.*

☆ Ask: *What could we tell someone about bats so they would stop being scared? We could say that bats are timid.* Ask the children to TTYP to think of words and phrases to describe how shy bats are. Popcorn feedback, e.g. *shy, like to stay hidden.*

☆ Practise saying the sentences with the words, e.g. *Do not have a fright. Bats are shy. Do not have a fright. Bats are timid. Do not have a fright. Bats like to stay hidden.*

☆ Click on the next screen and model writing the sentences into the poster with one of the words, e.g. *Do not have a fright. Bats are shy.* using Set 1 and 2 sounds. Show how to copy *are* and *do* from the Red Word cards. Rub out/cover up *are shy* and repeat the process with the other choices.

☆ Rub out/cover up your writing and tell the children to write some sentences in the poster in their *Get Writing!* Book.

Orange Storybook 1   *Playday*

Introducing the story

> *jump for joy*   *bounce about*   *delight/delighted*   *surprise*

☆ Use these 'power words' when introducing the story during reading Activity 3. Write them on sticky notes so you remember to use them through the lesson/day.

*See Blueprint lesson plans for **Activity 5 Hold a sentence** and **Activity 7 Edit** on pp.25–26.*

Activity 8 Composition: picture prompts

Power words

☆ TOL (Think out loud) to relate back to the story: *It is so much fun to play. The children were **delighted** to have clay, sand and dressing up clothes to play with. If I had a playday I would be **delighted**!*

☆ Use MT/YT (My turn/Your turn) to repeat the 'power words'. *If I could play all day I would **jump for joy**. I would be so **surprised** and **delighted**.*

☆ Use MT/YT to extend the language. *I would be so **surprised** that I would **jump for joy**! I would be so **delighted** I would **bounce about** the room.*

Say the sentences

☆ TOL as you build up the sentences, orally, about having a playday.

☆ Use MT/YT every time you expand the sentence together. Do not make it look too easy as you think of what to say. Encourage the children to help you so they take ownership of the sentence.

☆ Once you have decided upon the final sentence, use actions and facial expressions to help the children remember the sentence. Use MT/YT each time you expand on the sentence stem until they can all say it after you, e.g. ***If I had a playday** I would jump for joy and bounce about!* ***If I had a playday** I would jump for joy and bounce about as I made a castle in the sand.*

☆ Use the 'power words' and stems from the sentences you have built in this activity throughout the session and day e.g. *The gorgeous sunshine makes me want to **jump for joy**!*

Write the sentences

a) *What are the children saying?*

☆ Show the image of the child on **CD** (file 1.2). See p.3 of the *Get Writing!* Book for this activity.

☆ Ask the children to TTYP to tell their partner how they might feel if they could play all day. Ask the children to Popcorn ideas, e.g. *jump for joy, bounce about.*

☆ Ask the children to TTYP to tell their partner what they might do if they could play all day. Ask the children to Popcorn ideas, e.g. *dress up as a monkey, dig in the sandpit, play with the clay, swing on the swings.*

☆ Drag and drop the picture prompts next to the girl and practise saying the sentence with the phrases. *If I had a playday I might jump for joy as I dig in the sandpit. If I had a playday I might dress up as a monkey and hoot and shout. If I had a playday I might have a huge smile as I swing on the swings.*

☆ Model writing the sentence with one of the choices, e.g. *If I had a playday I might dress up as a monkey and hoot and shout.* TOL and ask children to help as you sound out each word using Set 1 and 2 sounds. Model how you re-read the sentence after writing each word to check it makes sense, leave spaces between words, and how you start with a capital letter and finish with a full stop. Rub out/cover up the words *dress up as a monkey and hoot and shout* and repeat the process with the other choices.

Orange

☆ Rub out/cover up your writing and tell the children to write some sentences in the speech bubbles in their *Get Writing!* Book, using either their own ideas or yours, if they need the support.

b) *What are the children going to do?*

☆ Display **CD** (file 1.3) and show the image of the three children dressing up as Batboy, a witch, and playing the sand. See p.4 of the *Get Writing!* Book for this activity.

☆ Ask the children: *What would you like to play?*

☆ Ask the children to TTYP and think of ideas. Take feedback, e.g. *We would play with clay.*

☆ Ask children to TTYP and describe what the children in the pictures are doing. Popcorn feedback, e.g. *dressing up as a witch/Batboy, playing in the sand tray.*

☆ Practise saying the sentence with the words, e.g. *I shall dig in the sand box. I shall dress up as Batboy/a witch.*

☆ Model writing the sentence with the words *I shall dress up as Batboy.* TOL and ask children to help as you sound out each word and then write it. Use current phonic knowledge to write the words. Model how you re-read the sentence after writing each word to check it makes sense. Rub out/cover up the sentence and repeat the process with the other choices.

☆ Rub out/cover up your writing and tell the children to write some sentences in the speech bubbles in their *Get Writing!* Book (p.4).

Orange Storybook 2   *I think I want to be a bee*

Introducing the story

creep   sneak   hunt   crouch   flit

☆ Use these 'power words' when introducing the story during reading Activity 3. Write them on sticky notes so you remember to use them through the lesson/day.

*See Blueprint lesson plans for **Activity 5 Hold a sentence** and **Activity 7 Edit** on pp.25–26.*

Activity 8 Composition: picture prompts

Power words

☆ TOL to relate back to the story: *The girl was having a marvellous daydream. Imagine being a bee that could dart from flower to flower!*

☆ Use MT/YT to repeat the 'power words'. *I would like to be a fox that can **crouch** and **hunt** in the long grass. I might like to be an ant that could scuttle and **creep** to safety. If I were a bat I'd **flit** at night and **hunt** for bugs! If I were a crab I'd **sneak** about in the rock pool all day.*

Which word?

☆ Ask the children to TTYP and decide which words/phrases they would use. Choose children to feed back. *Does the crab **sneak** or scuttle in the rock pool? Does the bat dart or **flit** in the night sky? Does the fox **creep** or **hunt** in the dark as it crouches in the long grass?*

Say the sentences

☆ TOL as you build up the sentences together, orally, about daydreaming.

☆ Use MT/YT each time you expand on the sentence stem until they can all say it after you. ***I think I want to be** a bat. **I think I want to be** a bat that darts and flits. **I think I want to be** a bat that darts and flits in the dark night sky!*

Write the sentences

What do the children want to be?

☆ Show one of the images of the children on **CD** (file 2.2). See p.6 in the *Get Writing!* Book for this activity.

☆ Drag one of the animals into the thought bubble. TOL as you do so, describing what they do. *A bat that darts and flits. A fox that creeps and hunts. A crab that crouches and scuttles. A rat that sneaks and creeps. A hen that pecks and hunts for slugs*, etc.

☆ Ask the children to TTYP to decide which animals they would like to be and describe how it moves. Ask the children to Popcorn ideas, e.g. *a bat that flits and hunts in the night, a hen that pecks and clucks in the grass.*

☆ Practise saying the sentences e.g. *I think I want to be a rat that creeps and scuttles in the kitchen. I think I want to be a hen that pecks and clucks in the grass. I think I want to be a bat that flits and hunts in the night. I think I want to be a fox that creeps and hunts in the dark.*

☆ Display **CD** (file 2.3) and model writing the sentence with one of the choices, e.g. *I think I want to be a fox that creeps and hunts in the dark.* using Set 1 and 2 sounds. Remember to model rereading for sense, and checking word spaces and punctuation. Show how to copy *want, to, be* and *the* from the Red Word cards. Rub out/cover up the words *fox that creeps and hunts in the dark* and repeat the process with the other choices.

☆ Rub out/cover up your writing and tell the children to write some sentences in the speech bubbles in their *Get Writing!* Book, using either their own ideas or yours, if they need the support.

Orange Storybook 3   *A bad fright*

Introducing the story

> *foul   horrid   ghastly   up to tricks*

☆ Use these 'power words' when introducing the story during reading Activity 3. Write them on sticky notes so you remember to use them through the lesson/day.

*See Blueprint lesson plans for **Activity 5 Hold a sentence** and **Activity 7 Edit** on pp.25–26.*

Activity 8 Composition: picture prompts

Power words

☆ TOL to relate back to the story: *Have you ever dressed up as a witch or wizard? It is fabulous fun! This girl has a whole outfit. In the end she pretends to be a vile witch **up to tricks**!*

☆ Use MT/YT to repeat the 'power words'. *With her sticky out teeth and her black hat she is a **ghastly** looking witch!*

☆ Use MT/YT to extend the language. *Dressed up as witch she is **up to tricks**. She pretends to be a **foul, horrid** witch. What vile tricks will she play?*

Say the sentences

☆ TOL as you build up the sentences together, orally, about the witch.

☆ Use MT/YT each time you expand on the sentence stem until they can all say it after you. ***I am a*** *wicked witch!* ***I am a*** *ghastly wicked witch.* ***I am a*** *ghastly wicked witch up to awful tricks!* ***I have my*** *black hat on.* ***I have my*** *black hat and sticky-out teeth on.* ***I have my*** *black hat covered in cobwebs and sticky-out teeth on.*

☆ Use the 'power words' and stems from the sentences you have built in this activity throughout the session and day, e.g. *It looks like we will have **ghastly** weather today! My brother used to play vile tricks on me like putting a frog in my bed. He was **foul**!*

Write the sentences

a) *What does the child put on?*

☆ Show the image of the child on **CD** (file 3.2). See p.8 of the *Get Writing!* Book for this activity.

☆ TOL as you describe the girl and what she is wearing, e.g. *black hat, big teeth, black tights, long nightdress, cobwebs.*

☆ Ask the children to TTYP to think of other words to describe the dressing up clothes. Ask the children to Popcorn ideas, e.g. *high/black hat, sticky-out teeth, long black tights, green nightdress, dusty cobwebs.*

☆ Click on the next screen and show the connectives. Practise saying sentences about dressing up using the connectives *first, then, next* and *last* to order each phrase, e.g. *First I put on my long green nightdress. Then I put on my sticky-out teeth.*

☆ Click on the next screen and model writing the sentence with one of the choices, e.g. *First, I put on my long green nightdress.* using Set 1 and 2 sounds. Remember to model rereading for sense, and checking word spaces and punctuation. Show how to copy *put* and *my* from the Red Word cards. Rub out/cover up the words *First* and *long green nightdress* and repeat the process with the other choices.

☆ Rub out/cover up your writing and tell the children to write some sentences around the child dressed up as a witch in their *Get Writing!* Book, using either their own ideas or yours, if they need the support.

b) *What is the girl saying?*

☆ Show the image of the witch on **CD** (file 3.3) and listen to the audio. See p.9 of the *Get Writing!* Book for this activity.

☆ Click on the next screen. The girl in the story says, "I am a wicked witch." TOL to describe other ways she could describe herself: *I am a foul witch. I am a ghastly witch,* etc.

☆ Ask the children to TTYP in role as the witch to think what else they might say. Popcorn feedback, e.g. *terrible, vile, mischievous, naughty.*

☆ Practise saying the sentence with the words, e.g. *Look at me, I am a foul witch. Look at me, I am a witch up to tricks. Look at me, I am a horrid witch.*

☆ Model writing the sentence with one of the words, e.g. *Look at me, I am a horrid witch.* using Set 1 and 2 sounds. Remember to model rereading for sense, and checking word spaces and punctuation. Rub out/cover up *horrid* and repeat the process with the other choices.

☆ Rub out/cover up your writing and tell the children to write in the speech bubbles in their *Get Writing!* Book.

> **Orange Storybook 4**   *Follow me!*

Introducing the story

> *thoughtful   glum   over the moon*

☆ Use these 'power words' when introducing the story during reading Activity 3. Write them on sticky notes so you remember to use them through the lesson/day.

*See Blueprint lesson plans for **Activity 5 Hold a sentence** and **Activity 7 Edit** on pp.25 – 26.*

Activity 8 Composition: picture prompts

Power words

☆ TOL to relate back to the story: *Dizzy Duck wanted to teach her three ducklings to swim but one duckling just could not do it. That duckling was so lucky because a kind crow helped him out!*

☆ Use MT/YT to repeat the 'power words'. *When he could not swim the duckling felt* **glum**. *He was left out whilst the other ducklings swam about. Oh dear, he looked so miserable.*

☆ Use MT/YT to extend the language. *But the duckling was so lucky because the helpful crow had a plan. The big-hearted crow gave the duckling a tow and the duckling quacked with glee! The* **thoughtful** *crow made the duckling feel* **over the moon** *with happiness!*

Say the sentences

☆ TOL as you build up the sentences together, orally, about how the crow helped the duckling.

☆ Use MT/YT each time you expand on the sentence stem until they can all say it after you. **The duckling was sitting on the bank**. Ask: *How was he feeling?* TTYP and take feedback.

☆ Say the new sentence using a couple of the children's ideas. **The duckling was sitting on the bank** *feeling left out and miserable.*

☆ Ask: *Why was he feeling that way?* TTYP and feed back. Say the new sentence using a couple of the children's ideas. **The duckling was sitting on the bank** *feeling left out and miserable because he could not swim.*

The crow helped the duckling. The *kind-hearted* **crow helped the duckling. The** *kind-hearted* **crow helped the duckling** *and then he was over the moon!*

☆ Use the 'power words' and stems from the sentences you have built in this activity throughout the session and day, e.g. *What a* **thoughtful** *idea.*

Write the sentences

a) *What is the duckling saying?*

☆ Show the image of Duckling 3 and the crow sitting on the riverbank on **CD** (file 4.2). See p.11 of the *Get Writing!* Book for this activity.

☆ Act out being Duckling 3 being fed-up. Say, in a fed up voice: *All the other ducklings can swim but I can't. I have to sit on the bank and watch them have fun!* In role, ask the children: *Do you have any idea how I'm feeling?* Ask children to TTYP and then Popcorn their ideas, e.g. *left out, fed up, miserable, glum.*

☆ Say: *Yes! That is exactly how I'm feeling. I am fed up/miserable/glum/left out. But then the crow helped me. It was wonderful! Do you have any idea how I'm feeling now?* Ask children to TTYP and then Popcorn their ideas, e.g. *over the moon, delighted, full of joy.*

☆ Say: *Yes! That is exactly how I'm feeling now. I was fed up but now I am quacking with glee!*

☆ Practise saying the sentences, e.g. *I was fed up but now I am over the moon. I was left out but now I am full of joy,* etc.

☆ Click on the next screen (Crow helping the duckling). Model writing the sentence, e.g. *I was fed up but now I am over the moon.* using Set 1 and 2 sounds. Remember to model rereading for sense, and checking word spaces and punctuation. Rub out/cover up *fed up* and *over the moon* and repeat the process with the other choices.

☆ Rub out/cover up your writing and tell the children to write the sentences into the speech bubbles in their *Get Writing!* Book, using either their own ideas or yours, if they need the support.

b) *What is Crow like?*

☆ Click on the next screen (Crow looking kind and wise). See p.11 of the *Get Writing!* Book for this activity.

Orange

☆ Ask the children to act in role as the duckling after the crow has helped him. Pretend to be a reporter and ask the children to say how they would describe the crow's actions. Ask the children to Popcorn ideas, e.g. *kind, helpful, wonderful.*

☆ Practise saying the sentence with the words, e.g. *What a kind/helpful/wonderful/gentle/thoughtful crow.*

☆ Model writing the sentence with one of the choices, e.g. *What a kind crow.* using Set 1 and 2 sounds. Show how to copy *what* from the Red Word cards. Rub out/cover up the word *kind* and repeat the process with the other choices.

☆ Rub out/cover up your writing and tell the children to write some sentences in their *Get Writing!* Book.

Orange Storybook 5   *Too much!*

Introducing the story

down in the dumps   scrawny   vast   enormous

☆ Use these 'power words' when introducing the story during reading Activity 3. Write them on sticky notes so you remember to use them through the lesson/day.

*See Blueprint lesson plans for **Activity 5 Hold a sentence** and **Activity 7 Edit** on pp.25 – 26.*

Activity 8 Composition: picture prompts

Power words

☆ TOL to relate back to the story: *This girl is feeling like nothing is right. She does seem fed up.*

☆ Use MT/YT to repeat the 'power words'. *She seems **down in the dumps** – she is annoyed her clothes don't fit.*

Say the sentences

☆ TOL as you build up the sentences together, orally, about how the girl feels about her pets and clothes.

☆ Use MT/YT each time you expand on the sentence stem until they can all say it after you. *Her dress is huge **but the** cap is tiny. Her cat is skinny **but the** dog is enormous. She is down in the dumps **but the** hug from her mum makes it all better.*

☆ Repeat with other sentence stems, e.g. **I wish my dog were** *not so huge!* **I wish my dog were** *not huge like a balloon!* **I wish my dog were** *not huge like a vast balloon that is about to explode!*

☆ Use the 'power words' and stems from the sentences you have built in this activity throughout the session and day e.g. *The hall is huge **but the** cupboard is tiny.*

Write the sentences

Write a letter to Jill.

☆ Show the image of the girl looking glum on **CD** (file 5.2). See p.13 of the *Get Writing!* Book.

☆ Act in role as the girl saying: *Oh I feel so glum. Everything is going wrong. Nothing seems right. I'm annoyed that my clothes don't fit. I'm down in the dumps about my pets. I feel really gloomy about my scooter. I wish someone could help me and give me some advice.*

☆ Tell the children that they are going to write a letter to Jill to help her cheer up.

☆ Ask the children to TTYP to tell their partners what the girl feels glum about.

☆ Click on the next screen (thin cat and fat dog). Ask the children to Popcorn ideas of how to solve the pet problems, e.g. *Don't feel glum about your pets. Feed the cat more and take the dog for a walk.*

☆ Click on the next screen (girl in long dress, small cap and tight shoes). Ask the children to Popcorn ideas of how to solve the problem, e.g. *Go shopping with Mum. Wear a belt with the dress. Swap your hat for a bigger one.*

☆ Click on the next screen and do the same for the scooter problem. Ask the children to Popcorn ideas of how to solve the problem, e.g. *oil the wheels, go down hill, get a push.*

☆ Practise saying the sentences. *Do not feel glum. Feed your tiny cat so it grows. Do not feel down. Make your enormous/vast dog go for a run. Do not feel gloomy. Go to the shops with your Mum.*

☆ Click on the next screen (letter writing frame) and model writing the sentences with one of the choices, e.g. *Do not feel glum. Feed your cat so it grows.* using Set 1 and 2 sounds. Remember to model rereading for sense, and checking word spaces and punctuation. Show how to copy *do, your* and *so* from the Red Word cards. Rub out/cover up the words *feel glum. Feed your cat so it grows* and repeat the process with the other choices.

☆ Rub out/cover up your writing and tell the children to write the letter in the writing frame in their *Get Writing!* Book, using either their own ideas or yours, if they need the support.

☆ Encourage children, where possible, to write some more of their own ideas to help the girl cheer up.

Orange Storybook 6   *A good cook?*

Introducing the story

> disaster   delicious   scent   whiff

☆ Use these 'power words' when introducing the story during reading Activity 3. Write them on sticky notes so you remember to use them through the lesson/day.

See Blueprint lesson plans for **Activity 5 Hold a sentence** and **Activity 7 Edit** on pp.25–26.

Activity 8 Composition: picture prompts

Power words

☆ TOL to relate back to the story: *It took Dad all day to cook but finally the **delicious** scent of the pasta made everyone hungry. But then there was a **disaster**. Dad dropped the dish. Oh well, chips for tea!*

☆ Use MT/YT to repeat these 'power words'. *We smelled the **delicious scent** of the pasta. We smelled the **whiff** of the pasta cooking. We could not wait to eat the chewy cheesy pasta. Yum!*

☆ Ask the children to TTYP to talk about what happened to the pasta.

☆ Use MT/YT to extend the language. *Dad made a mistake and the pasta ended up being a **disaster**! Dad mixed the pasta so it was salty and cheesy and it smelled **delicious**.*

Say the sentences

☆ TOL as you build up the sentences together, orally, about Dad's cooking.

☆ Use MT/YT each time you expand on the sentence stem until they can all say it after you. ***Can you smell the*** *scent of pasta cooking?* ***Can you smell the*** *delicious scent of pasta cooking?* ***Can you smell the*** *whiff of delicious pasta cooking?*

☆ Repeat with other sentence stems, e.g. ***We could not wait*** *to chew the delicious cheesy pasta.* ***We could not wait*** *but Dad had a cooking disaster!*

☆ Ask: *What might Dad say as he tastes the pasta as he cooks? Mmmm, too salty. Add some cheese. Mmmm, too cheesy. Add some milk. Mmmm, too crunchy. Add more water.*

☆ Use the 'power words' and stems from the sentences you have built in this activity throughout the session and day, e.g. *What a **disaster**. I smell the **whiff** of burnt toast!*

Write the sentences

What can you cook?

☆ Show the image of Dad on **CD** (file 6.2). See p.15 of the *Get Writing!* Book for this activity.

☆ Act out being Dad. *I just love cooking but I don't often get the chance. I love to cook pasta, pizza, cake and chips. What would you cook for your family?*

☆ Ask the children to TTYP and discuss what they would like to cook. Ask them to Popcorn their answers, e.g. *chocolate cake, fish and chips, cheesy pasta!*

☆ Use MT/YT to practise saying the sentences using some of the children's ideas, e.g. *I can cook crunchy hot chips. I can cook sweet jam tarts. I can cook cheesy pasta.*

☆ Click on the next screen (menu template) and model writing the sentence with one of the choices, e.g. *I can cook crunchy hot chips.* using Set 1 and 2 sounds. Remember to model rereading for sense, and checking word spaces and punctuation. Rub out/cover up the words *crunchy hot chips.*

☆ Rub out/cover up your writing and tell the children to write a sentence into the family dinner menu in their *Get Writing!* Books, using either their own idea or yours, if they need the support.

☆ Repeat with other meal ideas.

Orange Storybook 7   *Come on, Margo!*

Introducing the story

> *fabulous   massive   tatty   smart   plenty*

☆ Use these 'power words' when introducing the story during reading Activity 3. Write them on sticky notes so you remember to use them through the lesson/day.

*See Blueprint lesson plans for **Activity 5 Hold a sentence** and **Activity 7 Edit** on pp.25–26.*

Activity 8 Composition: picture prompts

Power words

☆ TOL to relate back to the story: *Margo was in the smallest car but she was the winner. She is a fantastic driver!*

☆ Use MT/YT to repeat the 'power words'. *Margo is a **fabulous** driver. Margo is fantastic in her **tatty**, tiny go-kart!*

Say the sentences

☆ TOL as you build up the sentences together, orally, about Margo.

☆ Use MT/YT each time you expand on the sentence stem until they can all say it after you. **Margo is a** *star.* **Margo is a** *fabulous fast racing star.* **Margo is a** *fantastic go-kart driver. Margo had a tiny go-kart **but the** others had massive cars. The others sped around and crashed **but the** winner was fantastic Margo! The others had massive smart cars **but the** tatty go-cart won!*

☆ Use the 'power words' and stems from the sentences you have built in this activity throughout the session and day e.g., *What **fabulous**, fast work!*

Write the sentences

a) *Can Margo win?*

☆ Show the image of Margo and the cars on **CD** (file 7.2). See p.17 of the *Get Writing!* Book for this activity.

☆ Ask the children to TTYP to describe what they can see. Popcorn feedback, e.g. *a red smart car, a big green car, a bright yellow car.*

☆ Act in role as a race commentator asking questions to describe the car race, e.g. *Can the smart red car rush past Margo? No! Can the flash green car zoom past Margo? No! Can the bright yellow car swerve past Margo? No! Margo wins!*

☆ Ask the children to TTYP in role as a sports commentator to choose a car and describe it trying to get past Margo. Popcorn feedback, e.g. *Can the fast red car slip past Margo?*

☆ Practise saying the sentence with the words, e.g. *Can the flash red car rush past Margo? Can the green sports car zoom past Margo?*

☆ Model writing a sentence with one of the phrases, e.g. *Can the green sports car get past Margo?* using Set 1 and 2 sounds. Remember to model rereading for sense, and checking word spaces and punctuation. Show how to copy *the* from the Red Word cards. Rub out/cover up the sentence and repeat the process with the other choices.

☆ Rub out/cover up your writing and tell the children to write the sentences next to the cars in their *Get Writing!* Book, using either their own ideas or yours, if they need the support. They can also write what the commentator says at the end next to the final picture.

b) *What is Margo like?*

☆ Show the image of Margo on **CD** (file 7.3). See p.18 in the *Get Writing!* Book for this activity.

☆ Ask the children how they would describe Margo. Popcorn feedback, e.g. *fabulous, a star, fantastic.*

☆ Practise saying the sentence with the words, e.g. *Margo is fantastic. Margo is a go-kart star. Margo is the go-kart winner.*

☆ Model writing the sentence with the words, e.g. *Margo is a go-kart star.* using Set 1 and 2 sounds.

☆ Rub out/cover up your writing and tell the children to write into the labels next to the picture of Margo in their *Get Writing!* Book.

Orange Storybook 8   *My sort of horse*

Introducing the story

> glossy   shaggy   crunch   munch

☆ Use these 'power words' when introducing the story during reading Activity 3. Write them on sticky notes so you remember to use them through the lesson/day.

See Blueprint lesson plans for **Activity 5 Hold a sentence** and **Activity 7 Edit** on pp.25–26.

Activity 8 Composition: picture prompts

Power words

☆ TOL to relate back to the story: *There are so many horses in the book. Some can do crazy things like wearing clothes or playing the piano. But I think the best horse is the one the little girl loves.*

☆ Use MT/YT to repeat the 'power words', e.g. *One greedy horse* **crunches** *and* **munches** *on corn all day long. I think the smart horse would have a neat,* **glossy** *mane, not a* **shaggy***, untidy one!*

☆ Use MT/YT to extend the language. *There is a horse with a* **glossy** *coat that is a crazy singer. There is a lazy horse with a* **shaggy** *mane that snores as it sleeps.*

Say the sentences

✫ TOL as you build up the sentences together, orally, about the horses.

✫ Use MT/YT each time you expand on the sentence stem until they can all say it after you. **The best horse has** a glossy coat of hair. **The best horse has** a soft, glossy coat of hair. **The best horse has** a soft, glossy coat of hair, which is like velvet to touch.

✫ Use the 'power words' and stems from the sentences you have built in this activity throughout the session and day e.g. *I saw you playing* **crazy** *games at playtime. You were not just hungry you were a* **crunching, munching** *eating machine at lunch!*

Write the sentences

a) *What can horses do?*

✫ Show the image of the girl on **CD** (file 8.2). See p. 20 of the *Get Writing!* Book for this activity.

✫ Drag the different horses next to the girl. TOL as you do so, describing what they can do. *This horse can pull a cart. This horse can munch and crunch corn. This horse can sing. This horse can snore.*

✫ Ask the children to TTYP to choose one horse and describe what it can do. Encourage the children to use the 'power words' to describe what the horses are like. Popcorn ideas, e.g. *This horse can sing in a dress. This greedy horse can munch lots of corn.*

✫ Practise saying the sentences, e.g. *This greedy horse can munch and crunch corn. This funny horse can sing in a dress. This lazy horse can snore as it sleeps. This strong horse can pull a cart.*

✫ Display **CD** (file 8.3) and model writing the sentence with one of the choices, e.g. *This strong horse can pull a cart.* using Set 1 and 2 sounds. Remember to model rereading for sense, and checking word spaces and punctuation.

✫ Repeat the process with the other choices/screens.

✫ Rub out/cover up your writing and tell the children to write some sentences next to the different horses in their *Get Writing!* Book, using either their own ideas or yours, if they need the support.

b) *Write about your best horse.*

✫ Show the image of the girl and her horse on **CD** (file 8.4). See p.21 of the *Get Writing!* Book for this activity.

✫ TOL to describe the horse, e.g. *It crunches apples. It has glossy hair. It has velvet ears. It gallops across the hills,* etc.

✫ Ask the children to describe their ideal horse. Popcorn feedback, e.g. *quick, black and glossy.*

✫ Practise saying the sentence with the words, e.g. *My horse crunches apples. My horse gallops across the hills. My horse has soft shaggy hair.*

✫ Model writing the sentence with the words, e.g. *My horse crunches apples.* using Set 1 and 2 sounds.

✫ Rub out/cover up your writing and tell the children to write some sentences around the picture of the horse in their *Get Writing!* Book.

Orange Storybook 9   *Haircuts*

Introducing the story

scruffy   untidy   grubby   smart   stylish

✫ Use these 'power words' when introducing the story during reading Activity 3. Write them on sticky notes so you remember to use them through the lesson/day.

See Blueprint lesson plans for **Activity 5 Hold a sentence** *and* **Activity 7 Edit** *on pp. 25 – 26.*

Activity 8 Composition: picture prompts

Power words

☆ TOL to relate back to the story: *This book has lots of fabulous haircuts! Some are so **smart** and others are a great big mess! Which one do you like best?*

☆ Use MT/YT to repeat the 'power words'. *The messy hair looks **untidy**. The **stylish** hair looks **smart**. The witchy hair was green and **grubby**.*

☆ Use MT/YT to extend the language. *I'd love my hair to be **smart, stylish** and just fabulous! I cannot stand messy **scruffy** hair. It is not **smart** at all! What **untidy** hair. It looks like a nest!*

Say the sentences

☆ TOL as you build up the sentences together, orally, about the haircuts.

☆ Use MT/YT with sentence stems, e.g. **I would like a** wig. **I would like a** stylish wig. **I would like a** wonderful stylish wig to wear to parties!

☆ Use the 'power words' and stems from the sentences you have built in this activity throughout the session and day e.g. *What **smart, stylish** plaits. Oh no! My hair is so **scruffy and untidy** it looks like a nest!*

Write the sentences

a) *What sort of hair do the children want?*

☆ Show the image of the girl with short hair on **CD** (file 9.2). See p.23 of the *Get Writing!* Book for this activity.

☆ Drag the different haircuts onto her head. TOL as you do so, describing what they look like, e.g. *smart black hair, frizzy hair, scruffy untidy hair.*

☆ Ask the children to TTYP to decide which haircut they like best and why. Ask the children to Popcorn ideas, e.g. *I like the messy hair because I don't like to brush it.*

☆ Practise saying the sentences using some of the children's ideas, e.g. *I want scruffy, messy hair that I do not brush. I want smart hair to go to a party. I want witchy hair to frighten Mum!*

☆ Display **CD** (file 9.3) and model writing the sentence with one of the choices, e.g. *I want posh smart hair to go to a party.* using Set 1 and 2 sounds. Remember to model rereading for sense, and checking word spaces and punctuation. Show how to copy *I, want, to* and *go* from the Red Word cards. Rub out/cover up the words *posh smart hair to go to a party* and repeat the process with the other choices/screens.

☆ Rub out/cover up your writing and tell the children to write some sentences in the speech bubbles in their *Get Writing!* Book, using either their own ideas or yours, if they need the support.

b) *Draw haircuts on the heads and describe them.*

☆ Ask the children how they would describe their hair. Popcorn feedback, e.g. *curly, frizzy, wonderful, funny, messy.* See p.24 of the *Get Writing!* Book for this activity.

☆ Practise saying the sentence with the words, e.g. *My hair is curly. My hair is frizzy. My hair is…*

☆ Display **CD** (file 9.4) and draw a hairstyle onto one of the figures using your whiteboard pen. Model writing a sentence to describe the hair with the words above, e.g. *My hair is curly.* using Set 1 and 2 sounds. Rub out/cover up the sentence and repeat the process with the other choices.

☆ Rub out/cover up your writing and tell the children to draw some haircuts onto the characters in their *Get Writing!* Books, and write some sentences to describe the styles into the speech bubbles.

Introducing the story

> grubby   tatty   squish   smear   sling/slung

✩ Use these 'power words' when introducing the story during reading Activity 3. Write them on sticky notes so you remember to use them through the lesson/day.

*See Blueprint lesson plans for **Activity 5 Hold a sentence** and **Activity 7 Edit** on pp.25 – 26.*

Activity 8 Composition: picture prompts

Power words

✩ TOL to relate back to the story: *Have you ever had to dress up for a special occasion? It can be hard to stay clean and behave. This boy and his friend Kirsty got up to mischief: they had a food fight. In the end the stylish shirt was very **grubby** and not smart at all!*

✩ Use MT/YT to repeat the 'power words'. *Before my stylish shirt was clean and smart. After it was a **grubby** mess! Mum was cross when she saw my **grubby** shirt. Kirsty squirted me so I **smeared** her with jelly!*

Drama

✩ Use MT/YT to extend the language. Ask the children to mime being the boy and Kirsty. Tell them how to move as they role-play the food fight e.g., *First squirt the ketchup and mustard on each other. Now **sling** some jelly at them and **smear** it into their top.*

Say the sentences

✩ TOL as you build up the sentences together, orally, about the food fight.

✩ Use MT/YT each time you expand on the sentence stem until they can all say it after you.
***Before** I was smart but **after** I was a grubby mess.* ***Before** I felt smart in my shirt but **after** I felt like a smeary, grubby mess.* ***Before** I felt smart in my blue shirt but **after** I was smeared with food and I was a grubby mess.*
***First Kirsty** squirted ketchup.* ***First Kirsty** squirted ketchup and smeared it in on me.* ***First Kirsty** squirted ketchup and smeared it onto my smart shirt.*

✩ Use the 'power words' and stems from the sentences you have built in this activity throughout the session and day e.g. ***Squirt** the glue carefully. What **grubby** hands!*

Write the sentences

a) *What happened in the food fight?*

✩ Show the images of the children having a food fight on **CD** (file 10.2). See p.26 of the *Get Writing!* Book for this activity.

✩ Work together to drag the four pictures of the food fight into order. Change the order of your choices until you are happy, and TOL as you do: *What happened in the food fight? First came the ketchup, next the mustard, then the lemon drink and last of all the green jelly.*

✩ Ask the children to TTYP to describe the food fight to each other. Ask them to think of 'power words' to describe the children's actions and Popcorn feedback.

✩ Click on the next screen to show the connectives. Practise saying the sentence using the connectives *first, then, next,* and *last* to order each phrase, e.g. *First Kirsty squirted the ketchup. Then I threw the mustard. Next Kirsty splashed the lemon drink and slung it at me. Then I got the jelly to squish it on her dress!*

Orange

☆ Display **CD** (file 10.3) and model writing a sentence to begin describing the food fight with one of the choices, e.g. *First Kirsty squirted the ketchup.* using Set 1 and 2 sounds. Remember to model rereading for sense, and checking word spaces and punctuation. Show how to copy *the* from the Red Word cards. Rub out/cover up the sentence and repeat the process with the other choices/screens.

☆ Rub out/cover up your writing and tell the children to write sentences using connectives next to the pictures in their *Get Writing!* Book, using either their own ideas or yours, if they need the support.

b) *What is the boy like now?*

☆ Show the image of the boy in his grubby shirt on **CD** (file 10.4). See p.27 of the *Get Writing!* Book for this activity.

☆ Ask the children how they would describe the boy. Popcorn feedback, e.g. *grubby, a mess.*

☆ Practise saying the sentence with the words, e.g. *I am a sticky mess. I am in a dirty, grubby shirt.*

☆ Model writing some sentences with the words, e.g. *I am a sticky mess.* using Set 1 and 2 sounds.

☆ Rub out/cover up your writing and tell the children to write some sentences into their *Get Writing!* Book. Ask them to write how he feels in the *feeling* bubble.

Orange Storybook 11   *Look out!*

Introducing the story

> scuttle   creep   dart   dash

☆ Use these 'power words' when introducing the story during reading Activity 3. Write them on sticky notes so you remember to use them through the lesson/day.

See Blueprint lesson plans for **Activity 5 Hold a sentence** *and* **Activity 7 Edit** *on pp.25–26.*

Activity 8 Composition: picture prompts

Power words

☆ TOL to relate back to the story: *The house is in uproar because there is a mouse* **scuttling** *about! The cat wants to pounce but Mum just wants it out!*

☆ Use MT/YT to repeat the 'power words'. *Mum is scared of the mouse but I like its sniffly snout. I like the way it* **scuttles** *and nips across the floor!*

Drama

☆ Tell the children that they are mice and you are Mum. They must move in the way Mum describes.

☆ Use MT/YT to extend the language. *Oh no! A mouse! Watch it* **scuttle** *across the room. Look, it is* **creeping** *towards me! Oh no! It is* **dashing** *towards the door. Oh good! It has* **darted** *out the house!*

Say the sentences

☆ TOL as you build up the sentences together, orally, about the mouse.

☆ Use MT/YT each time you expand on the sentence stem until they can all say it after you.
Watch the mouse *nip about.* **Watch the mouse** *nip and dash about the house.* **Watch the mouse** *nip and dash about the house and scuttle out the door.*
Look at the mouse *with its long sniffly snout.* **Look at the mouse** *with its long, sniffly snout and soft thick fur.* **Look at the mouse** *with its long, sniffly snout and soft thick fur as it darts at you!*

☆ Use the 'power words' and stems from the sentences you have built in this activity throughout the session and day, e.g. *The burglar was* **creeping** *quietly towards the house when the dog started barking! The runners* **dashed** *to the finish line.*

Write the sentences

a) Where does the mouse dash?

☆ Display **CD** (file 11.2). See p.29 of the *Get Writing!* Book for this activity. Click through the screens and click 'Mouse' to see the mouse animation.

☆ Ask the children to TTYP to describe how the mouse moves around the house. Remind them to use some of the 'power words' they have been exploring. Popcorn feedback, e.g. *dash, dart, scuttle, creep.*

☆ Click through the screens and, in role as Mum, describe the mouse's dash, e.g. *The mouse crept past the sink/crept past my feet/crept past the cat/crept out the door of the house.*

☆ Ask the children to TTYP in role as Mum to describe the mouse going past different obstacles. Popcorn feedback, e.g. *It creeps by my feet. It nips to the sink.*

☆ Practise saying the sentence with the words, e.g. *The mouse creeps by my feet. The mouse darts round the sink. The mouse nips under the cat. The mouse scuttles out the door.*

☆ Model writing a sentence with one of the phrases e.g. *The mouse darts round the sink.* using Set 1 and 2 sounds. Remember to model rereading for sense, and checking word spaces and punctuation. Show how to copy *the* from the Red Word cards. Rub out/cover up the sentence and repeat the process with the other choices.

☆ Rub out/cover up your writing and tell the children to write some sentences next to the pictures in their *Get Writing!* Book, using either their own ideas or yours, if they need the support.

b) Describe the mouse.

☆ Show the image of the mouse with empty labels on **CD** (file 11.3). See p.29 of the *Get Writing!* Book for this activity.

☆ Look at each label and TOL to say what they are: *nose, feet, tail, teeth.*

☆ Ask the children to TTYP to describe each part of the mouse. Popcorn feedback: *sniffly/twitchy snout, pink/sweet/scurrying feet,* etc.

☆ Practise saying the phrases with the words, e.g. *a sniffly snout, quick pink feet, long pink tail, sharp nippy teeth.*

☆ Model writing one of the captions, e.g. *The mouse has quick pink feet.* using Set 1 and 2 sounds. Rub out/cover up the caption and repeat the process with the other choices.

☆ Rub out/cover up your writing and tell the children to write the captions for the mouse in their *Get Writing!* Book.

Orange Storybook 12　　*Hunt the tortoise*

Introducing the story

> *frantic   alarmed   panic   search   seek out*

☆ Use these 'power words' when introducing the story during reading Activity 3. Write them on sticky notes so you remember to use them through the lesson/day.

*See Blueprint lesson plans for **Activity 5 Hold a sentence** and **Activity 7 Edit** on pp.25–26.*

Orange

Activity 8 Composition: picture prompts

Power words

☆ TOL to relate back to the story: *Floyd was Troy's new pet but he got lost in the garden. Everyone hunted and **searched** but where had that tortoise got to?*

☆ Use MT/YT to repeat the 'power words'. *The family were **frantic**. They **searched** the garden for the tortoise. The got in a mad **panic** and rushed about hunting for Floyd. They split up to **seek out** Floyd.*

Say the sentences

☆ TOL as you build up the sentences together, orally, about the family hunting for Floyd.

☆ Use MT/YT each time you expand on the sentence stem until they can all say it after you. ***We are not just worried**, we are in a frantic panic! **We are not just worried**, we are rushing about in a frantic panic! **We are not just worried**, we are rushing about in a frantic panic, seeking high and low for Floyd!*

☆ Use the 'power words' and stems from the sentences you have built in this activity throughout the session and day, e.g. *You need to **search** for your missing cap. **Seek it out** in the playground.*

Write the sentences

a) *What are they saying?*

☆ Show the image of the tortoise on **CD** (file 12.2). See p.31 of the *Get Writing!* Book for this activity.

☆ Ask the children to act in role as one of the children looking for Floyd the tortoise. Give them verbal prompts to focus their role-play.

☆ Ask the children how they felt when they were searching for the tortoise. Ask them to TTYP to tell their partner how they felt. Ask the children to Popcorn ideas, e.g. *upset, full of worry, frantic, alarmed, in a panic.*

☆ Remind the children of the 'power words' they have been using to think of a replacement for the word *looked*. Ask them to TTYP and think of one synonym for *look*. Popcorn feedback: *hunt, search, seek out.*

☆ Practise saying a sentence with each phrase, e.g. *We are full of worry but we will seek out Floyd. We are in a panic but we will search the garden. We are frantic but we will hunt for Floyd.*

☆ Click on the next screen (characters from the book, looking worried) and model writing a sentence with one of the choices, e.g. *We are in a panic but we will search the garden.* using Set 1 and 2 sounds. Remember to model rereading for sense, and checking word spaces and punctuation. Show how to copy *are* from the Red Word cards. Rub out/cover up the words *in a panic but we will search the garden* and repeat the process with the other choices.

☆ Rub out/cover up your writing and tell the children to write the sentences into the speech bubbles in their *Get Writing!* Book, using either their own ideas or yours, if they need the support.

b) *Where did they look?*

☆ Show the image of Grandpa Roy and the pictures of various locations on **CD** (file 12.3). See p.32 of the *Get Writing!* Book for this activity.

☆ Explain that Grandpa Roy can't see well and needs their help to find the tortoise. Drag and drop him in the different locations that the family looked in: the greenhouse, the weeds, the sandpit and the picnic rug.

☆ Each time, tell the children to TTYP to tell Grandpa Roy what they see. Encourage the children to give Grandpa Roy exact locations. Ask the children to Popcorn ideas, e.g. *the greenhouse near the shed/at the bottom of the garden.*

☆ Practise saying the sentence using each phrase, e.g. *We looked in the thick weeds. No tortoise. We looked in the greenhouse at the bottom of the garden. No tortoise. We looked around the sandpit by the tree. No tortoise. We went back to the picnic rug and there was Floyd!*

- ☆ Display **CD** (file 12.4) and model writing the sentences with one of the choices, e.g. *We looked in the greenhouse. No tortoise.* using Set 1 and 2 sounds. Show how to copy *the* and *no* from the Red Word cards. Rub out/cover up the word *greenhouse* and repeat the process with the other choices.
- ☆ Rub out/cover up your writing and tell the children to write into the speech bubbles in their *Get Writing!* Book.

Orange Non-fiction Book 1   *Jam tarts*

Introducing the book

> *stinky   crispy   crunchy   delicious   sparkling*

- ☆ Use these 'power words' when introducing the book during reading Activity 3. Write them on sticky notes so you remember to use them through the lesson/day.

See Blueprint lesson plans for **Activity 5 Hold a sentence** *and* **Activity 7 Edit** *on pp.25–26.*

Activity 8 Composition: picture prompts

Power words

- ☆ TOL to relate back to the book: *When we go shopping it is great to have a shopping list. But I think Mum's list could be better. She needs to say exactly what she wants!*
- ☆ Use MT/YT to repeat these 'power words'. *Does she want* **stinky** *cheese or just mild cheese? Does she want soft bread rolls or* **crispy**, **crunchy** *bread rolls? Does she want still water or* **sparkling** *water?*

Say the sentences

- ☆ TOL as you build up the sentences together, orally, about the shopping trip.
- ☆ Ask the children to help you remember some of the 'power words'.
- ☆ Use MT/YT every time you expand the sentence together. Do not make it look too easy as you think of what to say. Encourage the children to help you so they take ownership of the sentence.
- ☆ Once you have decided upon the final sentence, use actions and gestures to help the children remember the sentence. Repeat until they can all say it after you. **I want** *delicious, chewy jam tarts.* **I want** *stinky, smelly, gooey cheese.* **I want** *fizzy, sparkling, sweet pop in a can.* **I want** *crunchy, crackling bread rolls.*
  The jam tarts are *delicious.* **The jam tarts are** *sweet and delicious.* **The jam tarts are** *sweet and delicious washed down with fizzy pop!*
- ☆ Relate back to the book, and ask: what shall we put in the trolley? **Pop in a** *packet of stinky green cheese.* **Pop in** *six crunchy delicious bread rolls.*
- ☆ Use the 'power words' and stems from the sentences you have built in this activity throughout the session and day, e.g. *What* **delicious crunchy** *apples. I love* **sparkling** *drinks.*

Write the sentences

My picnic shopping list.
- ☆ Show the image of the lady with a shopping trolley on **CD** (file NF1.2). See p.34 in the *Get Writing!* Book for this activity.
- ☆ Act out being Mum. *Right, we need to get some food for a picnic. Can you think what we might need?* Choose children to feed back, e.g. *cheese, rolls, crisps, pop, jam tarts.*
- ☆ Use MT/YT to expand the descriptions of the items to go on the list. TOL: *Not just cheese; stinky smelly cheese. Not just rolls; crispy crunchy rolls. Not just pop; cans of fizzy pop.*

- ✰ Practise saying the sentences to go on the shopping list, e.g. *1 packet of stinky smelly cheese, 4 crispy crunchy rolls, 3 cans of fizzy pop.*
- ✰ Click on the next screen and model writing the list with one of the phrases e.g. *1 packet of stinky smelly cheese.* TOL and ask children to help as you sound out each word using Set 1 and 2 sounds. Model how you re-read the sentence after writing each word to check it makes sense and leave spaces between words. Show how you copy *of* from the Red Word card.
- ✰ Rub out/cover up the phrase *1 packet of stinky smelly cheese* and repeat the process with the other choices.
- ✰ Rub out/cover up your writing and tell the children to write the sentences onto the shopping list in their *Get Writing!* Book, using either their own ideas or yours, if they need the support.

Orange Non-fiction Book 5   *Jim's house in 1874*

Introducing the book

different servants scullery mangle

- ✰ Use these 'power words' when introducing the book during reading Activity 3. Write them on sticky notes so you remember to use them through the lesson/day.

*See Blueprint lesson plans for **Activity 5 Hold a sentence** and **Activity 7 Edit** on pp.25–26.*

Activity 8 Composition: picture prompts

Power words

- ✰ TOL to relate back to the book: *This book is an information book. It tells you all about what it was like to live in a house in 1874.*
- ✰ Use MT/YT to repeat the 'power words'. *It was **different** then. They had **servants** to help them. There were **different** names for rooms, like the '**scullery**'.*
- ✰ Use MT/YT to extend the language. *They used a **mangle** then. The maid used the **mangle** in the **scullery**. They had **servants** like the cook and the maid.*

Say the sentences

- ✰ TOL as you build up the sentences together, orally, about Jim's house.
- ✰ Use MT/YT each time you expand on the sentence stem until they can all say it after you. ***They had different** toys.* ***They had different** toys to play with.* ***They had different** toys to play with in the sitting room.* ***They had different** ways of doing things.* ***They had different** ways of doing the washing.* ***They had different** ways of doing the washing using a mangle.*
- ✰ Use the 'power words' and stems from the sentences you have built in this activity throughout the session and day, e.g. *It was very **different** in the past. They had **different** ideas about people – they even had **servants**!*

Write the sentences

Write about Jim's house in 1874 and Jim's house now.
- ✰ Display **CD** (file NF5.2). See p.36 in the *Get Writing!* Book for this activity.
- ✰ Say you are going to write about the differences between the 1874 house and houses now.
- ✰ Focus on the mind map headings (Kitchen, bathroom and toys) and the picture prompts and TOL as you think back to Jim's house again and what it was like, e.g. *Jim's kitchen has a cook to make the food and another room called a scullery. There is a maid. The mangle is used to help wash clothes.*

☆ Ask the children to TTYP to compare their kitchen to Jim's. Popcorn feedback, e.g. *We do the cooking, a machine cleans the clothes, we do not have a cook or maid.* Make brief notes of key words on the mind map.

☆ Then ask them to compare their bathroom to Jim's house. Popcorn feedback again, e.g. *They had a lav in the garden. We have a toilet/loo in the bathroom. They had a bowl and jug to wash with. We have taps, a sink and a bath.*

☆ Ask children the TTYP and compare the kinds of toys they have now with the toys that Jim had. Take feedback and make notes.

☆ Click on the next screen (bathroom section of chart). Practise saying the phrases for this section, e.g. *Then: They had a lav in the garden. They had a bowl and jug to wash with. Now: We have a toilet/loo in the bathroom. We have taps, a sink and a bath.*

☆ Model writing the sentence with of one the choices onto the chart, e.g. *They had a lav in the garden.* using Set 1 and 2 sounds. Show how to copy *the* from the red word cards.

☆ Rub out/cover up the sentence and repeat the process with the other screens (kitchen, toys).

☆ Rub out/cover up your writing and tell the children to write some sentences under the headings in the Now and Then chart in their *Get Writing!* book. They can use their own ideas, or you could display the mind map again to help them if they need the support.

Yellow Storybook 1   *The duckchick*

Introducing the story

> shocked   alarmed   plunged   shook like a leaf   yelled

☆ Use these 'power words' when introducing the story during reading Activity 3. Write them on sticky notes so you remember to use them through the lesson/day, e.g. *The children yelled and screamed in the playground. You look very alarmed. What happened?*

*See Blueprint lesson plans for **Activities 1, 2, 3, 4 (Spelling)** and **Activity 5 Hold a sentence** on pp.23–25.*

Activity 6 Build a sentence

shocked

☆ Ask children to TTYP (Turn to your partner) and think of words that mean the same as (synonyms for) *shocked*. Offer words of your own.

☆ Ask children when and where they might use the word. TTYP and feedback, e.g. *When something you have worked hard at goes wrong or is ruined. When a friend is unkind to you. When you feel someone has been unfair to you.*

☆ TOL (Think out loud) as you try out an example of your own. MT/YT (My turn/Your turn) each time you develop it, e.g. *Mama hen was shocked that the egg was different to the others. How did she show that she was shocked? Mama hen made a shocked cluck because she was full of worry about the over-sized egg. How did she react when she saw the egg crack open? Mama hen's eyes went wide with alarm and shock when she saw a duckchick come out of the egg.*

☆ Mime the punctuation when you are happy with your sentence.

☆ Ask children to TTYP to try out sentences of their own using different words to describe *shock*. Listen carefully, then Choose Two to feedback.

☆ TOL as you build on one of the ideas and write the sentence. Ask children to help as you do this. Model re-reading for sense and punctuation.

☆ Ask children to develop a sentence of their own. Ask them to practise saying it before they write.

☆ Rub out/cover up your writing and tell the children to write their own sentence/s in their *Get Writing!* Books (p.3).

☆ Remember to follow this process every time you build a sentence with the children. Page references to this set of notes are given as a reminder.

*See Blueprint lesson plans for **Activity 7 Edit** on p.26.*

Activity 8 Composition: picture prompts

Write about how the duckchick is different from the chicks.

☆ Show the image of the duckchick and the chicks on **CD** (file 1.2). See p.4 of the *Get Writing!* Book. In this activity the children will complete a chart, writing sentences comparing the duckchick and the chicks.

☆ Remind the children that the duckchick is different from the other chicks. Focus on the picture of the duckchick. TOL as you describe him. *The duckchick is much bigger: his beak and wings are bigger, he is a duck, he can quack and swim, he eats crusts.*

☆ Focus on the pictures of the chicks. Ask the children to TTYP and think how the chicks are different from the duckchick. Popcorn feedback, e.g. *they are smaller and fluffier, they peck grubs, they are chicks, they cannot swim, they cheep.*

Yellow

- ✩ Click on the next screen (differences chart) and model choosing two descriptions that contrast with each other. *The duckchick is big and has a large yellow beak. The chicks are small and fluffy.*
- ✩ Ask the children to TTYP and think of two descriptions that contrast with each other. Popcorn feedback, e.g. *chicks peck grubs, duckchick eats crusts.*
- ✩ Practise saying the sentences to compare them, e.g. *He is big with a large yellow beak./They are small and fluffy. He pecks crusts in the water. They peck grubs in the mud./He is a duck and he quacks. They are chicks and they cluck./He loves to swim. They cannot swim.*
- ✩ Ask the children to TTYP to think of other things that they could contrast about the chicks and the duckchick.
- ✩ Model writing the contrasting descriptions with some of the choices, e.g. *He loves to swim. They cannot swim.* TOL as you sound out each word. Model re-reading for sense and punctuation.
- ✩ Ask the children to practise saying their description.
- ✩ Rub out/cover up your writing and tell the children to write the comparisons on to the chart in their *Get Writing!* Book.

Activity 9 Composition

a) *What happened? What did Mama hen do?*

- ✩ Explain to the children that they are going to retell the story, using exciting language. First, through role-play, you will tell the story out loud together, remembering what happened and how the chicks felt.

    Teacher role: Mama hen   Children's role: chicks

- ✩ Take on your role whole-heartedly throughout this activity so children adopt their role easily and enthusiastically.
  The most awful thing has happened, a fox popped up and scared my chicks and they all fell into the pond. I shook like a leaf as they flapped about. I clucked with alarm. I flapped about in a panic. Oh, it was terrible.
  Chicks, did you see the fox? Tell me what you saw.
  Popcorn feedback from the chicks.
  Chicks, did you hear my panic? Tell me what you heard.
  Popcorn feedback from the chicks.
- ✩ *Sentence 1:* Show the image of the chicks falling into the pond on **CD** (file 1.3). See p.5 of the *Get Writing!* Book for this activity.
- ✩ Tell the children that they are going to write this part of the story using lots of exciting language. *Let's build up the tension to describe the fox suddenly appearing. We'll collect lots of ideas before we start to write.*
- ✩ Click on the next screen (mind map for the fox). Scribe some of the children's ideas on it to use later.
- ✩ Ask: *What did the fox look like?* TTYP and feedback, e.g. *sly, hungry, wild.*
  How did it appear? TTYP and feedback, e.g. *all of a sudden/out of nowhere/from behind the bushes. Show me how Mama hen reacted,* e.g. *she flapped and panicked, she squawked in alarm.*
  Let's write all these words down on the mind map before we forget them. Let's use some of these words to try out a different opener for this part of the story. Point to the words as you choose them.
- ✩ TOL, e.g. *The fox popped out from the bushes… The sly fox suddenly popped out from behind the bushes.*
  What did Mama hen do?
  The sly fox suddenly popped out from behind the bushes and Mama hen squawked.
  How/why did she squawk?
  The sly fox suddenly popped out from behind the bushes and Mama hen squawked in alarm/with fear, etc.

☆ Ask partners to TOL to try out different openers. Listen carefully as they talk and select one sentence to model writing.

☆ Click on the next screen and model writing your opening about the fox appearing, and what Mama hen did. Model re-reading for sense and punctuation.

☆ Ask the children to practise saying their sentence before they write.

☆ Either cover up/rub out your writing and tell the children to write some sentences in their *Get Writing!* Books or leave your sentence up so that less confident writers can borrow bits of the sentence to use in their writing. Then repeat the process for modelling sentences about what Mama hen did, e.g. *Mama hen was so worried that … she shook like a leaf/she clucked in alarm/she flapped and panicked.*

b) *What did the chicks say? What did the duckchick do?*

☆ Return to the role as Mama hen: *When my chicks fell in the pond I was alarmed. I could not see them! Oh chicks, where are you? I can hear my chicks calling but where are you?*

☆ Respond to the chicks' calls for help by describing what you can hear, e.g. *Listen! I can hear you cry/shout/scream/yell for help. You are all safe! Thank goodness for duckchick. That was awful. Chicks, my dears, tell me how you felt? e.g. alarmed/frightened/scared.*

☆ Reflect and develop the responses back to the chicks: *Oh my poor/brave/scared chicks. Oh my tiny frightened chicks.*

☆ Show the image of the chicks and the duckchick after he has saved the day on **CD** (file 1.4). See p.5 of the *Get Writing!* Book for this activity.

☆ Sentence 1: TOL: *Do you remember the chicks called for help? What other words could we use for called? yelled/shouted/cried, etc.* TTYP and feedback.

☆ TOL as you try out sentences.
"Help!" cried/shouted/yelled/screamed the chicks.
How can we show that the chicks are really scared?
"Help!" yelled the chicks in alarm. "Help!" screamed the chicks in a panic.

☆ Click on the next screen and model writing.

☆ Ask children to TTYP to try out different sentences out loud and then to write their chosen sentence in their *Get Writing!* Books.

☆ Sentence 2: TOL: *Do you remember how the book described the duckchick coming to the rescue as quick as a flash? How else could we describe his movement? Quick as lightning, like a bullet?* TTYP and feedback.

☆ TOL as you try out sentences.
Quick as lightning, the duckchick zoomed to the rescue. Fast as a bullet, the duckchick plunged to the rescue.

☆ Ask children to TTYP to try out different sentences out loud and then to write their chosen sentences.

Yellow Storybook 2   *Off sick*

Introducing the story

> miserable   down in the dumps   moody   bounce/bouncing   full of glee

☆ Use these 'power words' when introducing the story during reading Activity 3. Write them on sticky notes so you remember to use them through the lesson/day, e.g. *The character in the story is miserable because they can't find a way to escape. You look full of glee – has something good happened today?*

See Blueprint lesson plans for **Activities 1, 2, 3, 4 (Spelling)** and **Activity 5 Hold a sentence** on pp.23–25.

Yellow

Activity 6 Build a sentence

miserable

☆ Ask children to TTYP and think of words that mean the same as (synonyms for) *miserable*. Offer words of your own.

☆ Ask children when and where they might use the word. TTYP and feedback, e.g. when they are disappointed or when something has gone wrong.

☆ TOL as you try out an example of your own. MT/YT each time you develop it e.g.,
I feel miserable.
I feel miserable, my best toy is broken and I will never be happy again!
When I feel miserable it is as if there is a gigantic black hole of sadness in my tummy!
Continue as for the lesson plan on p.96.

☆ Rub out/cover up your writing and tell the children to write their *own* sentence/s about a time they were very sad in their *Get Writing!* Books (p.7).

See Blueprint lesson plans for **Activity 7 Edit** *on p. 26.*

Activity 8 Composition: picture prompts

Write your own door signs.

☆ Explain to the children that they will be writing a door sign that shows how they are feeling and what they want to do. First, through role-play, they will think of sentences out loud to describe their feelings.

    Teacher role: annoying sibling   Children's role: sick child

☆ Take on your role whole-heartedly throughout this activity so children adopt their role easily and enthusiastically.

☆ Show the image of a door with a door handle sign on it saying *Keep out!* on **CD** (file 2.2). See p.8 of the *Get Writing!* Book for this activity.

☆ Go into role as an annoying sibling:
Wait a minute, this door sign says 'Keep out!' How rude! Why should I keep out, I wonder? Is it because you are ill, or grumpy? Are you feeling down in the dumps, or moody? Tell me why I should keep out. I want to come in and play with you. Why should I stay away?

☆ Popcorn feedback from the children and Paraphrase the children's responses.
You are feeling miserable and down in the dumps! MT/YT.
You do not want to play because you are in a foul mood! MT/YT.
You want me to keep out because I am an annoying pest! MT/YT.

☆ Model writing descriptions for the *Keep out!* side of the door handle sign with their choices, e.g. *Keep out! I am down in the dumps and I do not want to play!* Model re-reading for sense and punctuation.

☆ Ask children to practise saying their sentence.

☆ Rub out/cover up your writing and ask them to write their own *Keep out!* sign in their *Get writing!* Books.

☆ Click on the next screen and show the door handle sign saying *Come in!* Ask the children what games the children could play together, and Popcorn feedback, e.g. *robots, cars, beds, dens, fairies/ dolls, tea sets, schools.*
Oh, I see! You want to play now. Well, I'm not sure. Why should I play with you?

☆ Paraphrase the children's responses. TTYP and feed back: *Why should I play with you?* e.g. *I've got cool games, we can make a den, we can bounce on the beds.*

☆ TTYP and feed back. *Why should I come in and play with you?*

☆ TOL as you expand the description together, e.g. *We can bounce on the beds. We can bounce on the beds and fling ourselves in the air. We can bounce on the beds and fling ourselves in the air so high that we hit the ceiling!*

- ✫ Repeat the above with different games. Ask children to TTYP and feed back to think about how much fun they can make each game sound.
- ✫ Model writing the descriptions for the *Come in!* side of the door handle sign with some of their choices, e.g. *Come in and play dens with me. Come in and play schools with me.*
- ✫ Ask the children to practise saying their welcoming sentence.
- ✫ Rub out/cover up your writing and ask the children to write their door handle signs in their *Get Writing!* Books.

Activity 9 Composition

Write what the children are thinking and saying.
- ✫ Show the image of Sam and his sick sister in the bedroom on **CD** (file 2.3). See p.9 of the *Get Writing!* Book for this activity.
- ✫ Tell the children that they are going to zoom in and write speech and feelings for the characters Sam and his sick sister.
- ✫ Ask the children to TTYP to discuss the questions below and Popcorn the feedback. Ask them to help you write their ideas on the board. *What is Sam doing at the end of the bed? e.g. looking smug, bouncing, jumping, jigging.*
Why is he jigging about? e.g. because he is off to swim/because he is excited/because he is doing something his sister isn't!
How is Sam feeling? e.g. delighted/a bit mean/excited/full of glee.
How is Sam's sister feeling? e.g. annoyed/down in the dumps/miserable/grumpy/moody.
What does Sam's sister look like? e.g. sad/gloomy/she is hiding under the pillow/cross/annoyed.
- ✫ Click on the next screen and show the speech and thought bubbles for Sam.
Speech Bubble 1
You look really gloomy hidden under your pillow.
I'm sorry that you are feeling so miserable.
Thought bubble 1
Ha ha! You are stuck here and I'm off having fun!
I'm annoying you. But I don't care because I'm off to swim!
- ✫ Use MT/YT to practise saying the sentences out loud using the children's ideas.
- ✫ Ask the children to write their chosen sentence in Sam's thought and speech bubble in their *Get Writing!* Books.
- ✫ Click on the next screen and show the speech and thought bubbles for Sam's sister. Repeat the process for Sam's sister.
Speech Bubble 2
Sam, stop bouncing about. You are making me feel grumpier.
I wish I could swim with you. I am so miserable stuck in my bed.
Thought bubble 2
I wish he would stop bouncing, he is so excited and I am so fed up.
Sam is really annoying. I wish he would just stop jiggling about.
- ✫ Use MT/YT to practise saying their sentences out loud using the children's ideas.
- ✫ Ask the children to write their chosen sentence for Sam's sister's thought and speech bubbles in their *Get Writing!* Books.

Introducing the story

the size of   as small as   gigantic   massive   enormous

☆ Use these 'power words' when introducing the story during reading Activity 3. Write them on sticky notes so you remember to use them through the lesson/day, e.g. *That is a gigantic picture. Make your circle the size of a penny. This teddy is smaller than the enormous father bear! I feel as small as an ant when I am embarrassed.*

*See Blueprint lesson plans for **Activities 1, 2, 3, 4 (Spelling)** and **Activity 5 Hold a sentence** on pp.23–25.*

Activity 6 Build a sentence

gigantic

☆ Ask children to TTYP and think of words that mean the same as (synonyms for) *gigantic*. Offer words of your own.

☆ Show the image of the size barometer on **CD** (file 3.2) and drag and drop the size words and phrases on it. Model using each word or phrase so that the children are familiar with the meaning (*gigantic, massive, enormous, as small as a pea, the size of an eggcup, smaller than a man's thumb*).

☆ Ask children when and where they might use the word. TTYP and feed back, e.g. *to describe things much bigger than them/to make comparisons about size.*

☆ TOL as you try out an example of your own. MT/YT each time you develop it, e.g.
The plants seemed gigantic to Tom Thumb.
Tom Thumb was so small that the fish that gobbled him up seemed gigantic!
Tom Thumb climbed out of the gigantic pie and surprised the King!

☆ Continue as for the lesson plan on p.96.

☆ Rub out/cover up your writing and tell the children to write their own sentence/s about Tom Thumb's size in their *Get Writing!* Books (p.11).

*See Blueprint lesson plans for **Activity 7 Edit** on p. 26.*

Activity 8 Composition: picture prompts

Write the 'Lost' poster about Tom Thumb

☆ Explain to the children that through role-play they will write a *Lost* poster for Tom Thumb.
Teacher role: Tom Thumb's mum   Children's role: Tom Thumb's friends

☆ Take on your role whole-heartedly throughout this activity so children adopt their role easily and enthusiastically.

☆ Show the image of Tom Thumb on **CD** (file 3.3). See p.12 of the *Get Writing!* Book for this activity.

☆ Teacher in role as Tom Thumb's mum, *Oh, I am distraught! Tom Thumb – my tiny boy – is gone! He has disappeared. Have you seen him? Well, I'm going to have to make a Lost poster. Help me describe him.*

☆ Popcorn feedback. Respond to the children's feedback and encourage them to expand their descriptions.

☆ *So I think we have all the details about what he looked like. Let's check that I've got it right.*

☆ Say after me MT/YT – *Tom Thumb is the size of a man's thumb. He has a shiny red button cap. He has a soft pink coat with a belt. He is smaller than a frog. He is as small as a box of matches.*

☆ Ask the children to TTYP and feed back the most important pieces of information to include about Tom Thumb's appearance for the poster.

Yellow

☆ Click on the next screen and model writing the descriptions with some of their choices, e.g. *Tom Thumb is as big as a man's thumb.* Model re-reading for sense and punctuation.

☆ Ask the children to practise saying the first sentence.

☆ Rub out/cover up your writing and ask the children to write their *Lost* poster in their *Get Writing!* Books.

☆ In role: *Mmm, that is great. I know: if we can say where he likes to play, we can help people look for him. So where should people look for him?*

☆ Ask the children to TTYP and feed back: *Where does Tom Thumb like to play?* e.g. *down by the pond, in the long grass with the insects. What does he like to do there?*

☆ TOL as you expand the description together, e.g. *splash and play.*
Tom Thumb likes to play with the frogs down by the pond.
Tom Thumb likes to splash and play with the frogs down by the shady pond.

☆ Ask children to TTYP and feed back to think about how much detail they can add to where Tom Thumb likes to play.

☆ Click on the next screen and model writing the descriptions with some of their choices, e.g. *He likes to play in the long grass with the insects.* Model re-reading for sense and punctuation.

☆ Ask the children to practise saying the first sentence.

☆ Rub out/cover up your writing and ask the children to write their *Lost* poster in their *Get Writing!* Books.

Activity 9 Composition

Write about the King when he sees Tom Thumb.

☆ Show the image of the King just as Tom Thumb pops out of the pie on **CD** (file 3.4). See p.13 of the *Get Writing!* Book for this activity.

☆ Tell the children that they are going to zoom in and write an exciting description of the moment the King sees Tom Thumb appear out of the cake.
Ask the children to TTYP to discuss the questions below and Popcorn the feedback, e.g.
Nose: *What can he smell?* e.g. *He can smell the sweet smell of the delicious mouth-watering plum pudding. Yum!*

☆ TOL as you build up two or three sentences with the children. Take children's ideas as you write next to the symbol on the board.

☆ Ask children to TTYP to try out different sentences out loud.

☆ Ask them to write their chosen sentence next to the nose symbol in their *Get Writing!* Books.

☆ Repeat for the other symbols.
Eyes: *What does he see?* e.g. *All of a sudden/in a flash/ a tiny boy/a boy as small as my thumb popped/burst out of the pie.*
Mouth: *What does he say?* e.g. *My pie is alive! A boy in my pie, oh my!*
Legs: *What does he do?* e.g. *He roared with laughter/clapped his hands together/laughed out loud.*
Heart: *How does the King feel?* *surprised/it was very funny/what a good trick!*

☆ Celebration: Partner 1 says how the King feels to Partner 2. Partner 2 repeats the sentence back. Choose a few of the sentences to feed back to the class.

Introducing the story

> *sneaked away   sprinted   ran like the wind   plodded   cunning   crafty*

☆ Use these 'power words' when introducing the story during reading Activity 3. Write them on sticky notes so you remember to use them through the lesson/day, e.g. *He sped away like the wind but I just trudged behind. Ah! You can't sneak away…I can see you.*

See Blueprint lesson plans for **Activities 1, 2, 3, 4 (Spelling)** and **Activity 5 Hold a sentence** on pp.23–25.

Activity 6 Build a sentence

ran like the wind

☆ Ask the children to TTYP and think of words that mean the same as (synonyms for) *ran like the wind*. Offer words of your own.

☆ Show the image of the speed barometer on **CD** (file 4.2) and drag and drop the words on it. Model using each word so that the children are familiar with the meaning of each word: *sped, sneaked away, dashed, ran like the wind, plodded, trudged, lumbered.*

☆ Ask children when and where they might use the word or phrase. TTYP and feed back, e.g. *to say how fast they are running in a race, to say how slowly they are moving when they don't want to do something!*

☆ TOL as you try out an example of your own. MT/YT each time you develop it, e.g.
The gingerbread man ran like the wind.
The gingerbread man ran like the wind as he sped out of the kitchen.
Ask: *How else could the others run after the gingerbread man? They plodded, lumbered slowly, etc.*
The gingerbread man ran like the wind and the others trudged along after him.

☆ Continue as for the lesson plan on p.96.

☆ Rub out/cover up your writing and tell the children to write their own sentence/s about the chase in their *Get Writing!* Books (p.15).

See Blueprint lesson plans for **Activity 7 Edit** on p.26.

Activity 8 Composition: picture prompts

Write a report about what happened when the gingerbread man ran away.

☆ Explain to the children that following a role-play they will write a police report about the gingerbread man running away.
> *Teacher role: Police   Children's role: Seth and Anne, who chased the gingerbread man*

☆ Take on your role whole-heartedly throughout this activity so children adopt their role easily and enthusiastically. Make yours a very detail-obsessed policeman. Be very deliberate and fussy to get all the facts exactly right when using MT/YT!

☆ Show the image of the policeman's notebook on **CD** (file 4.3). See p.16 of the *Get Writing!* Book for this activity.
Say: *I'm here to gather evidence of a disappearing gingerbread man, who I believe was baked in this here house today. Right, so he jumped up and sneaked out of the house. And then what happened? How fast did he run? Would I be able to keep up with him? Would a dog be able to run fast enough? How fast exactly could he run?*

☆ Ask the children to TTYP and Popcorn feedback: *like a bullet, as quick as lightning, like the wind. Never! And how fast did you run after him? e.g. we sprinted/sped off/we dashed after him. I need to get this exactly right…Tell me how fast this biscuit ran and how exactly you followed after him.*

☆ Ask children to TTYP and feed back using Choose Two or Paraphrase, e.g. *So he ran like the wind and you sprinted after him.* Offer your own ideas too.

☆ As you go through each sentence use MT/YT to get each part of the report just right, using connectives (*first, soon, just then, at last*) to order the events.

☆ Start the report by writing about what happened first when the gingerbread man ran away, e.g. *First the gingerbread man ran off like the wind and Seth and Anne sprinted after him.* Model re-reading for sense and punctuation.

☆ Use MT/YT to practise saying sentences out loud using the children's ideas.

☆ Ask the children to write their chosen sentences.

☆ *Sentence 2: So, why didn't you catch him? Surely you could catch up with a biscuit! Did you slow down? Did you run out of puff?*

☆ Ask the children to TTYP to discuss the question. Paraphrase their feedback.

☆ TOL as you expand the description together: e.g. *slow down, lumbered along.*
Soon Seth and Anne began to slow down and they slowly lumbered along.
Soon Seth and Anne ran out of steam, they lumbered along and saw the gingerbread man run off.

☆ Model writing the next line of the report: *Soon Seth and Anne ran out of steam and lumbered along but the gingerbread man just sped off.* Then ask children to write.

☆ *Sentences 3 and 4: Say: I hear a fox appeared on the scene. What type of fox would you say it was? And what did it do?*

☆ Ask the children to TTYP to discuss the question. Paraphrase their feedback.
It was a crafty, sneaky, clever fox.
It gobbled/snaffled the gingerbread man – bit him in two – ate him in one huge gulp!
Just then Seth and Anne saw a cunning fox walk up to the gingerbread man.
It gobbled up the gingerbread man in one huge gulp!

☆ Use MT/YT to practise saying sentences out loud using the children's ideas. Ask the children to write their chosen sentence in their *Get Writing!* Books.

Activity 9 Composition

Write your ideas about the fox.
What is the gingerbread man thinking?

☆ Show the image of the fox and the gingerbread man on **CD** (file 4.4). See p.17 of the *Get Writing!* Book for this activity.

☆ Tell the children that they are going to write their own version of the ending of the story. They will prepare for this by making notes about the fox, and what the gingerbread man was thinking.

☆ Ask the children to TTYP to discuss the questions below and Popcorn the feedback. Ask them to help you write their ideas on the board.

☆ Use the nose and legs symbols, as well as the thought bubbles on screen to help ask questions.
Nose: *What can the fox smell?* e.g. *sweet tasty gingerbread/a delicious lunch/the warm grass.*
Legs: *How is the fox moving?* e.g. *trotting along, quickly so the gingerbread man has to run to keep up.*
Thought bubble: *What is the fox thinking?* e.g. *Any minute now I'll eat him up.*
Thought bubble: *What is the gingerbread man thinking?* e.g. *at last a friend, I like this fox.*

☆ *Sentence 1:* TOL as you build up sentences with the children. Click on the next screens and take their ideas as you write, e.g.
The fox smells sweet, tasty gingerbread.

☆ *Sentence 2:*
The fox trots along happily.

☆ *Sentence 3:*
The fox thought, Yummy, lunch-time!
I will gobble him up in two big bites!

☆ *Sentence 4:*
The gingerbread man is thinking Good, I am safe at last.

* Use MT/YT to practise saying their sentences out loud using the children's ideas. Ask children to TTYP to try out different sentences out loud.
* Then ask them to write their chosen sentences.

Now write an end to the story.
* Ask: *What do you think happened in the end?*
* Ask children to TTYP and feed back using Choose Two or Paraphrase, e.g. *The cunning fox snapped up the gingerbread man and one, two he was gone! The crafty fox tricked the gingerbread man and had him for his lunch.*
* Ask them to write their own ending to the story in their *Get Writing!* Books.

Yellow Storybook 5   *Robin Hood*

Introducing the story

> immense/immensely   gigantic   massive   plunge   confident

* Use these 'power words' when introducing the story during reading Activity 3. Write them on sticky notes so you remember to use them through the lesson/day, e.g. *I am immensely tired after all that running. I am confident that our team will win the football match today.*

*See Blueprint lesson plans for **Activities 1, 2, 3, 4 (Spelling)** and **Activity 5 Hold a sentence** on pp.23–25.*

Activity 6 Build a sentence

immensely
* Ask children to TTYP and think of words that mean the same as (synonyms for) *immensely*. Offer words of your own.
* Ask children when and where they might use the word. TTYP and feed back, e.g. as an adjective to show how *big/strong/clever/dark* something is, as a substitute for *very*.
* TOL as you try out an example of your own. MT/YT each time you develop it, e.g.
  He was called Little John but he was… immensely big/huge/large.
  Little John was immensely strong.
  Little John was so immensely strong that he could whack Robin Hood into the brook/could carry six men/could lift ten logs at once.
  Get the children to Popcorn other ideas that show how immensely strong Little John was and use them.
* Continue as for the lesson plan on p.96.
* Rub out/cover up your writing and tell the children to write their own sentence/s about how immensly strong Little John was in their *Get Writing!* Books (p.19).

*See Blueprint lesson plans for **Activity 7 Edit** on p. 26.*

Activity 8 Composition: picture prompts

Write about Little John.
* Explain to the children that they will be writing a detailed description of Little John.
* Show the image of Little John on **CD** (file 5.2). See p.20 of the *Get Writing!* Book for this activity.
* Use the heart, eyes, nose, ear symbols on the **CD** to help ask questions. Use TTYP to discuss each question and then Paraphrase feedback enriching or prompting children to add detail to their responses.
  Heart: *What is he feeling when he sees Robin Hood? Who is this tiny fellow?* e.g. *I know him, I'll show him that he's not so special.*
  Nose: *What does he smell like?* e.g. *wood smoke and forest, damp and dirty.*

Yellow

Ear: *What does his voice sound like?* e.g. *immensely loud and booming, surprisingly shrill and high.*

Eyes: Choose one item of clothing and describe it in detail, e.g. *his overcoat: grass green and tatty with food stains and rips in the back.*

☆ Click onto the next screen and model writing the descriptions with some of their choices, e.g. *Little John had a huge booming voice.* Model re-reading for sense and punctuation.

☆ Ask the children to practise saying their first description of Little John.

☆ Rub out/cover up your writing and ask the children to write their descriptions around the picture of Little John in their *Get Writing!* Books.

☆ Celebration: partners rehearse one descriptive sentence together and feedback in unison. Teacher chooses feedback.

Activity 9 Composition

a) *What are they saying? What are they thinking?*

Speech bubbles

☆ Show the image of Little John and Robin Hood on the wooden bridge with two speech bubbles on **CD** (file 5.3). See p.21 in the *Get Writing!* Book for this activity.

☆ Tell the children that they are going to write the dialogue/speech for the two characters and try to work out what they might be thinking too

☆ Remind the children how Little John stood up to Robin Hood when they met. Ask them to act out meeting on the bridge and practise speaking to each other. Ask the children to TTYP and choose the best two sentences from their role-play and practise them. Popcorn feedback.

☆ TOL as you build up the two sentences with the children. Take their ideas as you write into the large speech bubbles, e.g.

> Little John: *Who are you? You cannot come past.*
> Robin Hood: *I will come past! Let me come past, I say!*

☆ Use MT/YT to practise saying their sentences out loud using the children's ideas.

☆ Ask the children to write their chosen sentences into the speech bubbles in their *Get Writing!* Books.

Thought bubbles

☆ Tell the children that although the men might sound brave and proud they might be feeling surprised, shocked or scared as they face each other.

☆ Ask the children to TTYP to discuss how they felt during their role-play. Paraphrase their feedback.

☆ Click onto the next screen and TOL as you build up two or three sentences with the children. Take children's ideas as you write, e.g. *Oh, that is Robin Hood. He is smaller than I thought./Who is that massive man? I hope he'll let me past./What a surprise! Robin Hood trying to cross my bridge./He may be gigantic but I am confident that I can beat him in a fight!*

☆ Ask children to TTYP to try out different sentences out loud.

☆ Ask them to write their chosen sentence in the thought bubbles.

b) *What are they saying?*

☆ Click onto the next screen and show the image of Little John and Robin Hood falling off the wooden bridge. See p.22 of the *Get Writing!* Book for this activity.

☆ Ask: *What did they say to each other as they fought?* e.g. *I will whack you!/Help, I am plunging into the brook!*

☆ Ask children to TTYP and feed back using Choose Two or Paraphrase, e.g. *Come here and I'll whack you off the bridge with my massive stick. I shall defeat you with two whacks and you shall plunge into the brook!*

☆ Ask children to TTYP to try out different sentences out loud.

☆ Then ask them to write their chosen sentence in the large speech bubbles.

c) *What are they thinking?*

☆ Click on the next screen (Little John and Robin Hood after the fight). See p.22 of the *Get Writing!* Book for this activity.

☆ Tell the children that the two men must have had very different feelings after the fight. *Was Robin Hood surprised to lose? What did Little John feel now? Did he change his mind about Robin Hood?*

☆ Ask the children to TTYP to discuss the questions. Paraphrase their feedback.

☆ TOL as you build up the two sentences with the children. Take children's ideas as you write, e.g. *I am surprised. Robin Hood put up a good fight./Oh, I was confident I'd win. Now I'm soaking wet!*

☆ Ask children to TTYP to try out different sentences out loud.

☆ Ask them to write their chosen sentence in the thought bubble, e.g. *Ha! I beat Robin Hood. He is not so confident now! I am surprised and wet. I feel a bit silly.*

☆ Select some interesting sentences to read aloud to the class.

Yellow Storybook 6   *Lost*

Introducing the story

mischief   leap   pounce   bounce

☆ Use these 'power words' when introducing the story during reading Activity 3. Write them on sticky notes so you remember to use them through the lesson/day, e.g. *You look like you are full of mischief today – what are you up to?*

See Blueprint lesson plans for **Activities 1, 2, 3, 4 (Spelling)** and **Activity 5 Hold a sentence** on pp.23–25.

Activity 6 Build a sentence

full of mischief

☆ Ask the children to TTYP and think of words that mean the same as (synonyms for) *full of mischief.* Offer words of your own.

☆ Ask the children when and where they might use the word. TTYP and feed back, e.g. *when they talking about cheeky things they have done/to describe puppies and kittens/to describe their friends and siblings.*

☆ TOL as you try out an example of your own. MT/YT each time you develop it. Ask the children to help you think of ways that the kittens could get into trouble, e.g.
Catkin's kittens were full of mischief.
Catkin's kittens were full of mischief as they pounced and rolled on the string.
Catkin's kittens were full of mischief leaping and bouncing on Ray's bed.

☆ Ask: *What else could they do?* e.g. *hide under the covers/climb the curtains/pounce on each other and tumble about.*

☆ Continue as for the lesson plan on p.96.

☆ Rub out/cover up your writing and tell the children to write their own sentence/s about the different antics the kittens got up to in their *Get Writing!* Books (p.24).

See Blueprint lesson plans for **Activity 7 Edit** on p. 26.

Activity 8 Composition: picture prompts

Read the postcard from Ray. Then write a postcard from Kay to Ray.

☆ Explain to the children that they will write a postcard to reply to Ray about how the kittens have been behaving whilst he has been away on holiday.

☆ Show the postcard on **CD** (file 6.2). See p.25 of the *Get Writing!* Book for this activity.

☆ Read the postcard together.

☆ Ask the children to TTYP and feed back: *What do the kittens like to do?* e.g. *play and make mischief.*

☆ Click on the next screen (kittens on the bed). *Exactly what mischief have the kittens been up to on the bed?*

☆ TOL as you expand the description together, e.g. *pounce and leap.*
The kittens like to pounce on the bed and leap out at me.
The kittens like to pounce on the bed and leap out at me because they are cheeky monsters that are full of mischief!

☆ Repeat the above with different things the kitten could play with, e.g. *curtains, string, boxes, sofa.*

☆ Ask children to TTYP and feed back to think about how mischievous they can make the kittens sound.

☆ Click on the next screen (postcard writing frame) and model writing the descriptions with some of their choices, e.g. *The kittens have been very cheeky pulling string around the house.* Model re-reading for sense and punctuation.

☆ Ask the children to practise saying their first sentence for their postcard.

☆ Rub out/cover up your writing and ask the children to write their postcard in their *Get Writing!* Books.

☆ Celebration: Partners tell each other their favourite description of the kittens' antics, and practise it until they can say it clearly. Teacher then chooses a few children to feedback.

Activity 9 Composition

Write what Catkin is saying

☆ Explain to the children that they will be taking the role of Catkin and, in role, writing about what happened and how she felt when she had her kittens.
    Teacher role: Kay   Children's role: Catkin

☆ Take on your role whole-heartedly throughout this activity so children adopt their role easily and enthusiastically.

a)

☆ Show the image of Catkin nesting on **CD** (file 6.3). See p.26 of the *Get Writing!* Book for this activity.

☆ Teacher in role: *Catkin, I have been looking all over for you! Oh, what are you doing snuggled up in a box of straw at Ray's house? Catkin, what are you doing?*
Ask the children to TTYP to discuss. Popcorn the feedback and Paraphrase their answers, expanding their ideas by questioning, e.g. *You are nesting in the warm straw? But why, Catkin? Why did you go to Ray's? You are nesting in the warm straw because you needed a safe quiet place to stay. Why is that, Catkin? Because something important is about to happen…etc.*

☆ When you have all the information repeat it back to the children using the first person, e.g. *I am nesting in the warm straw because I need a safe quiet place to stay.*

☆ TOL as you build up a sentence with the children. Take their ideas as you write, e.g. *Sentence 1: I am nesting in a warm safe place so that I am ready for an important event. I have found a safe secret place to hide and get ready for a special event.*

☆ Use MT/YT to practise saying their sentences out loud using the children's ideas.

☆ Ask the children to write their chosen sentence into the speech bubble.

b)

☆ Click on the next screen (Catkin with her tiny kittens). Ask: *What has happened, Catkin?*

☆ Ask children to TTYP and feed back using Choose Two or Paraphrase, e.g. *Something wonderful! It is amazing. I had two tiny kittens last night.*

☆ Ask: *What are your kittens like?* Popcorn feedback, e.g. *they leap and bounce, they are full of mischief.*

☆ Ask children to TTYP to try out different sentences out loud.

☆ Then tell them to write their chosen sentence in the speech bubble. on p.26 of their *Get Writing! Books.*

Yellow Storybook 7   *Do we have to keep it?*

Introducing the story

squeal with delight   gurgle   chuckle   wail   howl

☆ Use these 'power words' when introducing the story during reading Activity 3. Write them on sticky notes so you remember to use them through the lesson/day, e.g. *What a terrible howling sound! Have you hurt yourself? When babies are happy they burble and chuckle but when they are unhappy they wail and yell.*

*See Blueprint lesson plans for **Activities 1, 2, 3, 4 (Spelling)** and **Activity 5 Hold a sentence** on pp.23–25.*

Activity 6 Build a sentence

gurgles

☆ Ask children to TTYP and think of words that mean the same as (synonyms for) *gurgles* – as well as words that mean the opposite (antonyms). Offer words of your own.

☆ Show the image of the noise barometer on **CD** (file 7.2) and drag and drop the noise words on it. Model using each word so that the children are familiar with the meaning of each word (*laugh, giggle, squeal with delight, gurgle, chuckle, burble, scream, wail, yell, howl*).

☆ Ask children when and where they might use the word. TTYP and feed back, e.g. *when they are playing with a baby/to describe the noises in the playground.*

☆ TOL as you try out an example of your own. MT/YT each time you develop it, e.g.
When I tickle the baby he gurgles.
The baby can wail and wail, then he is happy and gurgles and burbles.
Sometimes when he's yelling I tickle him and he gurgles with delight!

☆ Ask the children to think of other ways of making the baby giggle or describe its delighted happy noises.

☆ Continue as for the lesson plan on p.96.

☆ Rub out/cover up your writing and tell the children to write their own sentence/s to describe the noises a baby makes in their *Get Writing! Books* (p.28).

*See Blueprint lesson plans for **Activity 7 Edit** on p. 26.*

Activity 8 Composition: picture prompts

Write about how to make a baby happy.

☆ Explain to the children that they are going to write a list of top tips to stop a baby screaming and to get it to squeal with delight. First you will think up ideas in role. The top tips will be for a parenting book.
   Teacher role: Mum/Dad   Children's role: a new sibling

☆ Take on your role whole-heartedly throughout this activity so children adopt their role easily and enthusiastically. Make yours a confused and desperate parent. Be very deliberate and ask for exact responses when using MT/YT so you get it right!

☆ Show the image of a page from a parenting book called *How to make a baby giggle and gurgle* on **CD** (file 7.3). See p.29 of the *Get Writing!* Book for this activity.

☆ Say to the children: *Oh dear, the baby is yelling again. What shall I do? How could I stop that howling? What shall we do to help the baby get happy?*

☆ Take children's ideas and Paraphrase them back offering additional information or asking questions to elicit further details. *So I tickle the baby on the feet until he smiles. What else can I do to make the baby chuckle? If I play peep-po with the baby, what noises should I make to make him gurgle with delight?*

☆ Say that their ideas are really helpful and you would like to write them down to remember them.

☆ TOL as you expand the instruction together, e.g. *Tickle them so they giggle and gurgle.*
If your baby is howling, tickle their feet until they giggle and gurgle.
When your baby screams and won't stop, just tickle them gently and listen to them giggle and gurgle with delight.

☆ Continuing in role, model writing the descriptions with some of their choices, e.g. *If the baby is howling, get a rattle and shake it until the baby chuckles.* Model re-reading for sense and punctuation.

☆ Ask the children to practise saying the first instruction for their book.

☆ Rub out/cover up your writing and ask the children to write into the page of the parenting book in their *Get Writing!* Books.

☆ Repeat the above with different toys/activities.

Activity 9 Composition

What would be the best presents for the baby? Write about them.

☆ Open **CD** (file 7.4) and show the last page of the Storybook. See p. 30 of the *Get Writing!* Book for this activity.

☆ Read the line from the Storybook p.15, 'But I may get the baby a new toy, or a silly hat.'

☆ Tell the children that they are going to choose and describe the best present for a baby.

☆ Ask the children to TTYP to discuss what they think would be a great present for a baby and Popcorn the feedback. Click on the next screen to show the mind map, and ask them to help you write their ideas into it.

☆ TOL as you build up some descriptions of the toys with the children. Take their ideas as you write, e.g. *a bright shiny rattle/a soft camel with a wind-up hump that plays a song/a board book with fur and crinkly paper to touch.*

☆ Ask the children to TTYP to discuss which three toys they think are best. Use thumbs up to decide which three toys to write descriptions of.

☆ TOL as you build up three sentences with the children. Take their ideas as you write, e.g.
Sentence 1: I would buy a wooden box with shapes that the baby could post through the holes.
Sentence 2: I would buy a wind-up mouse that could dart about the room and make baby chuckle.
Sentence 3: I would buy a toy elephant with soft floppy ears for baby to snuggle.

☆ Use MT/YT to practise saying their sentences out loud using the children's ideas.

☆ Ask the children to write their chosen sentences in the present labels in their *Get Writing!* Books.

☆ Tell the children that they are going to choose one toy to buy the baby and they need to convince you why it is the best. Use a choice from the previous feedback as an example, e.g. *The teddy is the best because it is soft and cuddly.*

☆ Ask children to TTYP and feed back using Choose Two or Paraphrase, e.g. *The wind-up mouse is best because it will make the baby giggle. The rattle is best because the baby will like to chew on it.*

☆ TOL as you build up the final sentence with the children. Click on the next screen and take their ideas as you write, e.g. *The board book is best because the baby can feel all the different materials. The shape sorter is best because we can play with it together,* etc.

☆ Use MT/YT to practise saying their sentence out loud using the children's ideas.

☆ Ask the children to write their chosen sentence in their *Get Writing!* Books, next to the *Winner* rosette.

Yellow Storybook 8   *Danny and the Bump-a-lump*

Introducing the story

> terrifying   rustle   scuttle   creep   lurk

☆ Use these 'power words' when introducing the story during reading Activity 3. Write them on sticky notes so you remember to use them through the lesson/day, e.g. *Can you creep over to the office and scuttle back with the register?*

*See Blueprint lesson plans for **Activities 1, 2, 3, 4 (Spelling)** and **Activity 5 Hold a sentence** on pp.23–25.*

Activity 6 Build a sentence

terrifying

☆ Ask children to TTYP and think of words that mean the same as (synonyms for) *terrifying*. Offer words of your own.

☆ Ask children when and where they might use the word. TTYP and feed back, e.g. *to describe how scary something was, like a film or a book or a trick.*

☆ TOL as you try out an example of your own. MT/YT each time you develop it, e.g.
The terrifying Bump-a-lump is lurking under my bed.
The terrifying Bump-a-lump is hiding in the shadows under my bed.
The terrifying Bump-a-lump is hidden in the dark corners under my bed.

☆ Ask: *Where else could it be hiding?* Take the children's suggestions and try them out.

☆ Continue as for the lesson plan on p.96.

☆ Rub out/cover up your writing and tell the children to write their own sentence/s to describe how frightening a Bump-a-lump is in their *Get Writing!* Books.

*See Blueprint lesson plans for **Activity 7 Edit** on p. 26.*

Activity 8 Composition: picture prompts

a) *Write notes about the Bump-a-lump.*

☆ Explain to the children that following a role-play they will write a description of the Bump-a-lump so that later they can work out the best way to scare it off. See pp.33–34 of the *Get Writing!* Book for this activity.

> Teacher role: Mum/Dad   Children's role: children scared of a Bump-a-lump under their beds

☆ Take on your role whole-heartedly throughout this activity so children adopt their role easily and enthusiastically. Be meticulous in getting an accurate description of the Bump-a-lump so that the right guardian can be found to scare it away!

☆ Show the images of Danny and Mum, and of Danny imagining the Bump-a-lump on **CD** (file 8.2).

☆ Teacher in role as Mum/Dad: *Why have you come running in here so late at night? What is the matter? What have you seen?*

☆ Take children's ideas and Paraphrase them back with additional information or asking questions to elicit further details.

Yellow

☆ *Well, where was this terrible Bump-a-lump? Under you bed? Oh dear, that is a worry. Why do you think it is under your bed?*

☆ *Say after me 'I will defeat this nasty Bump-a-lump. It is a terrible frightening beast but I will not be scared any more!'*

☆ *I wonder what sort of scary creature it is. If we know what type it is we can work out what will scare it away! Tell me everything you know about it.*

☆ Click on the next screen (mind map with symbols: heart, ear, nose, eyes). See p.33 of the *Get Writing!* Book for this activity.

☆ Ask the children to TTYP to discuss the questions below and Popcorn the feedback. Use the mind map to collect ideas using the questions below.
Eyes: *What exactly does its face look like?* e.g. shaggy hair, rolling mad eyes, green warts, etc.
Nose: *What does it smell of?* e.g. rotten eggs, my dad's cheesy feet.
Ear: *What noises does it make under your bed?* e.g. the scuttle of legs, a rustle of dry bat wings.
Heart: *How does it make you feel?* e.g. terrified, panicked, frozen with fright.

☆ Tell the children to write their own notes about the Bump-a-lump into the mind map on p.33 of their *Get Writing!* Books.

b) *Now write a description of the Bump-a-lump.*

☆ Click on the next screen if you would like to model writing a description on the CD. Continuing in role, model writing a sentence for each section in turn with some of their choices, e.g. *It has green shaggy hair that sticks up and a warty nose.* Model re-reading for sense and punctuation.

☆ Ask the children to practise saying the first sentence, using their mind map to help them.

☆ Repeat this for each question until you have a full set of notes to describe the Bump-a-lump.

☆ Rub out/cover up your writing and ask the children to write their sentences into their *Get Writing!* Books (p.34).

☆ Celebration: Ask each child to describe their Bump-a lump to their partner. Can they listen carefully and repeat the description back? Choose two for feedback.

Activity 9 Composition

a) *Draw your Bump-a-lump scarer.*

☆ Show the image of a Paxicorn (a fierce type of unicorn) along with the note written to the Bump-a-lump on **CD** (file 8.3). See pp.34–35 of the *Get Writing!* Book for this activity.

☆ Tell the children that they are going to draw their Bump-a-lump scarer then write a letter to the Bump-a-lump about it.

☆ Ask the children to TTYP to discuss their Bump-a-lump and what animal or magical creature or thing they think could scare it away. Popcorn feedback. Ask them to help you write their ideas on the board, e.g. *a fierce dragon, a courageous fairy, a lightning sword.*

☆ Get the children to *quickly* draw their Bump-a-lump scarer in their *Get Writing!* Books (p.34).

☆ Ask the children to TTYP and discuss how their creature can defend them from the Bump-a lump. Ask them to help you extend their ideas on the board, e.g. *The fierce dragon could roar at the Bump-a lump and scare it away. The courageous fairy could cast a spell on the Bump-a-lump and turn it into a frog in a tutu!*

b) *Write a letter to Bump-a-lump. Tell him why you are not scared any more.*

☆ Click on the next screen (letter template). See p.35 of the *Get Writing!* Book for this activity.

☆ TOL as you build up two or three sentences with the children for their letter. Take their ideas as you write, e.g.
Sentence 1:
I will not be scared of you any more because I have Roar the Dragon to help me.
I will not hide under my covers any more because I have Tink the Terrible to keep you away.
Sentence 2:

You should be scared now because my Dragon can roar such enormous roars that your ears will fall off! You should be terrified because Tink the Terrible can cast a spell to turn you into a tiny pink hippo!

☆ Use MT/YT to practise saying their sentences out loud using the children's ideas.

☆ Ask the children to start their letter by writing some sentences, using their own ideas or yours, if they need the support.

☆ Click on the next screen (knight nightlight). Ask: *What made the knight so good at scaring the Bump-a-lump away?* e.g. *It was shiny and fierce. It was so shiny and fierce it made Danny feel safe.*

☆ Ask children to TTYP and think how would they tell the Bump-a-lump to beware of their scarer and feed back using Choose Two or Paraphrase, e.g. *My lightning sword can detect when Bump-a-lumps are near and split them in two. So look out! My magical ring lights up when Bump-a-lumps come near and blasts them away! So keep away.*

☆ Ask children to TTYP to try out different sentences out loud.

☆ Then ask them to write some more sentences to continue their letter.

Yellow Storybook 9   *Grow your own radishes*

Introducing the story

> smear/smeared   *dribbling*   *delicious*   *sweet*   *scrumptious*

☆ Use these 'power words' when introducing the book during reading Activity 3. Write them on sticky notes so you remember to use them through the lesson/day, e.g. *Be careful of the paint on your hands or you will smear it everywhere. What a delicious cake with sweet sticky icing on the top!*

*See Blueprint lesson plans for **Activities 1, 2, 3, 4 (Spelling)** and **Activity 5 Hold a sentence** on pp.23–25.*

Activity 6 Build a sentence

smeared

☆ Ask children to TTYP and think of words that mean the same as *smeared*. Offer words of your own.

☆ Ask children when and where they might use the word. TTYP and feed back, e.g. *to describe a painting or how they painted something, to describe how a mess looks, or how the marks on a window are made.*

☆ TOL (Think out loud) as you try out an example of your own. MT/YT each time you develop it, e.g.
I smeared sticky pear juice on my face.
Sticky oranges dribbled down my face and smeared on my top.
The delicious juice from the mango got on my hands and smeared on the walls!

☆ Continue as for the lesson plan on p.96.

☆ Rub out/cover up your writing and tell the children to write their own sentence/s about how messy you can get eating sticky fruit in their *Get Writing!* Books (p.37).

*See Blueprint lesson plans for **Activity 7 Edit** on p.26.*

Activity 8 Composition: picture prompts

Describe what the fruit and vegetables taste like.

NB! You will need to get a variety of fruit and vegetables for the children to taste for this activity.

☆ Display **CD** (file 9.2) and drag and drop different fruit and vegetables into the focus box (*cucumber, apple, pear, banana, cherry tomatoes, oranges*). Ask children to TTYP and discuss which one they like to eat best and why. Popcorn feedback.

☆ Show the Tasting Chart on **CD** (file 9.3). See p.38 of the *Get Writing!* Book for this activity.

☆ Give the children a piece of each fruit/vegetable and get them to TTYP to describe what it tastes like. Choose Two and Paraphrase feedback using questions if needed to add detail, e.g. *This banana is soft and creamy and very sweet. The cucumber is fresh and cool and refreshing.*

☆ TOL as you build up each description with the children. Take their ideas as you write, e.g.
The pear is sweet, juicy and delicious.
The scrumptious orange juice dribbled down my chin.

☆ Use MT/YT to practise saying the sentences out loud using the children's ideas.

☆ Ask the children to write their chosen sentences in the chart in their *Get Writing!* Book.

☆ Tell the children that they are going to choose one of the fruit or vegetables as their favourite. They need to convince you why it is the best, e.g. *The cucumber is best because it is cool and refreshing.*

☆ Ask children to TTYP and feed back using Choose Two or Paraphrase.

☆ Click on the next screen and TOL as you build up the final sentence with the children. Take their ideas as you write, e.g. *I like apples best because they are crunchy and sweet.*

☆ Use MT/YT to practise saying sentences out loud using the children's ideas.

☆ Ask the children to write their chosen sentence next to 'The winner' rosette in their *Get Writing!* Books.

Activity 9 Composition

Write a fruit and vegetable poem.

☆ Explain to the children that through role-play they will work as a market-stall seller describing their delicious fruit and vegetables for sale. They will then write a poem that the market-stall seller can use to call out to people and entice them to his stall.

    Teacher role: head market-stall owner   Children's role: apprentice fruit and vegetable sellers

☆ Take on your role whole-heartedly throughout this activity so children adopt their role easily and enthusiastically.

☆ Show the image of the fruit and vegetable stall on **CD** (file 9.4). See p.39 of the *Get Writing!* Book for this activity.

☆ Teacher in role as head stall owner: *Have you seen my delicious fruit? Come and get my ripe crunchy apples. Right, we need to sell all this fruit and I need you to help me. We need to make the fruit and veg sound amazingly delicious. So scrumptious and tasty that by the end of the day we have none left and we have made lots of money. Hurray!*
Say after me: 'Sweet juicy shiny red apples! Wonderful crunchy pears, look how they dribble with juice.'

☆ Focus on different pieces of fruit and vegetables (click on the next screens to see photos of these to inspire their writing). Ask the children to TTYP and feed back: *How can we make this banana sound delicious?* e.g. *sweet, firm and tasty.*
What does the banana look like?

☆ TOL as you expand the description together, e.g. *Ripe, yellow, sweet, firm and tasty. Forget the rest, come and buy the best! Nice and sweet, a real treat.*
Come and buy my huge bunches of tasty, yellow, ripe bananas, best in the market!
Sound bossier than you would normally on a TOL!

☆ Repeat the above with different items of fruit. Include some summary lines too, e.g. *Get them here, all your greens! Broccoli, cucumbers, or big runner beans.* or *Come and see my market stall. Apples, peaches, there's plenty for all.*

- ☆ Return to the first screen. Continuing in role, model writing the descriptions with some of their choices, e.g. *Come and buy my fresh, crunchy green cucumbers.* Model re-reading for sense and punctuation.
- ☆ Ask the children to practise saying the first line of the poem.
- ☆ Rub out/cover up your writing and ask the children to write their market-stall seller's poem in their *Get Writing!* Books.

Yellow Storybook 10 *The foolish witch*

Introducing the story

scrumptious   mouth-watering   stumble/stumbling   weary/wearily   desperate/desperately

- ☆ Use these 'power words' when introducing the story during reading Activity 3. Write them on sticky notes so you remember to use them through the lesson/day, e.g. *We've got scrumptious chocolate pudding on the lunch menu today. I adore scrumptious, crispy, juicy pears. You are looking weary today – you must have gone to bed late last night.*

See Blueprint lesson plans for **Activities 1, 2, 3, 4 (Spelling)** and **Activity 5 Hold a sentence** on pp.23–25.

Activity 6 Build a sentence

scrumptious
- ☆ Ask children to TTYP and think of words that mean the same as *scrumptious* – synonyms. Offer words of your own.
- ☆ Ask children when and where they might use the word. TTYP and feed back, e.g. *a lovely tea/fish and chip shop/cake shop.*
- ☆ TOL as you try out an example of your own. MT/YT each time you develop it, e.g. *These chips are scrumptious. These chips are so tasty and scrumptious I could eat them every night, forever and ever. These chips are so soft on the inside and crispy on the outside. Mmmmm!*
- ☆ Continue as for the lesson plan on p.96.
- ☆ Rub out/cover up your writing and tell the children to write their own sentence/s about scrumptious food in their *Get Writing!* Books (p.41).

See Blueprint lesson plans for **Activity 7 Edit** on p. 26.

Activity 8 Composition: picture prompts

a) *What happened to the children?*
- ☆ Show the image of Hansel and Gretel appearing from the forest on **CD** (file 10.2). See p.42 of the *Get Writing!* Book for this activity.
- ☆ Tell the children that they are going to write a new exciting opening for the story, by building up the tension just before Hansel and Gretel see the cottage.
- ☆ Ask the children to TTYP to discuss the questions below and Popcorn the feedback. Ask them to help you write their ideas on the board.
- ☆ Use the heart, eyes, nose, ear and legs symbols on screen to help ask questions.
   Heart: *How are they feeling? e.g. weary, miserable, worried, frightened, hungry, desperate. What do the woods feel like? e.g. dark, scary, gloomy.*
   Ear: *What can they hear? e.g. trees rustling, bats squeaking – eek! eek! eek!*
   Legs: *How are they moving? e.g. stumbling, trudging wearily.*
   Eyes: *What do they see as they come through the clearing? e.g. a little cottage covered in liquorice/*

gooey toffee, dripping with chocolate with icing flowers curled around the window.

☆ TOL and use MT/YT as you build up two or three sentences with the children. Click on the next screen and take their ideas as you write, e.g.
Sentence 1:
After many hours of trudging through the dark forest, Hansel and Gretel stumbled into a small clearing.
Hansel and Gretel were stumbling through the forest when suddenly they came into a small clearing, etc.
Sentence 2:
There in the clearing, they saw an amazing sight, a little cottage covered in scrumptious, mouth-watering food.

☆ Ask the children to write their chosen sentences.

b) What is Gretel saying?   c) What is Hansel saying?

☆ Click on the next screen (Hansel and Gretel eating the cottage). See pp.42–43 of the *Get Writing!* Book for this activity.

☆ Ask: *What did they say to each other as they started to eat the sweets?* e.g. *Mmm, this is so chewy isn't it?*
I've got soft, sticky candy stuck to my fingers (mime).

☆ Ask children to TTYP and feed back using Choose Two or Paraphrase, e.g. *This chocolate is so scrumptious. The apple pie is amazingly tasty. I am so hungry, I could eat the whole cottage.*

☆ Ask children to TTYP to try out different sentences out loud.

☆ Then ask them to write their chosen sentence in the large speech bubbles in their *Get Writing!* Books.

d) What is Gretal thinking?

☆ Click on the next screen and show the image of Gretel, alone, lying in a hard bed with a shabby blanket in the witch's cottage. See p.43 of the *Get Writing!* Book for this activity.

☆ Tell the children that while Hansel was being fattened up in the hut, Gretel slept upstairs, alone in the little bedroom. The witch took away the soft satin sheets and the soft mattress.

☆ Ask the children to TTYP to discuss the questions below. Paraphrase their feedback.

☆ Ask the children to help you write their ideas on the board.
Where did she sleep? e.g. *hard bed, hard wooden slats, cold bare bed.*
How did she feel lying there? e.g. *desperate, worried, miserable.*
What did she think? e.g. *'I must find a way of rescuing Hansel. What can I do?'*
How would she have said this? e.g. *whispered, muttered, mumbled.*

☆ TOL as you build up two or three sentences with the children. Take children's ideas as you write.

☆ Ask children to TTYP to try out different sentences out loud.

☆ Ask them to write their chosen sentence by the picture of Gretel on the bed, e.g.
Gretel lay miserably on the cold bed, mumbling to herself, 'I must rescue Hansel'.
Gretel crouched desperately on the cold, hard bed, whispering, 'How can I ever rescue Hansel?'

☆ Select some interesting sentences to read aloud to the class.

Activity 9 Composition

Write a menu of things the witch gives Hansel to eat.

☆ Explain to the children that following a role-play they will write a menu of things to make a skinny boy plump, like the witch plans to do in the story of Hansel and Gretel.
      Teacher role: witch   Children's role: little witches at witch school

☆ Take on your role whole-heartedly throughout this activity so children adopt their role easily and enthusiastically. Make yours a very strict witchy school. Be very deliberate and fussy when using MT/YT!

☆ Show the image of an old page from the witch's notebook on **CD** (file 10.3). See p.44 of the *Get Writing!* Book for this activity.

☆ Teacher in role as witch: *Today, my little witches, you are all going to learn how to make a skinny boy plump and mouth-wateringly scrumptious to eat. You are going to devise a very special menu. We know what children really like, don't we? Hahahaha!*
Say after me, I want to hear your witchy cackles: 'Little boys like yummy, delicious, mouth-watering things to eat! Little boys like puddings oozing with chocolate sauce. Hahahaha!'

☆ Focus on the pictures of the food items dotted around the menu.

☆ Ask the children to TTYP and feed back: *What do little boys like?* e.g. *chocolate eggs. What do little boys like about chocolate eggs?*

☆ TOL as you expand the description together: e.g. *crispy, creamy, sickly sweet.*
Little boys like chocolate eggs because they are crispy and creamy.
Little boys like chocolate eggs because they are crispy and creamy, sickly and sweet.
Sound bossier than you would normally on a TOL!

☆ Repeat the above with different items of food.

☆ Ask children to TTYP and feed back to think about how scrumptious they can make each item sound.

☆ Continuing in witchy role, model writing the descriptions with some of their choices, e.g. *crispy creamy.* Model re-reading for sense and punctuation.

☆ Ask the children to practise saying the first item on the menu.

☆ Rub out/cover up your writing and ask the children to write their menus in their *Get Writing!* Books.

Yellow Non-fiction Book 1   *In the park*

Introducing the book

zoom   slide   scramble

☆ Use these 'power words' when introducing the book during reading Activity 3. Write them on sticky notes so you remember to use them through the lesson/day, e.g. *Can you see Tom climb up the scramble net? Watch Zara swing on the rope. Can you slide down super fast?*

See Blueprint lesson plans for **Activities 1, 2, 3, 4 (Spelling)** and **Activity 5 Hold a sentence** on pp.23–25.

Activity 6 Build a sentence

scramble

☆ Ask children to TTYP and think of words that mean the same as (synonyms for) *scramble.* Offer words of your own.

☆ Ask children when and where they might use the word. TTYP and feed back, e.g. *to describe how they move when they climb and play.*

☆ TOL as you try out an example of your own. MT/YT each time you develop it. Involve the children in extending and developing the sentence using questions, e.g. *I scrambled up the net. Where did I scramble? I scrambled up to the very top of the net/up to the highest branches/through the tunnel.*
Why did I scramble? I quickly scrambled up to the very top of the net to win the game/to climb over to the other side/to beat my friend/as part of a game.

☆ Continue as for the lesson plan on p.96.

☆ Rub out/cover up your writing and tell the children to write their own sentence/s to describe how they would move in a playground in their *Get Writing!* Books (p.46).

See Blueprint lesson plans for **Activity 7 Edit** on p.26.

Activity 8 Composition: picture prompts

Write about how you move in the park.

☆ Go to a local park or onto the apparatus in the school hall. Tell the children that they are going to collect words to describe how they move. Ask them to climb and run and jump, etc. and try to remember all the different ways they moved as they played for when they return to the classroom.

☆ Show the image of the playground on **CD** (file NF1.2) and on p.47 in their *Get Writing!* Books.

☆ Zoom in on the different parts of the playground. Ask the children to TTYP to say how they moved on each thing and Popcorn the feedback.

☆ Click on the next screen and ask them to help you write their ideas on the mind map. TOL as you build up some descriptions of how they moved in the playground with the children. Take their ideas as you write, e.g. *you whooshed down the slide, you scrambled up the net, you crawled under the tunnel, you kicked your leg as you swung, etc.*

☆ Click on the next screen and show the image of the playground with labels.

☆ Choose one of the labelled parts (slide) and ask the children to TTYP to describe how they moved on it, e.g. *First I pushed off, then I zoomed down. I swung back and then I whooshed down.*

☆ TOL as you expand the description together, e.g. *push and whoosh.*
First I pushed off and then I went whoosh down the slide.
First of all I pushed my body back and then, whoosh, I zoomed down the slide.

☆ Repeat the above with different parts of the playground. Model re-reading for sense and punctuation.

☆ Ask the children to practise saying their sentences.

☆ Rub out/cover up your writing and ask the children to write their sentences next to the labels on the playground in their *Get Writing!* Books.

Activity 9 Composition

Choose and write about 5 things to go in your park.

☆ Show an image of an empty park on **CD** (file NF1.3). See p.48 of the *Get Writing!* Book for this activity.

☆ Tell the children that they are going to design a park.

☆ Ask the children to TTYP to discuss what they think they would have to have in a park and Popcorn the feedback.

☆ Discuss which of the items dotted around the picture (*playground, sandpit, trees, pond, benches, café, skate ramps*) you would add to the park as you drag and drop them. TOL as you build up some descriptions of the different items with the children. Take their ideas as you write, e.g. *big trees to sit under/grass to have picnics and play games on/playground with swings and slides/a sandpit to dig in.*

☆ Ask the children to TTYP to discuss which five things they think are best. Use thumbs up to decide which five things to write descriptions of.

☆ Open **CD** (file NF1.4). TOL and use MT/YT as you build up five sentences with the children. Take their ideas as you write into the empty park area, e.g.
Sentence 1: I would have a huge bit of grass because children love to play football and have picnics.
Sentence 2: I would have a pond because children love to go pond dipping and to feed the ducks.
Sentence 3: I would have a playground with swings and slides and net to scramble up, etc.

☆ Ask the children to write their chosen sentences in their *Get Writing!* Books, p.48.

☆ Celebration: Ask the Partners to choose their favourite of the five items and rehearse saying it together and feed back in unison. Choose some examples as feedback.

☆ Tell the children that they are going to choose one special item for the park and they need to convince you why it is the best. Use a choice from the previous feedback as an example e.g. *The pond is best because children love to feed the ducks.*

Yellow

☆ Ask children to TTYP and feed back using Choose Two or Paraphrase, e.g. *The big trees are best because they would give shade on sunny days/would be great to climb/scramble up.*

☆ TOL and use MT/YT as you build up the final sentence with the children. Take their ideas as you write, e.g. *The skate ramps are best because it is exciting zooming up and down. The playground is best because everyone loves to climb and slide, etc.*

☆ Ask the children to write their chosen sentence next to the 'Best in park' star award in their *Get Writing!* Books.

Yellow Non-fiction Book 5   *A mouse in the house*

Introducing the book

scuttle   scurry   chomp   alert   twitching

☆ Use these 'power words' when introducing the book during reading Activity 3. Write them on sticky notes so you remember to use them through the lesson/day, e.g. *I can see your nose twitch just like a rabbit's! Watch how the ants scurry away when they see our shadows near them.*

*See Blueprint lesson plans for **Activities 1, 2, 3, 4 (Spelling)** and **Activity 5 Hold a sentence** on pp.23–25.*

Activity 6 Build a sentence

scuttle

☆ Ask children to TTYP and think of words that mean the same as *scuttle* – synonyms. Offer words of your own.

☆ Ask children when and where they might use the word. TTYP and feed back, e.g. *to describe an insect moving: 'the ant scuttled out of the way'. When they talk about how a character might move in a book: 'The malicious spider scuttled back to his den…'*

☆ TOL as you try out an example of your own. MT/YT each time you develop it. Involve the children in extending and developing the sentence using questions, e.g. *The mouse scuttled across the floor. How did it scuttle? The mouse scuttled quickly into its hole. Why did it scuttle? The mouse scuttled quickly because the cat was chasing it/to get to safety/because it felt frightened, etc.*

☆ Continue as for the lesson plan on p.96.

☆ Rub out/cover up your writing and tell the children to write their own sentence/s about the mouse scuttling to safety in their *Get Writing!* Books (p.50).

*See Blueprint lesson plans for **Activity 7 Edit** on p.26.*

Activity 8 Composition: picture prompts

Label the mouse.

☆ Explain to the children that they are going to write an entry for a book called 'All you need to know about keeping a mouse'. It will describe what a mouse looks like using labels.

☆ Show the image of the mouse on **CD** (file NF5.2). See p.51 of the *Get Writing!* Book for this activity.

☆ Choose one of the labelled parts (*nose, eyes, whiskers, tail, feet*) and ask the children to TTYP to describe it, e.g. *small pointed nose, alert twitchy nose.*

☆ TOL as you expand the description together: e.g. *alert twitchy nose:*
The mouse has an alert, twitchy nose.
The mouse has an alert, twitchy nose, which it uses to sniff for danger.
The mouse has an alert, twitchy nose, which snuffles at everything.

The mouse has an alert, twitchy nose, which is black and always moving.

☆ Repeat the above with different parts of the mouse (*eyes, whiskers, tail, feet*).

☆ Ask children to TTYP and feed back to think about how they can add additional information to the sentence to tell the reader more about the mouse.

☆ Model writing the descriptions with some of their choices, e.g. *The mouse has a long strong tail, which it uses to balance.* Model re-reading for sense and punctuation.

☆ Ask the children to practise saying sentences for their labels.

☆ Rub out/cover up your writing and ask the children to write their labels on the mouse in their *Get Writing!* Books.

Activity 9 Composition

Write about what a mouse likes to do.

☆ Explain to the children that they are going to write another entry for a book called *All you need to know about keeping a mouse.* It will describe what a mouse enjoys doing.

☆ Display **CD** (file NF5.3). See p.52 of the *Get Writing!* Book for this activity.

☆ Ask the children to TTYP and feed back: *What do mice like to do?* e.g. *scurry and run/chomp up food/scuttle about/snuggle up in their nest.*

☆ Click on the next screen (mouse in wheel). Say: *Tell me exactly what the mouse likes to do on its wheel.*

☆ TOL as you expand the description together, e.g. *scurry and zoom. Mice like to scurry and zoom on their wheel. Mice like to scurry up and down on their wheel and zoom around and around. Mice like to scurry quickly around their wheel zooming so fast they are like a blur.*

☆ Click on the next screen (mouse eating) and repeat the above.

☆ Model writing the descriptions with some of their choices, e.g. *Mice chew and chomp their food.* Model re-reading for sense and punctuation.

☆ Ask the children to practise saying their sentences for their label explanation.

☆ Rub out/cover up your writing and ask the children to write their label explanations about what mice like doing in their *Get Writing!* Books. Discuss ideas for the other picture prompts in the pupils' book (e.g. *Mice like to scuttle over to their water bottle and take a sip; mice like to scamper and scoot around their cage; mice like to scrape together bedding and make a cosy nest.*)

☆ Celebration: Partners tell each other their favourite description of what mice like to do and practise it together until they can say it in unison. Choose some children to feed back to the class.

Blue Storybook 1   *Barker*

Introducing the story

> gobble   ruin   attack

☆ Use these 'power words' when introducing the story during reading Activity 3. Write them on sticky notes so you remember to use them through the lesson/day, e.g. *Oh no, I've spilt coffee down me and ruined my top! Watch the greedy hamster gobble up the nuts. The cold weather has killed all the plants and ruined my garden!*

See Blueprint lesson plans for **Activities 1, 2, 3, 4 (Spelling)** and **Activity 5 Hold a sentence** on pp.23–25.

Activity 6 Build a sentence

ruin

☆ Ask the children to TTYP (Turn to your partner) and think of words that mean the same as *ruin* – synonyms. Offer words of your own (*spoil, mess up, destroy*).

☆ Ask the children when and where they might use the word. TTYP and feed back, e.g. *when things get ruined/when they are left in the rain/when we don't care for things/when something goes wrong, like when we feel we have ruined a painting/when we drop or spill things.*

☆ TOL (Think out loud) as you try out an example of your own. MT/YT (My turn/Your turn) each time you develop it, e.g.
You ruined our game!
When you came in and kicked over our Lego building you ruined all our hard work.
Oh, I felt so angry when my little brother ruined my picture by scribbling on it!

☆ Ask the children to TTYP to try out sentences of their own using their own experiences of when something was messed up and ruined. Listen carefully, then Choose Two to feed back.

☆ TOL as you build on one of the ideas and write the sentence. Ask the children to help as you do this. Model re-reading for sense and punctuation.

☆ Ask the children to develop a sentence of their own. Ask them to practise saying it before they write.

☆ Remember to follow this process every time you build a sentence with the children. Page references to this set of notes are given as a reminder.

☆ Rub out/cover up your writing and tell the children to write their own sentence/s in their *Get Writing!* Books (p.3).

See Blueprint lesson plans for **Activity 7 Edit** on p.26.

Activity 8 Composition: picture prompts

What is the boy saying?

☆ Explain to the children that through role-play they will write a conversation between Barker's owner and his mum/dad and that Mum/Dad is rather annoyed with Barker right now!
    Teacher role: Mum/Dad (annoyed with Barker's antics)   Children's role: Barker's owner

☆ Take on your role whole-heartedly throughout this activity so children adopt their role easily and enthusiastically. Make your parent very annoyed and make sure you repeat and elaborate on the child's excuses slowly and carefully as if weighing each one up as you do MT/YT!

Blue

- ☆ Show the image of Mum looking cross on **CD** (file 1.2). See p.4 of the *Get Writing!* Book for this activity.
- ☆ Teacher in role as Mum/Dad: *Barker! Barker! Where is that dog? I cannot believe the mess he has made. I'm so cross! He has chewed Grandad's slippers to pieces, they are soggy and holey. What a mess!*
- ☆ Ask the children to TTYP and feed back: *Why should I forgive that awful dog for chewing Grandad's slippers?* e.g. *he made a mistake/he was hungry/he thought they were food.*
- ☆ TOL as you expand the response/explanation to Mum together. Use MT/YT to practise the sentences, e.g. *He was hungry.*
  Barker chewed up the slippers because he was hungry.
  Barker chewed up the slippers because he was starving hungry and thought they looked tasty.
  Barker didn't mean to ruin the slippers but he was so hungry he could not help himself!
- ☆ Ask the children to TTYP and feed back to think about how sorry they can sound. Model writing the dialogue with some of their choices, e.g. *Mum, I'm so sorry Barker ruined the slippers but it was only because he was starving hungry.* Model re-reading for sense and punctuation.
- ☆ Ask the children to practise saying the first reply to Mum.
  Oh no! What now? Have you seen what that dog has done? I'm livid. I'm furious. I'm going to explode! Arggghh!
  Click on the next screens *(images of Barker: gobbling up food he shouldn't have/sitting on the bed).*
- ☆ Repeat the above for Barker's different misdemeanours.
- ☆ Rub out/cover your writing and tell the children to write their dialogue in their *Get Writing!* Books, using either their own ideas or yours, if children need the support.

Activity 9 Composition

a) Make notes about Barker.
- ☆ Show the image of Barker barking at night on **CD** (file 1.3). See p.5 of the *Get Writing!* Book for this activity.
- ☆ Tell the children that they are going to zoom in and write about the climax of the story.
- ☆ Ask the children to TTYP to discuss the questions below and Popcorn the feedback. Ask them to help you write their ideas on the board.
- ☆ Focus on the symbols alongside the picture of Barker as you ask questions (ear, eye, legs, heart). Ask the children to make notes of key words next to the symbols in their *Get Writing!* Books.
  Ear: *What did Barker hear?* e.g. *a rustling outside/a scraping at the window/the window being smashed,* etc.
  Eye: *What did Barker see?* e.g. *a foot emerging from the night/a mean face peeping in,* etc.
  Legs: *What did he do?* e.g. *he barked his head off.*
  Heart: *What did he feel in the end?* e.g. *Like a real hero/At last I got it right! Brilliant!*

b) Now write The bark in the dark.
- ☆ Click on the next screen. TOL as you build up three or four sentences with the children to tell the story. Take their ideas as you write, e.g.
  Sentence 1:
  In the middle of the night a rustling broke the quiet and a huge foot emerged from the darkness into the kitchen.
- ☆ Rub out/cover your writing and tell the children to write their sentences in their *Get Writing!* Books, using either their own ideas or yours, if they need the support.
  Sentence 2:
  There was more rustling and then a black figure padded towards Barker. What should he do? etc.
- ☆ Use MT/YT to practise saying their sentences out loud using the children's ideas.
- ☆ Carry on using MT/YT to compose sentences in this way until you have told the story of *The bark in the dark!*
- ☆ Select some interesting sentences to read aloud to the class.

Introducing the story

scornful   insult   ignore   miserable   triumphant   thoughtful

☆ Use these 'power words' when introducing the story during reading Activity 3. Write them on sticky notes so you remember to use them through the lesson/day, e.g. *Cinderella was feeling lonely and ignored when her family went off to the ball and left her behind. Later on she was thoughtful as she cleaned the dirty kitchen. When her fairy godmother arrived she felt hopeful.*

*See Blueprint lesson plans for **Activities 1, 2, 3, 4 (Spelling)** and **Activity 5 Hold a sentence** on pp.23–25.*

Activity 6 Build a sentence

miserable/miserably

☆ Ask the children to TTYP and think of words that mean the same as *miserable* – synonyms. Offer words of your own.

☆ Show the image of the feelings barometer on **CD** (file 2.2) and drag and drop the words on it. Model using each word so that the children are familiar with the meaning of each word (*scorned, insulted, ignored, miserable, triumphant, hopeful, lonely*).

☆ Ask the children when and where they might use the word. TTYP and feed back, e.g. *Cinderella felt miserable when she couldn't go to the ball/Hansel and Gretel felt miserable when they realised they had been tricked by the witch/Mama hen felt miserable when she thought her chicks would drown in the pond…*

☆ TOL as you try out an example of your own. MT/YT each time you develop it, e.g.
I feel miserable because Tara laughed at my new haircut.
I feel miserable and left out when the others won't play with me.
It is miserable sitting out of swimming when I forget my kit and I watch my friends having fun.

☆ Continue as for the lesson plan on p.121.

☆ Rub out/cover up your writing and tell the children to write their own sentence/s about a time when they felt left out and miserable in their *Get Writing!* Books (p.7).

*See Blueprint lesson plans for **Activity 7 Edit** on p.26.*

Activity 8 Composition: picture prompts

Think about some advice for a friend. Write some notes.

☆ Explain that you are going to think of some good advice to give to someone who feels upset because people have been mean to them. First you will build some sentences aloud by remembering how the goose felt. See p.8 of the *Get Writing!* Book for this activity.

☆ Show the picture of the goose looking sad on **CD** (file 2.3). Ask: *How were they mean to the goose?* Ask the children to TTYP and feed back: *They thought she was silly, they called her names.*

☆ Ask: *How did that make her feel?* Ask the children to TTYP and feed back: e.g. *insulted, miserable, angry.*

☆ TOL as you expand the sentence together:
The horse and the sheepdog were mean to the goose and they called her names and that made her feel miserable. The horse and the sheepdog were horrible to the goose and they called her names and that made her feel lonely and sad.

☆ Ask the children to imagine that someone has been mean to a friend of theirs. Ask them to think of advice they could give to the friend. Tell them to quietly tell their partner what happened, how they felt, and their advice. Feed back and Paraphrase their responses.

Blue

☆ Tell the children that they are going to write some advice for their friend and show their friend they understand how they felt.

☆ Click to the next screen and model writing a sentence with some of their choices, e.g. *The person was mean to my friend and called them a nasty name.* Then discuss how the friend felt and their advice to them. Model re-reading for sense and punctuation.

☆ Rub out/cover up your writing and tell the children to write their sentences in their *Get Writing!* Books (p.8), using either their own ideas or yours, if they need the support.

Activity 9 Composition

Tell the story from the goose's point of view

☆ Explain to the children that through role-play they will tell the story from the goose's point of view.

> *Teacher role: agony aunt   Children's role: goose*

☆ Take on your role whole-heartedly throughout this activity so children adopt their role easily and enthusiastically.

a)

☆ Teacher in role as agony aunt: *Goose, I'm here to help you. I have heard that you have a problem with the horse and the sheepdog. I have heard that they have been unkind to you.*

☆ Show the image of the goose, the horse and the sheepdog on **CD** (file 2.4). See p.9 of the *Get Writing!* Book for this activity.

☆ Teacher in role: *Goose, this is a picture of when the horse and the sheepdog were mean to you. Do you remember how you felt when they were mean to you and said you couldn't win? I imagine you are feeling sad about this. I bet you don't just feel sad…*

☆ Ask the children to TTYP and discuss how they felt at this moment. Popcorn the feedback, e.g. *miserable, lonely, fed up.* Ask them to help you write their ideas on the board.

☆ Continue in role: *So, Goose, this is how you felt, but what did you do? Did you break down and cry or did you hide feelings so those meanies didn't know how much you were hurting?*

☆ Ask the children to TTYP and discuss how they felt when the horse and sheepdog were mean. Popcorn the feedback, e.g. *I smiled to hide my sadness/I looked away/I pretended I couldn't hear.* Ask them to help you write their ideas on the board.

☆ TOL and use MT/YT as you build up two or three sentences with the children. Take their ideas as you write, e.g.
Sentence 1:
I could hear them calling me names, but I just smiled even though they made me feel lonely.
Sentence 2:
I looked at them as they laughed at the idea of me winning the race and began to feel annoyed! etc.

☆ Rub out/cover up your writing and tell the children to write their sentences next to the picture in their *Get Writing!* Books, using either their own ideas, or yours, if children need the support.

b)

☆ Click on the next screen (other animals running off). Ask: *What did you think to yourself as you saw them run off?*

☆ Ask the children to TTYP in role as the goose and feed back using Choose Two or Paraphrase, e.g. *I thought, good, now they have gone I shall think of a way to win. I can beat them. Now, think, Goose, think!*

☆ Ask the children to TTYP to try out different sentences out loud.

☆ Then ask them to write their chosen sentence in the large thought bubble in their *Get Writing!* Books.

c)

☆ Click on the next screen (goose by the barn as she wins the race).

☆ Ask the children to TTYP to discuss the questions below in role as the goose. Paraphrase their feedback.

☆ Ask the children to help you write their ideas on the board.

What was your plan? e.g. *to soar up in the sky and fly to the barn/to zoom in the air to the barn,* etc.

How did you feel as you flew? e.g. *hopeful, excited, a flutter of hope.*

What did you think in the end? e.g. *I am triumphant, I've shown those meanies.*

☆ TOL as you build up two or three sentences with the children. Take children's ideas as you write.

☆ Ask the children to TTYP to try out different sentences out loud.

☆ Ask them to write their chosen sentence by Picture 3 in their *Get Writing!* Books, e.g.

As I soared gracefully into the sky, I felt a flutter of hope. Then, when I landed, I saw that I was first. 'I am triumphant!' I cried.

☆ Select some interesting sentences to read aloud to the class.

Blue Storybook 3   *Hairy fairy*

Introducing the story

disaster   despair   embarrassed

☆ Use these 'power words' when introducing the story during reading Activity 3. Write them on sticky notes so you remember to use them through the lesson/day, e.g. *I was so embarrassed when I forgot my mum's birthday. The dinner I cooked was a disaster – the meat was burnt and the gravy was a gungy embarrassment.*

*See Blueprint lesson plans for **Activities 1, 2, 3, 4 (Spelling)** and **Activity 5 Hold a sentence** on pp.23–25.*

Activity 6 Build a sentence

despair

☆ Ask the children to TTYP and think of words that mean the same as *despair* – synonyms. Offer words of your own.

☆ Ask the children when and where they might use the word. TTYP and feed back, e.g. *when something has gone really wrong, when there is no hope of winning a game or race, Mama Hen when her chicks fell in the pond and she thought they would drown.*

☆ TOL as you try out an example of your own. Use MT/YT each time you develop it, e.g.

Gretel lay on her cold hard bed. 'We will never escape,' she despaired.

Gretel felt her despair change to hope as she realised she could get rid of the wicked witch.

'Do not despair,' she cried to Hansel, 'the witch is gone, we are free!'

☆ Continue as for the lesson plan on p.121.

☆ Rub out/cover up your writing and tell the children to write their own sentence/s in their *Get Writing!* Books (p.11).

*See Blueprint lesson plans for **Activity 7 Edit** on p.26.*

Activity 8 Composition: picture prompts

Write a newspaper report about what happened to the hairy fairy.

☆ Explain to the children that through role-play they will write a newspaper report about the hairy fairy's problems.

Teacher role: interviewer   Children's role: hairy fairy

☆ Take on your role whole-heartedly throughout this activity so children adopt their role easily and enthusiastically. Make sure that you get all the facts exactly right. Be very deliberate and fussy when using MT/YT!

☆ Show the image of a page from the reporter's notebook on **CD** (file 3.2). See pp.12–13 of the *Get Writing!* Book for this activity.

☆ Teacher in role as interviewer: *Hello, hairy fairy, I am so glad to meet you today and delighted that you agreed to do an interview for the Fairy Voice newspaper. Can I ask my first question? Good! I have heard that you are having a terrible time getting a job. Why is that, do you think?*

☆ Ask the children to TTYP and feed back. Choose Two and write their ideas down on the notepad on screen.

☆ Ask the children to TTYP to discuss the questions below and Popcorn the feedback. Ask them to help you write their ideas on the board.
What other jobs have you had and how have they gone wrong? e.g. *A tooth fairy but I think they thought I was too ugly.*
Have you ever tried to sort out your hair? e.g. *Yes, but it only grows back.*
How has the Fairy Queen reacted to you not having a job? e.g. *She is in despair, she says I have one more chance!*
How do you feel now? e.g. *Terrible, embarrassed, miserable, useless.*
What would be your ideal job? e.g. *I love magic and working with children.*

☆ Scribe the heading *No job joy!* onto the notebook page. Tell the children you are going to write a couple of sentences about the hairy fairy's job disasters.

☆ TOL as you build up two or three sentences with the children. Take their ideas as you write, e.g. *Hairy fairy has had a mountain of jobs, but sadly he has been sacked from them all. He says it is terrible and that he feels embarrassed. 'I was told I was too scary to be a tooth fairy. It really is awful,' he despaired.*

☆ Continuing in role, model writing a couple of sentences under the heading with some of their choices. Model re-reading for sense and punctuation.

☆ Ask the children to practise saying the sentences for the first heading *No job joy!*

☆ Rub out/cover up your writing and tell the children to write their newspaper reports in their *Get Writing!* Books, using either their own ideas or yours, if children need the support.

☆ Repeat the process with two other headings, *Hair despair* and *Fairy Queen quietly furious*.

Activity 9 Composition

a) *Make notes about a perfect fairy and the hairy fairy.*

☆ Show the image of the hairy fairy and a perfect fairy on **CD** (file 3.3). See pp.14–15 of the *Get Writing!* Book for this activity.

☆ Tell the children that the Fairy Queen has organised a meeting with the hairy fairy to help him be more like a proper fairy.

☆ Ask the children to TTYP to help the Fairy Queen explain to the hairy fairy how he should look and where he is going wrong! Popcorn the feedback.

☆ Point to the fairy's hair and say: *A real fairy has clean, bouncy, neat hair.* Ask the children to TTYP and explain how his hair is wrong, e.g. *messy, thick, sticks out, dull, dirty, bird's nest, filthy.* Click on the next two screens and model writing notes about the perfect fairy, then the hairy fairy, in the callout boxes.

☆ Ask them to make notes about the features of a perfect fairy and the hairy fairy in the boxes in their *Get Writing!* Books.

b) *What does the Fairy Queen say a real fairy should be like?*

☆ Click on the next screen. TOL and use MT/YT as you build up some sentences that the Fairy Queen might say with the children. Take their ideas as you write, e.g.
A real fairy should have bouncy, shiny hair but your hair is dull, dirty and looks like a bird's nest!
A real fairy should have beautiful, sweet smelling hair but your hair is filthy and sticks out like twigs!

- ✫ Use MT/YT to practise saying the sentences out loud using the children's ideas.
- ✫ Rub out/cover up your writing and tell the children to write their sentences into the speech bubbles in their *Get Writing!* Books (p.15), using either their own ideas, or yours, if they need the support.
- ✫ Repeat the process to describe: the perfect fairy's legs (e.g. *long, pretty, clean*); wings (e.g. *silver, gorgeous, sparkling*); wand (e.g. *clean, filled-up with magic, full of wishes*); dress (e.g. *beautiful, sparkly, frilly*). Encourage the children to gain independence by describing both fairies as they write what the Fairy Queen might say.

Blue Storybook 4   *King of the birds*

Introducing the story

quarrel   argue   gorgeous   dull   ordinary

- ✫ Use these 'power words' when introducing the story during reading Activity 3. Write them on sticky notes so you remember to use them through the lesson/day, e.g. *The children dressed up as gorgeous princesses but then quarrelled about who should be queen. What gorgeous pictures, I cannot decide which one I like best! School uniform can feel so dull and ordinary that it makes me want to wear something fantastic.*

*See Blueprint lesson plans for **Activities 1, 2, 3, 4 (Spelling)** and **Activity 5 Hold a sentence** on pp.23–25.*

Activity 6 Build a sentence

quarrel
- ✫ Ask the children to TTYP and think of words that mean the same as *quarrel* – synonyms. Offer words of your own.
- ✫ Ask the children when and where they might use the word. TTYP and feed back, e.g. *to describe a fight they had about something/when they fight with their siblings about wanting to watch different things on TV, etc.*
- ✫ TOL as you try out an example of your own. MT/YT each time you develop it, e.g.
  I quarrelled with Mum because I wanted to wear my beautiful dress to the farm and she thought I should not. Lucy and Shawn quarrelled about who should go next on the swings. One day I had an enormous quarrel with my sister and I was so cross with her that I wanted to run away from home!
- ✫ Continue as for the lesson plan on p121.
- ✫ Rub out/cover up your writing and tell the children to write their own sentence/s in their *Get Writing!* Books (p.17).

*See Blueprint lesson plans for **Activity 7 Edit** on p.26.*

Activity 8 Composition: picture prompts

a) *Write about the birds.*
- ✫ Explain to the children that through role-play they will work out which of the birds should be king. They will make notes about the strengths and attributes of the different birds, write a persuasive statement saying which one they think should win/be king, then record the result of a class vote.
  Teacher role: owl, the judge   Children's role: jury

☆ Take on your role whole-heartedly throughout this activity so children adopt their role easily and enthusiastically. Make your meeting very ordered. Be deliberate and fussy when using MT/YT!

☆ Show the image of the birds huddled on a branch at the meeting on **CD** (file 4.2).

☆ Teacher in role as the judge: *Order! Order! Order! Today we come together to decide which of you birds should be king. Each one of you who wants to be considered for king can say why you would be best! Think carefully, as only one bird can be king. In the end, the jury and I will decide.*
Say after me, MT/YT: 'The king of the birds will rule over us all, but who will be king? Who? Who? Who?'

☆ Click on the next screen to show the images of the different birds: *hummingbird, cockatoo, parrot, crow*. See pp.18–19 of the *Get Writing!* Book for this activity.

☆ Ask the children to TTYP and feed back in role as jury:
Why should this bird be king? e.g. It is small and beautiful./It can dart and see things others can't./It has special skills.
Give me all the reasons why you think it should be king.

☆ TOL and use MT/YT as you expand the description together, e.g. *clever, tiny, fantastic skills.*
Hummingbird is tiny and can get into the smallest spaces. Its fantastic hovering skills mean it can zoom in and help other birds in trouble.
Hummingbird is clever because he is so small and quick witted, that is a skill that is useful to everyone.
Sound more careful than you would normally on a TOL!

☆ Continuing in role, model writing the descriptions with some of their choices, e.g. *Hummingbird is bright and beautiful and can hover anywhere.* Model re-reading for sense and punctuation. Rub out/cover up your writing and tell the children to write their sentences for that bird in the relevant boxes in their *Get Writing!* Books, using either their own ideas, or yours, if children need the support.

☆ Repeat the above with each of the birds.

b) *Who do you think should be King of the birds?*   c) *Who is the winner?*

☆ Ask the children to TTYP and feed back to think about how they can persuade the meeting of the birds that each bird is best.

☆ Celebration: Tell the children to work in pairs and choose the bird that they think is best and practise a sentence saying why together. Tell them to write it out and say it in unison to the class. Once the class has voted for the king of the birds, write a final sentence saying why that bird was chosen.

Activity 9 Composition

Write about Crow and the other birds.

☆ Show the image of Crow on **CD** (file 4.3). See p.19 of the *Get Writing!* Book for this activity.

☆ Tell the children that they are going to write about how Crow saw himself compared to the other birds. They will fill in a chart comparing Crow and the other birds, to collect their ideas.

☆ Ask the children to TTYP to discuss the questions below and Popcorn the feedback. Click on the next screen (Crow/other birds comparison chart) and ask them to help you write their ideas on the chart.
How do the birds behave/feel? e.g. quarrel, fight, bicker, boast that they are the most gorgeous.
How does Crow behave/feel? e.g. he feels ugly/not good enough/no hope of being picked.
What do the other birds sound like? e.g. they chirp, cheep, sing, trill.
What does Crow sound like? e.g. squawk, croak, screech.
How do the other birds move? e.g. twirl, whirl, flutter, display, zip, soar.
How does Crow move? e.g. hop, strut, lumber.
What do the other birds look like? e.g. like rainbows of colour/like beautiful flashes of light.
What does Crow look like? e.g. as dull as a dark day/as black as night.

- Review each set of ideas on the chart as you TOL and build up each sentence with the children. MT/YT each time you develop it. Play around with the ideas until you are happy. Take their ideas as you write, e.g. *All the birds quarrelled/argued/bickered about who was best. Crow didn't argue as he knew he had no chance/was too dull.*
- Rub out/cover up your writing and tell the children to write into the chart in their *Get Writing!* Books, using either their own ideas or yours, if they need the support.

Blue Storybook 5   *Our house*

Introducing the story

> *massive   heap   cramped   poky   overcrowded*

- Use these 'power words' when introducing the story during reading Activity 3. Write them on sticky notes so you remember to use them through the lesson/day, e.g. *I have a massive pile of books here. There were hundreds of people at the school fair, it was overcrowded. There isn't much room in here, it's cramped.*

See Blueprint lesson plans for **Activities 1, 2, 3, 4 (Spelling)** and **Activity 5 Hold a sentence** on pp.23–25.

Activity 6 Build a sentence

cramped
- Ask the children to TTYP and think of words that mean the same as *cramped* – synonyms. Offer words of your own.
- Ask the children when and where they might use the word. TTYP and feed back, e.g. *when they hide in a small place/when they feel they haven't enough room.*
- TOL as you try out an example of your own. MT/YT each time you develop it, e.g.
  This table is cramped, there are six children on it and there is only room for four!
  I was squashed next to my big brother, little sister and baby brother in the car. It was awful and cramped!
  I have hundreds of teddies around me when I sleep so it's cramped in my bed.
- Continue as for the lesson plan on p.121.
- Rub out/cover up your writing and tell the children to write their own sentence/s in their *Get Writing!* Books (p.21).

See Blueprint lesson plans for **Activity 7 Edit** on p.26.

Activity 8 Composition: picture prompts

Write a letter to a friend you are going to stay with. Ask about his or her bedroom.
- Explain to the children that following a role-play they will write a letter to a friend who is coming to stay, about their bedroom.
  Teacher role: friend   Children's role: themselves
- Take on your role whole-heartedly throughout this activity so children adopt their role easily and enthusiastically.
- Show the picture of a bedroom on **CD** (file 5.2). See p.22 of the *Get Writing!* Book for this activity.
- Teacher in role as friend: *I'm sooo excited about coming to stay with you. I've packed my overnight bag and have got my teddy. Tell me all about your room. I want to know everything, so I'm going to ask some questions. Firstly, where will I sleep and should I bring a sleeping bag?*

☆ Ask the children to TTYP to discuss the question, and Popcorn the feedback (e.g. *on the pile of cushions, in the big messy bed, on the fluffy rug*). Ask them to help you write their ideas on the board.

☆ TOL as you expand the description together, e.g. *big messy bed, huge pile of cushions.*
My bed is messy but very big so you could sleep down the other end and share it with me.
If you like, we could pile up all the pillows to make a huge pillow bed!

☆ Use MT/YT to practise saying the sentence out loud using the children's ideas.

☆ Click on the next screen (letter writing frame) and model writing the sentence with some of their choices, e.g. *You could bring a sleeping bag and we will use a huge pile of cushions so you are comfy.* TOL as you sound out each word. Model re-reading for sense and punctuation.

☆ Rub out/cover up your writing and tell the children to write their first sentence of the letter in their *Get Writing!* Books, using either their own ideas or yours, if they need the support.

☆ Repeat the above using TTYP and feedback to help you build up an answer with each of the prompts below.
Tell me everything about your bedroom! For example, do you share it with your brother or sister?
I also need to know, do you have any special toys? I'm bringing Tatty Ted. Do you have a special bedtime friend?
OK, last of all. What is your favourite thing about your bedroom?

☆ Celebration: Tell the children to work in pairs and compose a final welcoming sentence to their friend and practise it together. Tell them to write it out and say it in unison to the class.

Activity 9 Composition

Write about living in a small house, like the boy in the story.

☆ Show the image of the house on **CD** (file 5.3). See p.23 of the *Get Writing!* Book for this activity.

☆ Tell the children that they are going to use different sentence starts to help them write about living in a small house.

☆ Ask the children to TTYP to discuss each of the sentence starts below and Popcorn the feedback. Ask them to help you write their ideas on the board so that you build up a description of the house, e.g. *My house is so cramped that…* (*we all eat on the floor/the TV is on top of the fridge/you can't use the loo when someone is in the bath/I have to share my room with the baby, a parrot and the dog!* etc.)

☆ Click on the next screen (writing frame with 'My house is so cramped that…' sentence start). TOL as you build up a sentence with the children. Use MT/YT as you develop it. Take their ideas as you write, e.g.
My house is so cramped that when you open the door all you can see is my toys covering the floor!
My house is so cramped that I have to share my room with the cat, the dog, the goldfish, my sister and her teddies!

☆ Rub out/cover up your writing and tell the children to write their sentences in their *Get Writing!* Books.

☆ Click through the following screens and repeat the above for the sentence starts below.
Although my house is overcrowded…(*we have lots of fun/Mum knows where everything is/friends are always welcome/I can still find a quiet place even if it is in the loo!*)
At times I wish my house were bigger, then…(*I wouldn't have to share/we could have a gigantic TV/it wouldn't be so poky,* etc.)
When everyone is in the house…(*it can feel very poky/it can be fun,* etc.)

Introducing the story

elated   devastated   terrible   foolish   despair

☆ Use these 'power words' when introducing the story during reading Activity 3. Write them on sticky notes so you remember to use them through the lesson/day, e.g. *The weather is terrible today – I feel full of despair! You must have been devastated when you realised that your pet dog had gone missing… and then elated when you found him again!*

*See Blueprint lesson plans for **Activities 1, 2, 3, 4 (Spelling)** and **Activity 5 Hold a sentence** on pp.23–25.*

Activity 6 Build a sentence

elated

☆ Ask the children to TTYP and think of words that mean the same as *elated* – synonyms. Offer words of your own.

☆ Display the feelings barometer on **CD** (file 6.2) and drag and drop the words on to it. Model using each word so that the children are familiar with its meaning (*excited, elated, feeling wonderful, feeling brilliant, devastated, feeling terrible, despairing, feeling foolish*).

☆ Ask the children when and where they might use the word. TTYP and feed back, e.g. *when they have won a race/when the teacher reads out their work to the class/when they have spoken in assembly/when they are given a wonderful present.*

☆ TOL as you try out an example of your own. MT/YT each time you develop it, e.g.
I was elated when I won the race.
I was so elated when I won the race that I jumped up and punched the air!
I was so elated when I won the race that I ran around the race-track and then I hugged my teacher!

☆ Continue as for the lesson plan on p.121.

☆ Rub out/cover up your writing and tell the children to write their own sentence/s in their *Get Writing!* Books (p.25).

*See Blueprint lesson plans for **Activity 7 Edit** on p.26.*

Activity 8 Composition: picture prompts

Write an advert for the perfume…

☆ Explain to the children that through role-play they will create an advert for a perfume made with the poor man's oil. The advert will start with a tempting description of how the perfume smells, and will end with a persuasive statement telling us the name of the perfume and how it will make the wearer feel. You will need lots of fruit, chocolate and strong-smelling foods for the children to smell and taste to give them ideas about the smells of this extraordinary perfume.
   Teacher role: poor man   Children's role: perfume makers

☆ Take on your role whole-heartedly throughout this activity so children adopt their role easily and enthusiastically. Be very deliberate and fussy when using MT/YT!

☆ Show the image of the mysterious looking perfume bottles on **CD** (file 6.3). See p.26 of the *Get Writing!* Book for this activity.

☆ Teacher in role as poor man: *Oh, Mr and Mrs Perfume makers! I have some gorgeous sweet smelling oil that I want to sell, but I need your help. I have heard that you are the best in the business and that you create wonderful names for perfumes and fantastic labels and descriptions of perfumes so that everyone wants to buy the perfumes you create. Please help me, please.*
   Say after me, MT/YT: 'Bottles, labels, scents and names, I'll make you rich and bring you fame!'

Blue

☆ Let the children smell and taste the different foods you have brought in. Do this one food at a time. Ask the children to TTYP to describe the smells and to Popcorn feedback.

☆ Tell the children to choose their favourite smells to make the amazing and unusual perfume. Ask the children to TTYP and feed back: *What does the perfumed oil smell of? What can you smell?*

☆ Click on the next screen (*smells like… notes page*). Paraphrase their feedback, adding adjectives, e.g. *chocolates (sweet delicious), oranges (juicy sweet), apples (fresh sour).*
How shall we describe the perfume?

☆ TOL as you expand the description together for an advert, e.g. *sweet sticky chocolate, sharp juicy oranges.*
Enjoy the aroma of sweet sticky chocolate. It smells like juicy fresh oranges.

☆ Ask the children to TTYP and feed back to think about how they can make the person buying the perfume imagine its smell.

☆ Click on the next screen (perfume bottle writing frame). Continuing in role, model writing the description with some of their choices. Model re-reading for sense and punctuation.

☆ Ask the children to practise saying what the perfume smells of.

☆ Rub out your writing and tell the children to write their description next to the bottle in their *Get Writing!* Books, using either their own ideas, or yours, if children need the support.

☆ Teacher in role as poor man: *My perfume needs a name, all the best perfumes have a name, some are cool like 'Jazz', 'Shizzam', or 'OK'; some make you think of the smell of the perfume like 'Citrus', or 'Chocolate'; some say how you feel when you wear the perfume like 'Happiness' or 'Laughter'.*

☆ Ask the children to TTYP to discuss a name for the perfume and feed back.

☆ *How shall we describe what it is like to wear the perfume?* TOL as you expand the description together for an advert for the perfume, e.g. *wonderful, cool, smart.*
Wear 'Happy' and escape boredom and feel wonderful! 'Jazz' – it's smart, just like you!

☆ Continuing in role, model writing the name and strap line with some of their choices. Model re-reading for sense and punctuation. There is also an example advert on the final screen of **CD** (file 6.3) as a model to provide extra ideas.

☆ Ask the children to practise saying what the perfume smells of.

☆ Rub out/cover up your writing and ask the children to write the name of their perfume and how it makes you feel at the end of the advert in their *Get Writing!* Books.

Activity 9 Composition

Write thinking and happening bubbles about the story.

☆ Explain to the children that through role-play they will write about the poor man's story.
    Teacher role: interviewer   Children's role: poor man

☆ Take on your role whole-heartedly throughout this activity so children adopt their role easily and enthusiastically. Make sure that you get all the facts exactly right.

☆ Show the image of a page from the reporter's notebook on **CD** (file 6.4).

☆ Teacher in role as interviewer: *Hello! I am so glad to meet you today and delighted that you agreed to speak to me. I have heard that you have had some great fortune. What has happened?*

☆ Ask the children to TTYP and feed back. Choose Two and write their ideas down on the notepad on screen.

☆ Ask the children to TTYP to discuss the questions below and Popcorn the feedback. Ask them to help you write their ideas on the board.
How did you feel when you got the oil? e.g. *excited, elated, wonderful, brilliant.*
What did you plan to spend your money on? e.g. *amazing food/getting married/buying beautiful things.*
What will you do now? e.g. *go back to how I was before, learn to live with the regret.*
How did you feel as you dropped the oil? e.g. *awful, devastated, terrible, foolish.*

☆ Tell the children that now they have had the interview they can retell the story using the thinking bubbles and happening bubbles in their *Get Writing!* Books.

☆ Ask them to TTYP using the notes you have made together and feed back: *How did the poor man feel when he got the oil?* e.g. *excited, elated, wonderful, brilliant.*

☆ Click on the next screen (man with 'thinking bubble'). Tell the children you are going to write a couple of sentences about what the poor man was thinking.

☆ TOL as you build up two or three sentences with the children. Take their ideas as you write, e.g. *I cannot believe how lucky I am. I am so elated to have this huge jar of oil, everything is going to change now.*

☆ Model writing a couple of sentences for the thinking bubble with some of their choices, e.g. *Ha ha! I am so excited. This jar of oil will change my life! Oh, how wonderful, now I can stop work and be rich!* Model re-reading for sense and punctuation.

☆ Ask the children to practise saying the sentences for the thinking bubble.

☆ Rub out/cover up your writing and tell the children to write their sentences in their *Get Writing!* Books, using either their own ideas or yours, if they need the support.

☆ Click through the next screens (man knocking over jar with happening bubble; man at end of the story with thinking bubble). Repeat the process for the other thinking bubble and the happening bubble.

Blue Storybook 7   *Jade's party*

Introducing the story

delicious   exciting

☆ Use these 'power words' when introducing the story during reading Activity 3. Write them on sticky notes so you remember to use them through the lesson/day, e.g. *We are going to have an exciting party for… Mmmm, let's gobble up this delicious party food.*

See Blueprint lesson plans for **Activities 1, 2, 3, 4 (Spelling)** and **Activity 5 Hold a sentence** on pp.23–25.

Activity 6 Build a sentence

delicious

☆ Ask the children to TTYP and think of words that mean the same as (synonyms for) *delicious*. Offer words of your own.

☆ Ask the children when and where they might use the word. TTYP and feed back, e.g. *a lovely tea/ fish and chips/a cake shop.*

☆ TOL as you try out an example of your own. MT/YT each time you develop it, e.g.
This chocolate cake is so delicious I could gobble it all up!
Mmmmm, let me have some more of those delicious sandwiches, they are so tasty.
What smells so delicious? Is it cheesy pizza for tea?

☆ Continue as for the lesson plan on p.121.

☆ Rub out/cover up your writing and tell the children to write their own sentence/s in their *Get Writing!* Books (p.29).

See Blueprint lesson plans for **Activity 7 Edit** on p.26.

Activity 8 Composition: picture prompts

Write about what type of class party you will have.

☆ Explain to the children that through role-play they will write a plan for a party. Your plan could fit in with what's happening at school, e.g. an end of term party, a Christmas party, a Hanukkah party.
  Teacher role: party planner   Children's role: themselves

Blue

- ✿ Take on your role whole-heartedly throughout this activity so children adopt their role easily and enthusiastically. Make sure that your plan is exact. Be very deliberate and fussy about details when using MT/YT!
- ✿ Show the image of a party planner on **CD** (file 7.2). See p.30 of the *Get Writing!* Book for this activity.
- ✿ Teacher in role as party planner: *OK everyone, don't worry, I am here to sort out your party. As you can see I have my planner and if you give me exact details I can plan the most perfect party with the most fabulous theme and the most delicious scrumptious food and yes, the best decorations and games. So let's go...What exactly is the theme of your party?* Focus on the different picture prompts for themes and model describing them, e.g. *A fabulous dressing up party, come as your favourite hero/a wonderful wild west party, dress up as cowboys and cowgirls/a goodbye to Mrs X party with the theme of chocolates because she loves them.*
- ✿ Ask the children to TTYP and feed back: *What should be the theme for our party?*
- ✿ TOL as you expand the description of the theme together, e.g. *fantasy, dressing up. A fantastic dressing up party with a fantasy theme – come dressed up as a magical creature. An amazing magical theme party – dress up as a fantastic fantasy creature.*
- ✿ Say you are now ready to complete the first part of the party planner writing frame (*Theme* section). Continuing in role, model writing the descriptions with some of their choices, e.g. *An extraordinary space-themed party – dress up as an alien or astronaut.* Model re-reading for sense and punctuation.
- ✿ Ask the children to practise saying the first item on their party planner. Rub out/cover up your writing and tell the children to write it in their planners in their *Get Writing!* Books, using either their own ideas or yours, if they need the support.
- ✿ Click through the following screens (*Food, Games, Decoration*) and repeat the above with different headings. Save/print your party planner as you will need it in the next activity.

Activity 9 Composition

Write an invitation for your class party.

- ✿ Display the party planner form that you completed in Activity 8. See p.31 of the *Get Writing!* Book for this activity.
- ✿ Tell the children that they are going to write an invitation for their class party.
- ✿ Ask the children to TTYP to discuss the questions below and Popcorn the feedback. Open **CD** (file 7.3) and ask them to help you write their notes/ideas on the board under the questions.
  What time (start and end) and date is the party? Where is the party? What is the theme and reason for the party? What should you wear? Will there be food and what is it?
- ✿ TOL as you build up the notes for the invitation with the children. Click on the next screen (party invitation writing frame). Take their ideas as you write the invitation.
- ✿ Use MT/YT to practise saying each sentence out loud using the children's ideas.
- ✿ Rub out/cover up your writing and tell the children to write their sentence into the invitation in their *Get Writing!* Books, using either their own ideas or yours, if they need the support.
- ✿ Encourage them to use the exciting descriptive language from their planner in their invitation.
- ✿ Select some interesting sentences to read aloud to the class.
- ✿ Celebration: Ask the partners to think of a short sentence to end the invitation that really shows that they want their guests to come. Choose some examples as feedback.

Introducing the story

> *perfect　amazing　slimy*

☆ Use these 'power words' when introducing the story during reading Activity 3. Write them on sticky notes so you remember to use them through the lesson/day, e.g. *I can see the amazing scales on the snake. I thought it would feel slimy but it was rough and dry. What a lot of children sitting in the perfect partner position!*

*See Blueprint lesson plans for **Activities 1, 2, 3, 4 (Spelling)** and **Activity 5 Hold a sentence** on pp.23–25.*

Activity 6 Build a sentence

perfect

☆ Ask the children to TTYP and think of words that mean the same as *perfect* – synonyms. Offer words of your own.

☆ Ask the children when and where they might use the word. TTYP and feed back, e.g. *when they have done an amazing job/scored a brilliant goal/are sitting in the perfect partner position!*

☆ TOL as you try out an example of your own. MT/YT each time you develop it, e.g.
Perfect Pete got everything right all the time.
I would hate to have a friend that was perfect at everything because I would never win anything.
Some artists can draw a perfect circle without any lumps or bumps.

☆ Continue as for the lesson plan on p.121.

☆ Rub out/cover up your writing and tell the children to write their own sentence/s in their *Get Writing!* Books (p.33).

*See Blueprint lesson plans for **Activity 7 Edit** on p.26.*

Activity 8 Composition: picture prompts

Decide which would be good pets and write a reply to the letter.

☆ Explain to the children that following a role-play they will give some advice to the little girl who wants a pet. They will write a letter with this advice.
　　Teacher role: agony aunt　　Children's role: little agony aunts at agony aunt school

☆ Take on your role whole-heartedly throughout this activity so children adopt their role easily and enthusiastically. Make yours a very strict agony aunt school. Be very deliberate and fussy when using MT/YT.

☆ Show the image of a letter from the little girl in the book on **CD** (file 8.2). See pp.34–35 of the *Get Writing!* Book for this activity.

☆ Teacher in role as agony aunt (reads the letter aloud): *Look at this letter. What a problem. A pet problem. Well, we can help her. We can work out the best advice.*
Say after me, MT/YT, I want to hear your sympathetic sighs: 'A perfect pet is hard to find, but solving problems is our line!'

☆ Click on the next screen (pictures of different pets).

☆ TOL as you build up some descriptions of the pets with the children. Take their ideas as you write and add in adjectives yourself, e.g. *croaky slimy frogs/a lion with a cuddly mane/a mischievous weasel.*

☆ Ask the children to TTYP to discuss which three pets they think are best. Use thumbs up to decide which three pets to write descriptions of. Ask the children to list the pets, 1 to 3, in their *Get Writing!* Books. Then ask them to write a short sentence about what makes their first choice the best in the 'Best pet' section.

- ☆ Ask the children to TTYP and feed back: *What makes this pet perfect?* e.g. *(frog) it is small, has a friendly croak, can live outdoors, easy to keep.*
- ☆ Ask the children to TTYP and feed back: *What might not be good about this pet?* e.g. *(frog) hard to cuddle, might escape, a bit slimy.*
- ☆ TOL as you expand the advice together, e.g. *small and friendly but slimy.*
  A frog would be a perfect pet because it is small and friendly, but it might be too slimy to cuddle!
- ☆ Ask the children to TTYP and feed back to check that their advice says what is good and bad about the pet.
- ☆ Click on the next screen (letter writing frame) and TOL as you build up three sentences for the letter with the children. Take their ideas as you write, e.g. *A puppy is perfect because you can walk it and play with it, but it is a lot of work and might chew up your toys.*
- ☆ Rub out/cover up your writing and tell the children to write the first piece of advice in their letter in their *Get Writing!* Books, using either their own ideas or yours, if they need the support.
- ☆ Celebration: Ask the partners to choose their favourite of the three pets and rehearse saying the advice together and feed back in unison. Choose some examples as feedback.
- ☆ Tell the children that they are going to choose one pet and they need to convince you why it is the best. Use a choice from the previous feedback as an example.
- ☆ Ask the children to TTYP and feed back using Choose Two or Paraphrase, e.g. *The snake is the best pet because it is easy to keep and is fascinating to watch./The hamster is the best pet because you can look after it all by yourself.*
- ☆ TOL and use MT/YT as you build up the final sentence with the children. Take their ideas as you write.
- ☆ Ask the children to write their chosen sentence in their *Get Writing!* Books.

Activity 9 Composition

Write a poem asking for the perfect pet.
- ☆ Show the image of the little girl on **CD** (file 8.3). See p.36 of the *Get Writing!* Book for this activity.
- ☆ Tell the children that they are going to write a poem begging Mum for a pet. Click on the next screen and read the first lines of the poem: *Please, please let me have a pet…*
- ☆ Focus on the thought bubble from the girl, with pictures of different pets.
- ☆ Ask the children to TTYP and feed back: *Why do you want this pet?* e.g. *(snake) it is beautiful and clever and can catch mice, it moves in the most fantastic ways, its scales are in an amazing pattern.*
- ☆ TOL as you expand the line of poetry together, e.g. *patterned scales*
  A snake would be great with its amazing patterned scales,
  A snake would be brilliant with its shining patterned scales, etc.
- ☆ Check your TOL for rhythm and rich images.
- ☆ Use MT/YT to practise saying their sentences out loud using the children's ideas.
- ☆ Model writing the line of poetry with some of their choices, e.g.
  A snake would be exciting as it strikes at its prey,
  A snake would be perfect to keep mice away.
  Model re-reading for sense and rhythm.
- ☆ Repeat the process with the other pets. Once you have written your lines, play around with the order until you are happy with the structure of the poem.
- ☆ Rub out/cover up your writing and tell the children to write their poems in their *Get Writing!* Books, using either their own ideas, or yours, if they need the support.
- ☆ Encourage the children to continue editing and moving the lines around until they are happy with how it sounds.

Introducing the story

> *like lightning   as quick as a bullet   gloom/gloomy   pitch black   dim   murky*

☆ Use these 'power words' when introducing the story during reading Activity 3. Write them on sticky notes so you remember to use them through the lesson/day, e.g. *She is fast, she can run like lightning. That idea came to you as quick as a bullet! In the winter the afternoons are murky and a gloomy light comes down and soon we are in the pitch black of night!*

See Blueprint lesson plans for **Activities 1, 2, 3, 4 (Spelling)** and **Activity 5 Hold a sentence** on pp.23–25.

Activity 6 Build a sentence

murky

☆ Ask the children to TTYP and think of words that mean the same as (synonyms for) *murky*. Offer words of your own.

☆ Ask the children when and where they might use the word. TTYP and feed back, e.g. *when Hansel and Gretel stumbled through the dark murky woods/to describe the grey light of an overcast day/the pond that the princess lost her ball in was full of weeds and had green murky water.*

☆ TOL as you try out an example of your own. MT/YT each time you develop it, e.g.
I reached my hand into the cold murky water to try to find my ring. It was so green and slimy that I had to feel for it.
The evil pixie had green murky eyes without any sparkle or shine.
The fog came down and wrapped us in a silent murky hug.

☆ Continue as for the lesson plan on p.121.

☆ Rub out/cover up your writing and tell the children to write their own sentence/s using their own murky settings (e.g. *woods at night, foggy park*) in their *Get Writing!* Books (p.38).

See Blueprint lesson plans for **Activity 7 Edit** on p.26.

Activity 8 Composition: picture prompts

Write the poem: in the darkness

☆ Drama: you will need a large open space for this activity. Either clear away the tables and chairs, or use the hall or playground.

☆ Tell the children that they are going to do a 'trust' activity in pairs. Explain that they will take turns to be blindfolded and walk across the room without bumping into anyone else. The 'seeing' partner will guide the blindfolded partner with words and only step in to touch them if they are about to bump into anything. Ask the children to think about how it feels to walk about without sight as they do the exercise. At the end of the first blindfolded walk ask the partners to swap around.

☆ Show the image of fox stumbling around in the darkness on **CD** (file 9.2). See p.39 of the *Get Writing!* Book for this activity.

☆ Ask the children to TTYP to discuss the questions below and Popcorn the feedback. Focus on the symbols as you ask the questions, and model writing notes.
Legs: *How did you move? stumble/fumble/trip/slowly*
Eyes: *What could you see? darkness/hints of light/gloom/murky shadows, etc.*
Heart: *How did you feel? scared/alone/worried, etc.*
Ear: *What could you hear? every rustle/my partner breathing/my own movements, etc.*

☆ Ask the children to TTYP and feed back: *How did you move in the darkness?* e.g. *I stumbled, shuffled, patted the ground to make sure it was safe.*
Why did you move like that? Because I was scared I'd fall/because it was impossible to see/so I didn't hurt myself.

☆ Explain you are going to play around with the words and ideas they have come up with to write a line of poetry.

☆ TOL as you try out a few lines of poetry together, e.g.
Stumble, shuffle, fumble, stumble, pat… pat… pat…
Fumble fingers, stumble toes, careful… pat… pat… pat…
Slowly creeping, cautious feeling, stumble onwards, pat, pat, pat.

☆ Say the lines in different ways to make different rhythms, explaining the effects you are making: *If I say it fast it sounds as if I'm moving faster, maybe I'm scared or worried. If I say it slower then it sounds like I'm moving slowly, perhaps because I'm somewhere that is hard to walk easily on like on the edge of a cliff, near water, etc.*

☆ Repeat the above exploring what you can see, hear and feel. Choose one word or sound to repeat to give the poem rhythm.

☆ Click onto the next screen and model writing the descriptive lines with some of the children's choices, e.g. *A rustle in the wind, a crunch by my feet, cold breaths by my ear, shh… shh… shh…* Model re-reading for sense and punctuation.

☆ Ask the children to practise saying the first line of the poem.

☆ Rub out/cover up your writing and tell the children to write their poem in their *Get Writing!* Books, using either their own ideas or yours, if they need the support.

☆ Celebration: In pairs choose one line of the poem and practise it together. Write it out and say it in unison to the class.

Activity 9 Composition

Write the end of the story from Fox's point of view.

☆ Explain to the children that through role-play they will write about the moment that the Sun was released from the Fox's point of view. First they will make notes about what happened (in role) and then they will write on account of the beginning, middle and end of the story from Fox's point of view.
  Teacher role: interviewer   Children's role: Fox

☆ Take on your role whole-heartedly throughout this activity so children adopt their role easily and enthusiastically. Make sure that you get all the facts exactly right.

☆ Show the image of a page from the reporter's notebook on **CD** (file 9.3). See p.40 of the *Get Writing!* Book for this activity.

☆ Teacher in role as interviewer: *Hello Fox. You are my hero. I don't know if I can thank you enough because without you we would still be living in a murky gloom. I would like to find out about your amazing experience. Can I ask my first question? How exactly did you find the box?*

☆ Ask the children to TTYP and feed back. Choose Two and write their ideas down on the notepad on screen, e.g. *I crept up/I scrambled up silently.*

☆ Ask the children to TTYP to discuss the questions below and Popcorn the feedback. Ask them to help you write their ideas on the board.
  What did the box look like? e.g. *glimmers of light/small and glowing/shining in the dark.*
  What did you do with the box? e.g. *grabbed it and hid it/snatched it and ran.*
  How did you feel as you began to open the lid? e.g. *nervous, excited, butterflies in my tummy.*
  Think carefully and tell me exactly how the light escaped from the box. e.g. *There was a blast of light/it shot out as quick as lightning.*
  I believe you told Kestrel to 'Fetch the light'. What happened next? e.g. *He flew and flew but never reached the blazing light/He soared up into the sky but the ball of fire was always higher than he was.*

☆ Tell the children that now they have had the interview they need to organise the ideas into a story structure. Ask them to TTYP using the notes they have made and feed back: *Which parts of the interview should we use for the beginning of the story?*

☆ Click onto the next screen to show the 'Beginning' heading. Tell the children you are going to write a couple of sentences to introduce the setting and start the story. Remind them that they will be writing in role as Fox.

- ☆ TOL as you build up two or three sentences for the beginning of the story with the children. Take their ideas as you write, e.g.
  Sentence 1:
  I crept up to the box in the murky gloom/I scrambled up the bank to where the box glowed in the darkness, etc.
  Sentence 2:
  I could make it out as it shimmered in the darkness and as I scrambled silently closer I could see a bright glow coming from inside it, etc.
- ☆ Continuing in role, model writing a couple of sentences with some of their choices, e.g. *I crept silently out of the darkness towards the glowing box.* Model re-reading for sense and punctuation.
- ☆ Ask the children to practise saying the sentences for the beginning of the story.
- ☆ Rub out/cover up your writing and tell the children to write their beginning in their *Get Writing! Books*, using either their own ideas or yours, if they need the support.
- ☆ Click onto the next two screens ('Middle' and 'End' headings) and repeat the process with the middle and the end of the story.

Blue Storybook 10   *The hole in the hill*

Introducing the story

> beg   demand   pity   entice

- ☆ Use these 'power words' when introducing the story during reading Activity 3. Write them on sticky notes so you remember to use them through the lesson/day, e.g. *'Can I join in?' begged Luca. 'I demand silence!' thundered the headteacher. We can entice the greedy birds into the garden with some bird seeds.*

See Blueprint lesson plans for **Activities 1, 2, 3, 4 (Spelling)** and **Activity 5 Hold a sentence** on pp.23–25.

Activity 6 Build a sentence

entice
- ☆ Ask the children to TTYP and think of words that mean the same as *entice* – synonyms. Offer words of your own.
- ☆ Ask the children when and where they might use the word. TTYP and feed back, e.g. *the wicked witch enticed Sleeping Beauty to eat the apple/the adverts entice you to buy things.*
- ☆ TOL as you try out an example of your own. MT/YT each time you develop it, e.g.
  The old hag held up the apple. 'Eat the sweet, juicy, delicious, red apple,' she said, enticing the girl to eat it.
  The doughnut shop had free samples of their new doughnuts to entice the customers to buy them.
  The scrumptious smell of cake cooking enticed me into the kitchen.
- ☆ Continue as for the lesson plan on p.121.
- ☆ Rub out/cover up your writing and tell the children to write their own sentence/s in their *Get Writing! Books* (p.42).

See Blueprint lesson plans for **Activity 7 Edit** on p.26.

Activity 8 Composition: picture prompts

Write a song to get the rats to follow you.

☆ Explain to the children that they are going to help the Pied Piper create the words for a song to get the rats to follow him.

> *Teacher role: Pied Piper   Children's role: Pied Piper's helpers*

☆ Take on your role whole-heartedly throughout this activity so children adopt their role easily and enthusiastically. Be quite stern and deliberate as the Pied Piper. Be very deliberate and fussy when using MT/YT!

☆ Show the image of the rats on **CD** (file 10.2). See p.43 of the *Get Writing!* Book for this activity.

☆ Teacher in role as the Pied Piper: *Right, my helpers, we have a new job. Do you see these foul rodents, these disgusting, scrabbling rats? Well, the King has said that if we can entice them away he will reward us with heaps of gold. So, what would entice a rat away from Hamelin?*
Say after me, MT/YT, I want to hear your most enticing, persuasive voices: 'Rats like delicious food to eat. Rats will scurry and scavenge delicious morsels of cheese and cake. Mmmmm. Come here rats, come here. We have all you need…'

☆ Ask the children to TTYP and feed back: *What do rats like? e.g. stinky cheese.*

☆ TOL as you expand the description together, e.g. *stinking, oozing cheese.*
Rats beg for stinky cheese that oozes and dribbles down the plate.

☆ Ask the children to TTYP to discuss the questions below and Popcorn the feedback. Ask them to help you write their ideas on the board:
What could make the rats leave their homes? e.g. a new rat-catcher coming/terrible traps.
What phrases could we use to entice the rats? e.g. come here dear rats, oh sweet rats have no fear, etc.

☆ Say that you have discovered a fabulous chorus (click on the next screen to display this) and that this will be part of the song. Use MT/YT to share it with the children:
'Scamper up! Clamber up!
Rats, oh rats!
Gobble up and leave your homes,
Rats of Hamelin come with me,
To a place where you'll be free…'

☆ Explain you are going to play around with the words and ideas they have come up with to write a line of poetry. Say you are going to try to make the song appeal to the rats by repeating words to make a fast rhythm and by trying to entice them.

☆ TOL as you try out a few lines of poetry together, e.g.
Run away from traps with jaws that snap!
Twitch, scuttle, creep, are you safe where you sleep?
There'll be cheese for you and warm nests too!
There'll be no traps and no big cats!
You'll be free to play and scamper all day!

☆ Say the lines in different ways to make different rhythms. Explain the effects you are making: *If I say it fast it sounds like rats scurrying. If I say parts slow and low then they sound more enticing.*

☆ Model writing the descriptions with some of their choices. Model re-reading for sense and punctuation.

☆ Ask the children to practise saying the first line of the song.

☆ Rub out/cover up your writing and tell the children to write their song in their *Get Writing!* Books, using either their own ideas or yours, if they need the support.

Activity 9 Composition

Write a letter, begging the Pied Piper to give the children back.

☆ Explain to the children that through role-play they will write a letter to the Pied Piper to beg him to release their brother or sister.

    Teacher role: Pied Piper   Children's role: the only child left in the village of Hamelin

☆ Take on your role whole-heartedly throughout this activity so children adopt their role easily and enthusiastically. Make the Pied Piper cruel and fussy – don't be easily persuaded. Be very deliberate and fussy when using MT/YT.

☆ Show the image of the Pied Piper looking very angry on **CD** (file 10.3). See p.44 of the *Get Writing!* Book for this activity.

☆ Teacher in role as the Pied Piper: *Go away! Your greedy King disgusts me! We made a deal and he thinks he can just lie to me and pay me as little as he likes! Ha! Now I have your brother or sister and I shall do with them as I wish. They can help me catch rats. You will never see them again... Tell me exactly why I should let even one child go home?*

☆ Ask the children to TTYP to discuss the question and Popcorn the feedback, e.g. *it's not their fault, it's the King's/I can pay you/I miss my sister so much.*

☆ Ask them to help you write their ideas on the board on the next screen.
    Well, that may be true but you will have to do better than that to persuade me that I should let your brother or sister go. Tell me exactly what you miss about them.

☆ Ask the children to TTYP to discuss the question and Popcorn the feedback.
    I miss playing games with them/I miss sharing toys with them.

☆ Ask the children to TTYP to discuss the questions below and Popcorn the feedback. Ask them to help you write their ideas on the board.
    Why should I let your brother or sister go? e.g. *because it wasn't their fault/because the town is silent and sad/because everyone misses their children/I hate being alone.*
    What is it like without your brother or sister at home? e.g. *terrible/empty/lonely.*
    What will you give me in return? e.g. *all the silver and gold I can find/all my toys/my favourite books.*

☆ Review the notes you have made. Click on the next screen (letter template) and TOL as you build up two or three sentences of the letter with the children. MT/YT each time you develop the sentence. Take their ideas as you write, e.g.
    Sentence 1:
    I beg you to let my sister go because I miss her so much. The house is empty and cold without her!/ Please release my brother. I am so lonely without him.
    Sentence 2:
    All of Hamelin is sad and lonely without the children./Please let them come home.

☆ Rub out/cover up your writing and tell the children to write their sentences in their *Get Writing!* Books, using either their own ideas or yours, if they need the support.

☆ Ask the children to continue writing the rest of their letter.

Blue Non-fiction Book 3   *On your bike*

Introducing the book

> wobble   worried   proud   difficult

☆ Use these 'power words' when introducing the book during reading Activity 3. Write them on sticky notes so you remember to use them through the lesson/day, e.g. *If you are worried and you don't understand something, ask for help. It was difficult to eat my jelly at lunch-time, it wobbled on my spoon so much. I am so proud of how well you have worked today!*

*See Blueprint lesson plans for **Activities 1, 2, 3, 4 (Spelling)** and **Activity 5 Hold a sentence** on pp.23–25.*

Activity 6 Build a sentence

proud

☆ Ask the children to TTYP and think of words that mean the same as (synonyms for) *proud*. Offer words of your own.

☆ Ask the children when and where they might use the word. TTYP and feed back, e.g. *to describe how they feel when something good has happened/when they have worked hard and achieved/when they have risen to a challenge.*

☆ TOL as you try out an example of your own. MT/YT each time you develop it.
   I was so proud when I won the medal that I beamed with delight.
   It was a proud moment for me when I finally tied my own shoelaces.

☆ Continue as for the lesson plan on p.121.

☆ Rub out/cover up your writing and tell the children to write their own sentence/s to describe a time when they were extremely pleased with something they had done in their *Get Writing!* Books (p.46).

See Blueprint lesson plans for **Activity 7 Edit** on p.26.

Activity 8 Composition: picture prompts

Write about learning to ride a bike.

☆ Show the image of a child on a bike on **CD** (file NF3.2). See p.47 of the *Get Writing!* Book for this activity. Tell the children they are going to write a recount about learning to ride a bike.

☆ *Can you ride a bike? What was it like when you were learning?* Ask the children to TTYP to say how they learned to ride a bike and Popcorn the feedback. Children who have not learned to ride a bike yet could write about learning to ride a scooter or a like-a-bike, etc.

☆ Click on the next screen and ask them to help you write their ideas on the mind map with sub-headings: *Who? Where? When? How?*

☆ TOL as you build up some descriptions of 'Where' they learned to ride their bike. Take their ideas as you write, e.g. *on the grass at the playground/outside my house/in my garden.*

☆ Ask the children to TTYP to discuss the questions below and Popcorn the feedback. Continue to make notes on the board, using their ideas.
   Who taught you to ride your bike? e.g. *a friend/my parent/an uncle.*
   When did you learn, can you remember the day? e.g. *last summer/a few days ago.*
   How did you feel as you tried? e.g. *it was difficult/I was thinking so hard my face went red.*
   How did it go when you did it on your own? e.g. *I wobbled a bit/I thought I would fall.*
   How did you feel afterwards? e.g. *I was really proud/I wanted to do it again/puffed out!*

☆ TOL as you expand the description using time connectives (e.g. *first, then, next, after that*) to help order the recount. Think carefully about the order that the information should be in. Use the recount planner on the next screen to order ideas.

☆ Click on the next screen and model writing the opening sentence of the recount with some of their choices, e.g. *When I learned to ride my bike I was scared at first, but my aunty was with me and she told me not to worry.* Model re-reading for sense and punctuation.

☆ Ask the children to practise saying the first sentence of their recount.

☆ Rub out/cover up your writing and tell the children to write their first sentence in their *Get Writing!* Book, using either their own ideas, or yours, if children need the support.

☆ Repeat the process so each child recounts their story of how they learned to ride, or are still learning.

☆ Celebration: In pairs ask the children to look back at how they felt that day and reflect about how it made them feel to learn to ride a bike. Encourage them to tell their partner so that they can repeat it back to them.

Activity 9 Composition

Write about how to take care of your bike.

☆ Show an image of a bike on **CD** (NF3.3). See p.48 of the *Get Writing!* Book for this activity.

☆ Tell the children that they are going to write a simple explanation that describes how to look after a bike. This will be in the form of labelling parts of the bike.

☆ Ask the children to TTYP to discuss which part of the bike they would need to keep clean and Popcorn the feedback, e.g. *you should clean the wheels if they get muddy, and the chain.*

☆ Zoom into different parts of the bike and TOL as you build up some descriptions of how that part of the bike might need to be taken care of. Take their ideas as you write, e.g. *the lights will need batteries to work, the chain needs to be oiled, the handlebars should be tight so they don't wobble, the tyres need to be checked for punctures.*

☆ Click on the next screen and ask the children to TTYP and think of exact verbs to describe how you could clean a muddy wheel. Popcorn the feedback, e.g. *hose it down, scrub the wheels, brush off the mud.*

☆ TOL and use MT/YT as you build up the first sentence with the children. Take their ideas as you write, e.g.
Sentence 1:
If your wheels are muddy you should clean off the mud using water and a brush and then check the tyres for punctures.

☆ Rub out/cover up your writing and tell the children to write their chosen sentence to describe how a bike's wheels can be cared for in their *Get Writing!* Books, using either their own ideas or yours, if they need the support.

☆ Click on the next screen (bike photo with 'Lights' label). Ask the children to TTYP and think why it is important to have lights on a bike. Choose Two or Paraphrase, e.g. *so you can ride at night safely/so people can see you when it is dark or foggy.*

☆ TOL as you build up the next sentence with the children. Take their ideas as you write, e.g.
Sentence 2:
Never go out in the dark without lights, and always check your batteries work before you go out.

☆ Ask the children to TTYP to try out different sentences out loud.

☆ Then ask them to write their chosen sentence in their *Get Writing!* Books.

☆ Repeat the format for *chain* and *handlebars*. Use MT/YT to practise saying the sentences out loud using the children's ideas.

☆ Ask the children to write their sentences in their *Get Writing!* Books.

Blue Non-fiction Book 5   *At the seaside*

Introducing the book

> predator   spicy   sticky

☆ Use these 'power words' when introducing the book during reading Activity 3. Write them on sticky notes so you remember to use them through the lesson/day, e.g. *The predator lay in wait for its prey. The spiciest food that I can eat is curry. This glue is so sticky that it has fixed the picture to my top!*

*See Blueprint lesson plans for **Activities 1, 2, 3, 4 (Spelling)** and **Activity 5 Hold a sentence** on pp.23–25.*

Activity 6 Build a sentence

predator

☆ Ask the children to TTYP and think of words that mean the same as *predator* – synonyms. Offer words of your own.

☆ Ask the children when and where they might use the word. TTYP and feed back, e.g. *to describe a lion or wolf/you could use the word predatory to describe how the wolf in Little Red Riding Hood smiled.*

☆ TOL as you try out an example of your own. MT/YT each time you develop it. Involve the children in extending and developing the sentence using questions, e.g.
  The lion is the greatest predator in Africa and it kills gazelle to feed its pride.
  Cats are predators too, as they hunt mice and other small animals.
  The wolf flashed a predatory smile as Little Red Riding Hood said, 'What big teeth you have.'

☆ Continue as for the lesson plan on p.121.

☆ Rub out/cover up your writing and tell the children to write their own sentence/s to describe animals that hunt in their *Get Writing!* Books (p.50).

*See Blueprint lesson plans for **Activity 7 Edit** on p.26.*

Activity 8 Composition: picture prompts

Write a list of the ingredients you need for a picnic.

☆ Explain to the children that they are going to write a list of ingredients for a family picnic at the beach so that Dad can go and buy everything they need.

☆ Show the image of the family having a picnic on **CD** (file NF5.2). See p.51 of the *Get Writing!* Books for this activity.
  What do you like to eat when you have a picnic? Ask the children to TTYP and feed back, e.g. *sandwiches, pies, crisps, drinks, samosas, cake, biscuits, fruit.*

☆ Say: *Tell me exactly the type and amount of sandwiches you need.*

☆ TOL as you expand the description together, e.g. *cheese and pickle.*
  We need enough bread, butter, cheese and pickle to make five sandwiches.

☆ Click on the next screen and model writing the ingredients needed for the sandwiches with some of their choices, e.g. *We need a big pot of jam, a jar of sticky sweet honey and a box of crackers.* Model re-reading for sense and punctuation.

☆ Ask the children to practise saying their first sentence for their list.

☆ Rub out/cover your writing and tell the children to write their list of ingredients for the picnic in their *Get Writing!* Books, using either their own ideas or yours, if they need the support.

☆ Repeat the above with different food to take on the picnic (e.g. *pies, crisps, drinks, samosas, cake, biscuits, fruit*). Make sure that each description is very clear and give the type and amount so Dad does not get it wrong!

☆ Celebration: Partners tell each other a description of eating their favourite picnic food and practise it together until they can say it in unison. Choose some children to feed back to the class.

Activity 9 Composition

Describe the things you can find in a rock pool.

☆ Explain to the children that they are going to write an entry for a book called *Sea life*. It will describe the habitat of the rock pool using information sentences which they will write in labels/ callout boxes.

☆ Show the image of the rock pool on **CD** (file NF5.3). See p.52 of the *Get Writing!* Book for this activity.

☆ Choose one of the drag and drop items (*crab, seaweed, starfish, shrimp*) and ask the children to TTYP to describe it, e.g. *seaweed, blue-green, swaying, a hiding place for small fish.*

☆ TOL as you expand the description together, e.g. *blue-green seaweed.*
  The blue-green seaweed is a hiding place for small fish.
  The blue-green seaweed sways in the rock pool and provides shade.

Blue

☆ Ask the children to TTYP and feed back to think about how they can add additional information to the sentence to tell the reader more about the rock pool habitat, e.g. *Most rock pools have seaweed.*

☆ Display **CD** (file NF5.4) and model writing the descriptions with some of their choices, e.g. *Most rock pools have seaweed which is a good place for small fish to hide from predators.* Model re-reading for sense and punctuation.

☆ Ask the children to practise saying the first label.

☆ Rub out/cover up your writing and tell the children fill in the label in their *Get Writing!* Books, using either their own ideas or yours, if they need the support.

☆ Repeat the above with different items (*crab, starfish, shrimps*).

Blue

Grey Storybook 1   *Rex to the rescue*

Introducing the story

minute   freedom   different

☆ Use these 'power words' when introducing the story during reading Activity 3. Write them on sticky notes so you remember to use them through the lesson/day, e.g. *I had a minute slice of the cake so that the others could have some too. We should all have the freedom to dance about at playtime if we want to. Look at all these different dogs. Which one do you like best?*

*See Blueprint lesson plans for **Activities 1, 2, 3, 4 (Spelling)** and **Activity 5 Hold a sentence** on pp.23–25.*

Activity 6 Build a sentence

minute

☆ Tell the children that *minute* meaning small and *minute* meaning sixty seconds of time are spelled the same way but said differently. Ask children to TTYP (Turn to your partner) and think of words that mean the same as (synonyms for) *minute* (small). Offer words of your own.

☆ Ask children when and where they might use the word. TTYP and feed back, e.g. *to describe Tom Thumb or perhaps a fairy/to show that something is absolutely tiny.*

☆ TOL (Think out loud) as you try out an example of your own. MT/YT (My turn/Your turn) each time you develop it, e.g.
   That was a minute serving of food so I am still hungry.
   Look at the minute insects and mini beasts in the pond, they are tiny.
   There are thirty minute tadpoles.

☆ Mime the punctuation when you are happy with your sentence.

☆ Ask children to TTYP to try out sentences of their own about tiny things. Listen carefully, then Choose Two to feed back.

☆ TOL as you build on one of the ideas and write the sentence. Ask children to help as you do this. Model re-reading for sense and punctuation.

☆ Ask children to develop a sentence of their own. Ask them to practise saying it before they write.

☆ Rub out/cover up your writing and tell the children to write their own sentence/s in their *Get Writing!* Books (p.3).

*See Blueprint lesson plans for **Activity 7 Edit** on p.26.*

Activity 9 Composition

a) *Write notes about what dogs need.*

☆ Explain to the children that through role-play they will plan and write a booklet about dogs for people who are thinking of getting a dog. You can use the RSPCA website to help you get extra information for this role. 'Animals and the law – the five freedoms' is especially helpful, as well as the information pages about dogs. Give the children time to read about the 'five freedoms' on the website before starting this activity.
   Teacher role: animal lover   Children's role: authors

☆ Take on your role whole-heartedly throughout this activity so children adopt their role easily and enthusiastically.

☆ Show the photos of the sad-looking dogs on **CD** (file 1.2). See p.4 of the *Get Writing!* Book for this activity.
Teacher in role as animal lover: *Today we are going to work together to think of how we can help people make good choices before they buy a dog. We want to help people think about all the different things a dog needs, what it costs, what they need to do to keep it healthy and happy and also how to choose the right dog for their home and family.*

☆ Ask the children to TTYP and feed back: *What different types of dogs are there?* e.g. *minute yappy dogs, racing dogs, guard dogs, huge dogs.*
What do these dogs like to do? e.g. *have lots of company, be petted, have lots of space to run.*

☆ Click on the next screen and ask the children to help you write their ideas on the board.

☆ Click on the next screen to show the small illustrations/vignettes that symbolise the five things a dog needs (these are adapted from the 'five freedoms'). Explain what each picture means (free from fear/distress, free from discomfort, free to express normal behaviour and exercise, free from hunger and thirst, free from pain, injury and disease).

☆ Ask the children to TTYP and think about what foods and drink a dog or puppy needs and Popcorn feedback, e.g. *tinned dog food, a bowl of water, enough food, puppy food chews and treats, bones.* Write short notes on the board next to the pictures.

☆ Rub out/cover up your writing and tell the children to write notes in their *Get Writing!* Books p.4, using either their own ideas, or yours, if children need the support.

☆ Repeat the above with the different pictures.

b) *Write sentences about what dogs need.*

☆ After the children have planned their booklet on p.4, help them to compose sentences for each section so that each of the five pictures depicting what a dog needs on p.5 is covered.

☆ Click through the screens and TOL as you expand the description together, e.g. *fresh water and dog food.*
Dogs need to have fresh water and the right sort of food for them.
Puppies need lots of fresh water and special puppy food to help them grow.

☆ Continuing in role, model writing sentences for 'Free from hunger and thirst' with some of their choices, e.g. *Dogs need to be fed every day and they need fresh water too.* Model re-reading for sense.

☆ Ask the children to practise saying their sentences before they write.

☆ Celebration: Ask the children to take turns to tell their partner which type of dog they like best and why. Can their partner repeat the sentence back to them?

Grey Storybook 2   *The lion's paw*

Introducing the story

terrified/terror   horrified/horror   punishment   courageous

☆ Use these 'power words' when introducing the story during reading Activity 3. Write them on sticky notes so you remember to use them through the lesson/day, e.g. *In one story the courageous lion was helped by a tiny mouse. I was terrified that the ferocious dog would snarl at me. I was horrified to find a spider in my sandwich.*

See Blueprint lesson plans for **Activities 1, 2, 3, 4 (Spelling)** and **Activity 5 Hold a sentence** on pp.23–25.

Grey

Activity 6 Build a sentence

horror/horrified

☆ Ask children to TTYP and think of words that mean the same as *horror/horrified* – synonyms. Offer words of your own.

☆ Ask children when and where they might use the word. TTYP and feed back, e.g. *when you realise you have made a huge mistake/when the seven dwarves found Snow White and they thought she was dead/when Little Red Riding Hood realised the wolf was not her Granny.*

☆ TOL as you try out an example of your own. MT/YT each time you develop it, e.g.
Mum was horrified when she saw the enormous mess left for her to clear up.
I was horrified when a dark, ghostly shadow crept across the tent and relieved when it turned out to be my brother playing a trick.

☆ Continue as for the lesson plan on p.146.

☆ Rub out/cover up your writing and tell the children to write their own sentence/s in their *Get Writing!* Books (p.7).

*See Blueprint lesson plans for **Activity 7 Edit** on p.26.*

Activity 9 Composition

a) *Make notes about Androcles.*

☆ Explain to the children that through role-play they will be interviewed as the character Androcles and explain how it felt to be in the Arena. First you will make notes as a class, on the board, following this interview. Then they will write their own notes (organised under headings) in their books.

    Teacher role: interviewer   Children's role: Androcles

☆ Take on your role whole-heartedly throughout this activity so children adopt their role easily and enthusiastically. Make sure that you get all the facts for your plan exactly right. Be very deliberate and fussy when using MT/YT!

☆ Show the image of a page from the reporter's notebook on **CD** (file 2.2). See p.8 of the *Get Writing!* Book for this activity.

☆ Teacher in role as interviewer: *Hello Androcles. You are a real hero! I am a reporter from the* Roman Times *and I wanted to write about your amazing experience in the Arena today. I have heard that you were there because you were being punished. What were you being punished for?*

☆ Ask the children to TTYP and feed back.

☆ If necessary remind them that Androcles was a slave who ran away from a wicked master. This was against the law.

☆ Model how you decide the questions you are going to ask before you meet Androcles. Use the bank of question words (*How? What? Can you tell me?*) on the screen to help you frame your questions. Use the heart, eyes, ear, legs and thought bubble symbols on the **CD** to help you focus your questions.

☆ If you wish to use pre-prepared questions, these can be found on the next screen of the **CD** file, and are listed below. As you role-play the interview, make notes of responses on the board.
Ear: *How did you hear what your punishment would be? e.g. from a cruel guard, when I was in prison, moments before I was sent into the Arena.*
Heart: *How did you feel about that? e.g. terrified, despairing, scared that it was too cruel.*
Thought bubble: *What did you think about as you entered the Arena? e.g. this is it!/that I had to escape/I gave up hope.*
Heart: *What was it like stepping out into the Arena? e.g. horrifying, appalling, there was a huge overwhelming noise.*
Eyes: *What did you see as you stepped out? e.g. a brilliant white light, the golden fur of an enormous beast, a sea of faces.*
Ear: *What could you hear? e.g. a deep rumbling roar, the snarls of wild beasts, the steady chants of the excited crowd.*
Eyes: *Can you tell me what happened next? e.g. I could hardly believe my eyes – my lion was there.*

At first I just saw a terrifying sight and then I realised…

Ear: *Can you tell me how the crowd reacted?* e.g. *they roared in disbelief, they called me a hero.*

Heart: *How are you feeling now?* e.g. *elated, ecstatic, overjoyed, overwhelmed, alive!*

☆ Tell the children that now they have had the interview they need to organise the ideas onto their plan in their books under the different headings.

☆ Remind the children of their ideas about Androcles' punishment. Tell the children you are going to write some notes about Androcles' punishment. Ask them to TTYP and feed back ideas about why he was punished and how he felt, e.g.: *because he was a runaway slave, because his master was cruel, he was thrown into prison and then thrown to the lions.*
Feelings: unfair, cruel, scared, terrified, despairing, etc.

☆ Model writing the notes with some of their choices. Model re-reading for sense.

☆ Ask the children to practise saying their first set of notes.

☆ Rub out/cover up your writing and tell the children to write their plans in their *Get Writing!* Books, using either their own ideas, or yours, if children need the support.

☆ Click on the next screens and repeat the process for the other headings: 'Stepping out into the Arena', 'In the Arena, and 'Safe at last'.

☆ Celebration: Ask the children to take turns to imagine that they are Androcles about to enter the ring. Ask them to tell their partner exactly how they feel. Can they repeat it back to their partner?

b) *You are Androcles. Write about what happened to you.*

☆ Click on the next screen to show the image of Androcles standing at the edge of the Arena. See p.9 of the *Get writing!* Book for this part of the activity.

☆ Tell the children that they are going zoom in to write a new atmospheric description of this part of the story in role as Androcles.

☆ Ask the children to TTYP to discuss the questions below and Popcorn the feedback. Ask them to help you write their ideas on the board.
Heart: *What are you feeling as you stand on the edge of the Arena?* e.g. *terrified, sweating with fear, breathless with terror.*
Ear: *What can you hear?* e.g. *the roar of the crowd/the growls and movement of the beasts/my heart thumping wildly.*
Legs: *How are you moving?* e.g. *trembling, staggering, hardly standing.*
Eyes: *What do you see as you enter the ring?* e.g. *a huge beast, a dark yellow shape, an enormous crowd.*

☆ Remind the children of the notes they have already taken to help them build each sentence. TOL as you build up two or three sentences with the children. Take their ideas as you write, e.g.
Sentence 1:
I could hardly stand as I trembled all over with terror, my heart beating like a runaway train as I was about to face my punishment.
Sentence 2:
There in the arena, something wild and dangerous moved, and its growls made my terror even worse.

☆ Use MT/YT to practise saying their sentences out loud using the children's ideas.

☆ Ask the children to write their chosen sentence in their *Get Writing!* Books. Ask them to continue to write their account of Androcles' experience in the Arena using their notes.

☆ Select some interesting sentences to read aloud to the class.

Introducing the story

cramped   crammed   squeezed

☆ Use these 'power words' when introducing the story during reading Activity 3. Write them on sticky notes so you remember to use them through the lesson/day, e.g. *We squeezed the present into the envelope to post it to Granny. I crammed a handful of fizzy sweets in my mouth! We were very cramped when the class next door shared our room for the day.*

See Blueprint lesson plans for **Activities 1, 2, 3, 4 (Spelling)** and **Activity 5 Hold a sentence** on pp.23–25.

Activity 6 Build a sentence

crammed

☆ Ask the children to TTYP and think of words that mean the same as *crammed* – synonyms. Offer words of your own.

☆ Ask the children when and where they might use the word. TTYP and feed back, e.g. *when there are lots of things squashed into a tight space, when they stuff loads of food in their mouth because they are so hungry.*

☆ TOL as you try out an example of your own. MT/YT each time you develop it, e.g.
We crammed into the wardrobe and tried not to giggle.
My pens were crammed so tightly into my pencil case that they all popped out when I opened up the zip!
Ryan crammed a huge slice of cream cake into his mouth.

☆ Continue as for the lesson plan on p.146.

☆ Rub out/cover up your writing and tell the children to write their own sentence/s in their *Get Writing!* Books (p.11).

See Blueprint lesson plans for **Activity 7 Edit** on p.26.

Activity 9 Composition

Have you ever played Hide and Seek or Sardines? How did you feel?

☆ Tell the children that they are going to write about a time they played a hiding game; what it was like waiting to be found, how other people found you and crammed into the space with you and how the game ended.

☆ Ask the children: *Have you ever played a game like Sardines where one person hides and everyone else has to find him or her? If you are the 'hider' you have to wait and wait until someone finds you and then they squeeze into the hiding space next to you. You have to be very quiet and try not to giggle. In the end you are all crammed in like sardines in a tin! The last person to find you is the 'hider' next time.*

☆ Ask the children to TTYP and discuss any hiding games that they have played. Popcorn feedback so you get an idea of the games and basic rules of the game.

☆ Show the image of a child hidden in a cramped space on **CD** (file 3.2). See p.12 of the *Get Writing!* Book for this activity.

☆ Ask the children to TTYP and feed back: *Have you ever been the hider in a game? What kind of places make good hiding places? e.g. cupboard, behind a door, under a bed, behind a curtain.*

☆ Ask the children to TTYP and feed back: *Close your eyes and imagine a place you have hidden. What was it like?*

☆ TOL as you expand the description together, e.g. *dark and dusty.*
It was dark and dusty under the bed; I tried hard not to sneeze.

- ☆ Ask the children to TTYP and tell their partner about a time that they were a 'hider' in preparation for the next part of the activity.
- ☆ Ask the children to TTYP to discuss the questions below and Popcorn the feedback. Ask them to help you write their ideas on the board.

    Heart: *How are you feeling as you wait alone?* e.g. *excited, bored, no one will ever find me, a bit scared. How do feel when the first person finds you?* e.g. *pleased because now I have someone to hide with/ annoyed it is not my best friend.*

    Ear: *What can you hear on your own?* e.g. *feet running by, whispers of the seekers. What noises do you make as you are hiding with the others?* e.g. *quiet giggles, hushed whispers.*

    Legs: *How do you move whilst you are waiting?* e.g. *fidget, wriggle, twitch, squirm. How do you fit in the space?* e.g. *too cramped to move, squeezed in tight, elbow in my ribs.*

    Eyes: *What do you see when you peep out of your hiding place?* e.g. *a pair of shoes, an empty room.*
- ☆ Click on the next screen. TOL as you build up two or three sentences for the start of the story with the children. Take their ideas as you write, e.g.

    I could hear the other children running right past me as I hid behind the old dusty curtain.

    By now I was bored and hoped someone would find me but then some feet stopped right by me – who was it?
- ☆ Model writing the descriptions with some of their choices, e.g. *Suddenly, the curtain was pulled back and my best friend squeezed in next to me giggling.* Model re-reading for sense and punctuation.
- ☆ Ask the children to think of how they are finally found and TTYP to describe the noises and movements they make as they leave the hiding place. Popcorn feedback, e.g. *we all fell out of the cupboard laughing/we crawled out from under the bed giggling/we jumped out of the curtain screaming,* etc. Ask children to TTYP to try out different sentences to end their story out loud.
- ☆ Encourage them to write their chosen sentences in their *Get Writing!* Books.
- ☆ Select some interesting sentences to read aloud to the class.

Grey Storybook 4   *Looking after a hamster*

Introducing the book

    scuttle   scurry   clamber   entice

- ☆ Use these 'power words' when introducing the book during reading Activity 3. Write them on sticky notes so you remember to use them through the lesson/day, e.g. *Please don't leave your bags on the floor, so I have to clamber over them. How can I entice you all to join the new club?*

See Blueprint lesson plans for **Activities 1, 2, 3, 4 (Spelling)** and **Activity 5 Hold a sentence** on pp.23–25.

Activity 6 Build a sentence

clamber

- ☆ Ask the children to TTYP and think of words that mean the same as (synonyms for) *clamber.* Offer words of your own.
- ☆ Ask children when and where they might use the word. TTYP and feed back, e.g. *when there are lots of things in your way and you have to clamber over them, when you are in adventure playground and you have to clamber up the nets.*
- ☆ TOL as you try out an example of your own. MT/YT each time you develop it, e.g.

    I had to clamber over the gate because it was locked.

    There was no other way in so I had to clamber over the high gate.

    I clambered over the high gate because it was locked and there was no other way into the field.

☆ Continue as for the lesson plan on p.146.

☆ Rub out/cover up your writing and tell the children to write their own sentence/s in their *Get Writing!* Books (p.14).

See Blueprint lesson plans for **Activity 7 Edit** on p.26.

Activity 9 Composition

Finish the poem about the hamster that escaped.

☆ Explain to the children that the hamster has escaped and that they are going to write a poem to try and entice it out of its hiding-place.

   Teacher role: teacher in a panic, having lost the hamster   *Children's role: helpers*

☆ Take on your role whole-heartedly throughout this activity so children adopt their role easily and enthusiastically. Be flustered and panicky, so that you need clear instructions from the children to help you. Be very deliberate and fussy when using MT/YT!

☆ Show the images of the hamster on **CD** (file 4.2). See p.15 of the *Get Writing!* Book for this activity.

☆ Teacher in role as a teacher in a fix: *Oh, no! Egbert the hamster has escaped. He's clambered out of his cage and disappeared. He's nowhere to be found. What shall I do!? What shall we do? I know – we'll entice him out with his favourite treats.*

   Say after me, MT/YT, I want to hear your most enticing persuasive voices: 'Egbert the hamster loves cheese to nibble and small juicy currants. Come out, Egbert, we have wonderful crunchy cornflakes and jam-smeared bread, mmmm…'

☆ Ask the children to TTYP and feed back: *What do hamsters like?* e.g. *nuts and raisins.*

☆ *Hamsters gobble up chewy raisins and crunchy nuts. Mmmm, delicious!* TOL as you expand the description together: e.g. *chewy crunchy delicious*
   Watch the greedy hamster munch and crunch on his delicious treats.

☆ Click on the next screen to show the questions below. Ask the children to help you find the hamster by telling them to TTYP and discuss the questions. Popcorn the feedback (add adjectives where needed). Write their ideas on the board:
   How did Egbert escape? e.g. *crept and clambered, climbed the cage, nudged the door.*
   Where could he be hidden? e.g. *under the dusty cupboards, behind the squeaky door, in the teacher's bag, among the coats hanging in the corridor.*
   What could make Egbert come back? e.g. *treats, a clean cage, a new toy.*
   What phrases could we use to entice Egbert? e.g. *don't be scared, Come out Egbert – I've got some treats!*

☆ Click on the next screen (hamster poem chorus). Say that you have discovered a fabulous chorus that will be part of the poem. Use MT/YT to share it with the children:
   We didn't lock the door
   We forgot to shut it tight,
   We should have all made sure,
   But our pet escaped last night!

☆ Explain you are going to play around with the words and ideas they have come up with to write a line of poetry. Say you are going to try to make the poetry appeal to Egbert, the escaped hamster, by repeating words to make a rhythm and by trying to entice him with things he likes.

☆ TOL as you try out a few lines of poetry together that describe Egbert's escape. Do not worry about rhyming necessarily, but emphasize good word choices and rhythm, e.g.
   A nudge and a push and he escaped from his cage
   Creeping and climbing, a night-time escape

☆ Say the lines in different ways to make different rhythms, explaining the effects you are making:
   If I say it fast, it sounds like Egbert escaped in a panic. If I say parts slow then it sounds like he sneaked out.

☆ Model writing the descriptions with some of their choices. Model re-reading for sense and punctuation.

- ☆ Ask the children to practise saying the first new line of the poem.
- ☆ Rub out/cover up your writing and tell the children to write their new verse in their *Get Writing!* Books, using either their own ideas, or yours, if children need the support.
- ☆ Repeat the above exploring places that the hamster would hide, e.g. *under things (cupboards, table, chairs), in things (bags, boxes, books), and what might entice him out,* e.g. *cheese, treats, a new toy.* Choose words/phrases to repeat to give the poem rhythm, e.g.

  Has he scuttled under the dusty cupboards?
  Has he scurried beneath the chairs?
  Where is Egbert, the great escaping hamster?
  Entice him out with sweet treats
  Entice him out with toys
- ☆ Once you have written your lines, show how you play around with the order until you are happy with the structure of the poem.
- ☆ Encourage the children to continue editing and moving the lines around until they are happy with how it sounds.
- ☆ Tell them to write the rest of their poem in their *Get Writing!* Books.
- ☆ Celebration: In pairs choose one line of the poem and practise it together. Write it out and say it in unison to the class.

Grey Storybook 5   *How silly!*

Introducing the story

ridiculous   nonsense   sensible   embarrassing/embarrassed

- ☆ Use these 'power words' when introducing the story during reading Activity 3. Write them on sticky notes so you remember to use them through the lesson/day, e.g. *It is a ridiculous idea to wear a swimsuit in the snow – instead it would be sensible to wear a snowsuit. What a wonderful nonsense poem full of ridiculous creatures and hilarious ideas! I was embarrassed when my mum called my friend by the wrong name and it was a girl's/boy's name!*

See Blueprint lesson plans for **Activities 1, 2, 3, 4 (Spelling)** and **Activity 5 Hold a sentence** on pp. 23–25.

Activity 6 Build a sentence

ridiculous
- ☆ Ask children to TTYP and think of words that mean the same as (synonyms for) *ridiculous*. Offer words of your own.
- ☆ Ask children when and where they might use the word. TTYP and feed back, e.g. *to describe something very silly, as an antonym for sensible.*
- ☆ TOL as you try out an example of your own. MT/YT each time you develop it, e.g.
  You look ridiculous in that tiny top and enormous pair of baggy trousers.
  That is the most ridiculously over-the-top cake I have ever seen, piled high with layers of cream and chocolate and strawberries.
  What silly nonsense, it is ridiculous to think that cows can jump over the Moon.
- ☆ Continue as for the lesson plan on p.146.
- ☆ Rub out/cover up your writing and tell the children to write their own sentence/s in their *Get Writing!* Books (p.17).

See Blueprint lesson plans for **Activity 7 Edit** on p.26.

Grey

Activity 9 Composition

a) *Make notes about when you were embarrassed.*

☆ Ask the children to TTYP and discuss any times that they have been embarrassed (in a funny way!). *What is the silliest thing you ever done? Have you ever been really embarrassed by something you've done? Or perhaps your brother or sister, mum or dad, have really embarrassed you?* Popcorn feedback so you all can share some embarrassing moments.

☆ Show the image of a child looking red faced with embarrassment wearing a fancy dress surrounded by children in school uniform on **CD** (file 5.2). See pp.18–19 of the *Get Writing!* Book for this activity.

☆ Ask the children to TTYP and feed back: *Have you ever been really embarrassed like this little boy? What did it feel like? e.g. I went all red and hot/I wanted to hide my face/I wanted to disappear/I went all sweaty.*

☆ TOL as you expand the description together: *e.g. red hot, disappear.*
When I realised I was wearing the wrong clothes I wanted to disappear.
I felt red hot with shame and wished I could disappear when I called the teacher Mum, etc.

☆ Tell the children that they are going to choose an embarrassing moment and write about it.

☆ Ask the children to TTYP and tell their partner about a time they have been embarrassed. For example, it could be a time when their parent/carer has embarrassed them, with another adult has embarrassed them, or when they've made a silly mistake themselves and got embarrassed.

☆ Click on the next screen and ask the children to TTYP to discuss the questions below and Popcorn the feedback. Ask them to help you write their ideas on the board.
Heart: *How do you feel when you get embarrassed? e.g. silly, ashamed, upset, awful.*
Legs: *What do you do or want to do when you are embarrassed? e.g. fidget, wriggle, twitch, squirm, want to hide, disappear, go home.*
Eyes: *What does your body look/feel like when you are embarrassed? e.g. red faced, hot and sweaty, butterflies in my tum.*

☆ Ask the children to use the planner in their *Get Writing!* Books to help them collect good words and phrases to use in their writing later on.

b) *Now write about what happened.*

☆ Tell the children they are going to use their notes and ideas to write in more detail about what happened when they were embarrassed.

☆ TOL as you build up two or three sentences with the children. Take their ideas as you write, e.g. *One day my dad was in charge and he gave me the wrong swimming things. When I tried them on I saw they were my big brother's and they were enormous.*

☆ Click on the next screen and model writing the descriptions with some of their choices. Model re-reading for sense and punctuation.

☆ Ask children to TTYP to try out different sentences out loud using some of the words they have collected to describe how they felt.

☆ Ask them to write their stories of embarrassment in their *Get Writing!* Books.

☆ Select some interesting sentences to read aloud to the class.

☆ Celebration: Ask the children to take turns to read their embarrassing story to their partner and each partner can feed back why they like it.

Grey

154

Introducing the story

> useless   foul   horrible   vile   mouldy

☆ Use these 'power words' when introducing the story during reading Activity 3. Write them on sticky notes so you remember to use them through the lesson/day, e.g. *What is this vile thing stuck to the bottom of my shoe? Let's clean all the mouldy cups from the staffroom! What a foul smell, it's like rotten eggs.*

*See Blueprint lesson plans for **Activities 1, 2, 3, 4 (Spelling)** and **Activity 5 Hold a sentence** on pp.23–25.*

Activity 6 Build a sentence

disgusting

☆ Ask the children to TTYP and think of words that mean the same as *disgusting* – synonyms. Offer words of your own.

☆ Ask children when and where they might use the word. TTYP and feed back, e.g. *to describe something really horrible or food that they hate to eat.*

☆ TOL as you try out an example of your own. MT/YT each time you develop it, e.g.
I am disgusted at this stinking pile of mouldy washing up.
It was a disgusting, squashed frog that the cat brought in and left on the kitchen floor – ew!
What a disgusting idea, I will not go swimming in the foul murky pond.

☆ Continue as for the lesson plan on p.146.

☆ Rub out/cover up your writing and tell the children to write their own sentence/s in their *Get Writing!* Books (p.21).

*See Blueprint lesson plans for **Activity 7 Edit** on p.26.*

Activity 9 Composition

Write a poem about what you can buy at Wailing Winny's car boot sale.

☆ Explain to the children that through role-play they will work as witches trying to describe revolting items in their car boot sale. They will then use their descriptions to write a poem.

☆ Collect some disgusting items to show and describe to the children before the activity to help them get ideas e.g. mouldy mugs, an overflowing rubbish bin, stinky trainers and other items from lost property.

> *Teacher role: head witch at a car boot sale*   *Children's role: apprentice witches*

☆ Take on your role whole-heartedly throughout this activity so children adopt their role easily and enthusiastically.

☆ Show the image of the car boot and all the disgusting things for sale (*mouldy mug, dirty clothes, mouldy trainers, rubbish bin, toenail clippings, snail slime in a jar*) on **CD** (file 6.2). See p.22 of the *Get Writing!* Book for this activity.

☆ Teacher in role as head witch: *Have you seen my wonderful mouldy mug? Look at the stains and blue mould floating about in the grey milky tea. Perfect for spell makers everywhere. Come and see the amazing things I have here at my car boot.*
Right, we need to sell all this stuff and I need you to help me. We need to make it all sound amazingly foul, disgusting and terrible because that's what witches like. So stinky, vile and horrible that, by the end of the day we will have none left and we have made lots of money. Ha, ha, ha, ha!
Say after me, MT/YT, I want to hear your witchy voices: 'Gorgeous, stinking, mouldy trainers with mud splashed all over them. Dirty, sweaty, old PE shorts with paint drips and rips! Ha, ha, ha!'

- ☆ Drag and drop a rubbish bin on screen. Ask the children to TTYP and feed back: *How can we make this rubbish bin sound attractive to witches?* e.g. *overflowing with foul rubbish. What does the bin look like?* e.g. *a bent bin overflowing with rubbish/a dirty grubby bin.*
- ☆ TOL as you expand the description together: e.g. *stinky, mouldy. Come and see my wonderful stinky bin filled to the brim with mouldy rubbish. Come and buy my broken, grubby bin filled with rotten fruits and smelly rubbish. Sound very witch-like!*
- ☆ Repeat the above with different items as you drag and drop them onto the car boot.
- ☆ Ask children to TTYP and feed back to think about how foul they can make each item sound.
- ☆ Display **CD** (file 6.3). Continuing in role, model writing the descriptions with some of their choices, e.g. *Come and buy my dirty, green, gooey, dripping snails' slime.* Model re-reading for sense and punctuation.
- ☆ Ask the children to practise saying their lines for their poem.
- ☆ Rub out/cover up your writing and tell the children to write their witch's car boot poem in their *Get Writing!* Books, using either their own ideas or yours, if children need the support.
- ☆ Celebration: In pairs choose one line of the poem and practise it together. Write it out and say it in unison to the class.

Grey Storybook 7   *Toad*

Introducing the story

loathsome   hideous   slimy   deceitful

- ☆ Use these 'power words' when introducing the story during reading Activity 3. Write them on sticky notes so you remember to use them through the lesson/day, e.g. *The Wicked Queen was a loathsome, evil character. It was hideous to tread on a slug! At the witches' ball everyone wore their ugliest clothes and vilest hats.*

See Blueprint lesson plans for **Activities 1, 2, 3, 4 (Spelling)** and **Activity 5 Hold a sentence** on pp.23–25.

Activity 6 Build a sentence

deceitful
- ☆ Ask the children to TTYP and think of words that mean the same as *deceitful* – synonyms. Offer words of your own.
- ☆ Ask children when and where they might use the word. TTYP and feed back, e.g. *when someone has told a lie or been untruthful.*
- ☆ TOL as you try out an example of your own. MT/YT each time you develop it, e.g.
  It was deceitful to tell a lie about your brother to get him in trouble.
  It was deceitful to cheat in the test so you got full marks.
- ☆ Continue as for the lesson plan on p.146.
- ☆ Rub out/cover up your writing and tell the children to write their own sentence/s in their *Get Writing!* Books (p.24).

See Blueprint lesson plans for **Activity 7 Edit** on p.26.

Activity 9 Composition

Write notes about what the characters did and thought.
- ☆ Explain to the children that they are going to think about some characters from familiar stories

that they have read and explore what they thought and did, and what lesson they learned.

☆ Show the images of Hansel and Gretel, Princess Joan, the King from the Pied Piper, Crow from the King of the Birds, with tags coming off them saying 'lesson learned' on **CD** (file 7.2). See p.25 of the *Get Writing!* Book for this activity.

☆ Click on the next screen to show a zoomed in picture of Princess Joan. Ask: *What do you know about her?* TTYP and Popcorn feedback e.g. *she lost a ball in a pond, she is a princess, she told a lie, she did not keep her promise.*

☆ Tell the children that you will be writing notes into the 'Notes about' section of the screen. Ask the children to TTYP and discuss how Joan tricked the toad.

☆ Ask the children to help you write their ideas on the board.

☆ Ask the children to TTYP and feed back: *What did Joan do that was deceitful?* e.g. *she tricked the toad.*
How did she trick the toad?

☆ TOL as you expand the notes together: e.g.
Joan made a promise that she did not intend to keep.
Joan told a lie so she could get her ball.

☆ Rub out/cover up your writing and tell the children to write their notes for Joan in their *Get Writing!* Books, using either their own ideas or yours, if they need the support.

☆ Click through the screens (Hansel and Gretel, King, Crow) and repeat the above with the different characters.

Write notes about what lessons the characters learned.

☆ Tell the children they will now think about the lessons these characters learned. Ask children to TTYP using their notes to help them and feed back to think about how Joan had changed by the end of the story, e.g. *she knew she had been mean to the toad, she said 'I won't be unkind again', she would not lie again.* See pp.26–27 of the *Get Writing!* Book for this activity.

☆ Click on the next screen (Joan with 'lesson learned' label) and model writing descriptions of Joan with some of their choices, e.g. *Princess Joan lied to the toad but she got found out. She will not lie again./Princess Joan was unkind to the toad, but she will not do that again.* Model re-reading for sense and punctuation.

☆ Ask the children to practise saying the lesson that Joan has learned.

☆ Rub out/cover up your writing and tell the children to write Joan's label in their *Get Writing!* Books, using either their own ideas or yours, if they need the support.

☆ Click through the next screens (Hansel and Gretel, King, Crow) and repeat the above with the different characters.

Grey Storybook 8   *Andrew*

Introducing the story

> disappear   terrified   horrified   scanned

☆ Use these 'power words' when introducing the story during reading Activity 3. Write them on sticky notes so you remember to use them through the lesson/day, e.g. *I scanned the staffroom to see if I could see my lost gloves, but no luck, they didn't seem to be there. Do not be terrified of a spider's web, it is only trying to make a trap to catch nasty flies.*

*See Blueprint lesson plans for **Activities 1, 2, 3, 4 (Spelling)** and **Activity 5 Hold a sentence** on pp.23–25.*

Activity 6 Build a sentence

disappeared

- ☆ Ask the children to TTYP and think of words that mean the same as *disappeared* – synonyms. Offer words of your own.
- ☆ Ask the children when and where they might use the word. TTYP and feed back, e.g. *when they've finished a big plate of food, when a magician performs a trick.*
- ☆ TOL as you try out an example of your own. MT/YT each time you develop it, e.g.
  The pile of chips disappeared – the hungry children gobbled them up!
  At last I had finished: the pile of reports had disappeared to nothing!
- ☆ Continue as for the lesson plan on p.146.
- ☆ Rub out/cover up your writing and tell the children to write their own sentence/s in their *Get Writing!* Books (p.29).

See Blueprint lesson plans for **Activity 7 Edit** *on p.26.*

Activity 9 Composition

a) *Make notes about what happened to you when you were lost at sea.*

- ☆ Tell the children that through role-play they are going to interview Andrew and make notes about his story. They are then going to use their notes to write a diary entry about the most exciting part of the story.
  Teacher role: interviewer   Children's role: Andrew
- ☆ Take on your role whole-heartedly throughout this activity so children adopt their role easily and enthusiastically. Make sure that you get all the facts exactly right. Be very deliberate and fussy when using MT/YT!
- ☆ Show the image of a page from the reporter's notebook on **CD** (file 8.2). See p.30 of the *Get Writing!* Book for this activity.
- ☆ Teacher in role as interviewer: *Hello, Andrew. I'm so sorry that you've had such an awful experience. Would you mind if I asked you a few questions about what happened to you today? I heard you were rescued by a lifeboat. Can you describe how you got lost at sea?*
- ☆ Ask the children to TTYP and feed back. Choose Two and write their ideas down on the notepad on screen.
- ☆ Now ask the children to TTYP to discuss the questions below (these are on the next screens of the **CD** file) and Popcorn the feedback. Ask them to help you write their ideas on the board.
  Take me back to the moment you realised you were in trouble… What was your first thought? e.g. *I was confused, I felt worried and then scared.*
  What did you see? e.g. *It was mainly sea, I saw some gulls, a huge wave.*
  What was the sea like? e.g. *The waves got bigger and began to lift me up.*
  Describe how far away the beach was. What did it look like? e.g. *The beach seemed far away, it was like a strip of yellow, the people were like dots.*
  How did you feel when you realised how far out you were? e.g. *Now I was really terrified, I started to shake with fear.*
  How did you feel when you saw the lifeboat? e.g. *frantic in case they hadn't seen me, hopeful/desperate that they get to me quickly.*
- ☆ Tell the children that now they have had the interview they need to organise the ideas onto their plan in their books under the different symbols.
- ☆ Click on the next screen and focus on the heart symbol. Tell the children you are going to write some notes about how Andrew felt when he realised he was lost. Ask them to TTYP using the notes on the whiteboard and feed back: *I was terrified, I shook with fear, I couldn't understand where I was, I became more and more anxious as time went by, etc.*
- ☆ Model writing the notes with some of their choices. Model re-reading for sense.
- ☆ Ask the children to practise saying their first set of notes.

- ✩ Rub out/cover up your writing and ask the children to write in their *Get Writing!* Books.
- ✩ Repeat the process for the other symbols: eyes (what he saw), legs (what he did), ears (what he heard).

b) *Write about what happened.*
- ✩ Click on the next screen (Andrew in the boat).
- ✩ Tell the children that they are going to zoom in to write a diary entry for this part of the story. They are going to use some of Andrew's words to help write the diary. See p.31 of the *Get Writing!* Book for this activity.
- ✩ Ask the children to TTYP to discuss the endings for the sentence starters on screen. (These are: *The first thing I remember is… The wind had blown up… The sea was… The beach disappeared… I scanned the shoreline…*) Popcorn the feedback. Click on the next screen and ask them to help you write their ideas on the board. Remind the children of the notes they have already taken to help them build each sentence.
- ✩ TOL and use MT/YT as you build up two or three sentences with the children that describe how Andrew realised that he had got lost at sea. Take their ideas as you write, e.g.
  Sentence 1:
  The first thing I remember is waking up to hear a seagull screeching next to my head!
  Sentence 2:
  The wind had blown up and I rocked from side-to-side as huge waves lifted me up.
- ✩ Rub out/cover up your writing and tell the children to write their chosen sentence in their *Get Writing!* Books, using either their own ideas or yours, if they need the support.
- ✩ Repeat the process for the other sentence starters.
- ✩ Click on the next screen to focus on the picture of Andrew again. You are going to write a dramatic conclusion to the diary entry! Ask: *What did he say as he saw the lifeboat? Look, here, please come and save me. Help me, I'm sinking, come quickly!* (mime).
  How would he have said this? e.g. *screamed, shouted, cried, bellowed.*
- ✩ Ask children to TTYP to try out different sentences out loud.
- ✩ Then ask them to write their chosen sentence, which finishes the dairy entry of Andrew being rescued.
- ✩ Select some interesting sentences to read aloud to the class.

Grey Storybook 9   *Dear Vampire*

Introducing the story

| *terrifying*   *horrifying*   *frightening*   *blood-curdling* |

- ✩ Use these 'power words' when introducing the story during reading Activity 3. Write them on sticky notes so you remember to use them through the lesson/day, e.g. *The thunderstorm was frightening. I find the thunder terrifying, it always makes me jump. I had a horrifying moment because I thought I had broken my mum's favourite mug, and she would be so upset. The children ran about making bloodcurdling, high-pitched screams.*

See Blueprint lesson plans for **Activities 1, 2, 3, 4 (Spelling)** and **Activity 5 Hold a sentence** on pp.23–25.

Activity 6 Build a sentence

terrifying
- ✩ Ask the children to TTYP and think of words that mean the same as (synonyms for) *terrifying*. Offer words of your own.
- ✩ Ask the children when and where they might use the word. TTYP and feed back, e.g. *when they had a scare.*

✫ TOL as you try out an example of your own. MT/YT each time you develop it, e.g.
The Horrordrop was a terrifying rollercoaster with lots of loops and sudden drops.
We screamed at the terrifying monster in the Haunted House ride and then laughed out loud when we saw it was just a man in a mask!

✫ Continue as for the lesson plan on p.146.

✫ Rub out/cover up your writing and tell the children to write their own sentence/s in their *Get Writing!* Books (p.33).

See Blueprint lesson plans for **Activity 7 Edit** on p.26.

Activity 9 Composition

a) Make notes for your writing.

✫ Explain to the children that through role-play they will give some advice to the vampire in the story about how to be more scary. Then they will use the notes to write a letter, giving advice.
     Teacher role: agony aunt   Children's role: little agony aunts at agony aunt school

✫ Take on your role whole-heartedly throughout this activity so children adopt their role easily and enthusiastically. Make yours a very strict agony aunt school. Be very deliberate and fussy when using MT/YT.

✫ Show the image of a letter from the vampire in the storybook on **CD** (file 9.2). See p.34 of the *Get Writing!* Book for this activity.

✫ Teacher in role as agony aunt reads the letter out loud. *Look at this letter. What a problem, a scaring-people problem from a vampire. Well we can help him, we can work out the best advice.*

✫ *Say after me, MT/YT, I want to hear your sympathetic sighs: 'It is hard to be a terrifying scarer but agony aunts can solve even the trickiest problem.'*

✫ Click on the next screen and show the image of the bat from the Storybook and a vampire with pointed glistening teeth, big scary eyes, a huge black cape and long twitching fingers.

✫ Tell the children that luckily the vampire who wrote the letter has included a picture so that they could give him some ideas about how to be more like a 'real' vampire.

✫ Ask the children to TTYP to help you explain to the bat how he should look and where he is going wrong! Popcorn the feedback. Ask them to help you write their ideas on the board.

✫ Point to the vampire's teeth and say: *A real vampire has sharp, glistening, scary fangs…* Ask the children to TTYP and explain how the bat's teeth are wrong, e.g. *fallen out, gummy, small, not sharp enough, dirty.*

✫ TOL and use MT/YT as you build up some notes with the children. Take their ideas as you write them next to the vampire and the bat, e.g.
bat: gummy with no fangs/useless blunt fangs
vampire: sharp, glistening, pointed fangs/terrifying, super-white fangs

✫ Ask the children to write their chosen notes into the perfect vampire and the bat boxes in their *Get Writing!* Books using either their own ideas or yours, if they need the support.

✫ Repeat the process to describe the vampire's eyes (*dark, crazy, sparkling,* etc.), hands (*long fingernails, twitching, strong,* etc.), cape (*black, velvet, swishing, long,* etc.), voice (*deep, blood-curdling, scary, frightening,* etc). Encourage the children to gain independence by making notes to describe both the bat and the vampire.

b) Write a letter to the vampire. Give him some good advice about how to be more scary.

✫ Click on the next screen (picture of the scary vampire with headings 'Looks', 'Moves', 'Says'). You will be describing why it is perfect! See p.35 of the *Get Writing!* Book for this activity.

✫ TOL as you build up some descriptions of the vampire using the heading 'Looks' with the children. Take their ideas as you write and add in adjectives yourself, e.g. *He has dark, scary eyes; long, pointed fangs; a wild, swishing, black, velvet cape.*

✫ Ask the children to TTYP and feed back: *What advice would you give the bat to help him look scarier?* e.g. *Get some sharp pointed fangs, buy a dark black swishing cape.*

☆ TOL as you expand the advice together, e.g.
  To scare people you need to look the part. Your blunt fangs are useless! Get yourself some sharp fangs and a massive swirling black cape.

☆ Ask children to TTYP and feed back to check that their advice says how the bat can be scarier.

☆ Click on the next screen (letter writing template). TOL as you build up two or three sentences with the children. Take their ideas as you write, e.g.
  To be really scary you need to look like a vampire. Right now you are too sweet to be scary. I think you should get some really sharp pointed fangs and a huge black cape.

☆ Rub out/cover up your writing and tell the children to write their first piece of advice in their letter in their *Get Writing!* Books, using either their own ideas or yours, if they need the support.

☆ Repeat the process, first describing how a vampire could move to scare people (*fly, appear suddenly, disappear in a flash, move quickly*, etc.) and what words the bat could use to scare people and how he could say them (*I'm a vampire, ahaha! Watch me turn into a bat!* etc.).

☆ Each time use MT/YT to practise saying their sentences out loud using the children's ideas.

☆ Ask the children to write their chosen sentences in their *Get Writing!* Books.

☆ Celebration: Ask the Partners to choose their favourite piece of advice and rehearse saying the advice together, then feed back in unison. Choose some examples as feedback.

Grey Storybook 10   *Vulture culture*

Introducing the book

> *cloak-like   wings   scavenger   capture   colony*

☆ Use these 'power words' when introducing the book during reading Activity 3. Write them on sticky notes so you remember to use them through the lesson/day, e.g. *The bat had cloak-like wings that flapped about Winny the Witch's head! The magpie is a scavenger looking for bright things to steal and hide in its nest. When you play 'stuck in the mud' you capture your friends and they have to stand still until someone lets them go. A colony of over one hundred birds came and nested in the mud banks.*

*See Blueprint lesson plans for **Activities 1, 2, 3, 4 (Spelling)** and **Activity 5 Hold a sentence** on pp. 23–25.*

Activity 6 Build a sentence

scavenge/scavenger

☆ Ask the children to TTYP and think of words that mean the same as (synonyms for) *scavenge/scavenger* (*hunt, search, forage*). Offer words of your own.

☆ Ask the children when and where they might use the word. TTYP and feed back, e.g. *to describe animals such as vultures, hyenas, foxes, crows, magpies/when you are searching for something.*

☆ TOL as you try out an example of your own. MT/YT each time you develop it, e.g.
  We were so hungry that we scavenged through the leftovers from our picnic hoping to find a biscuit or half-eaten packet of crisps.
  The seagulls followed the tractor to scavenge for any juicy worms that it turned over in the soil.
  The foxes knocked over the dustbins when they were out scavenging for tasty morsels of food.

☆ Continue as for the lesson plan on p. 146.

☆ Rub out/cover up your writing and tell the children to write their own sentence/s in their *Get Writing!* Books (p. 37).

*See Blueprint lesson plans for **Activity 7 Edit** on p. 26.*

Activity 9 Composition

a) *Write notes about the Marabou stork.*

☆ Explain to the children that they are going to write another entry for the vulture book they have just read. It will be a fact file describing a different sort of scavenger, the Marabou stork.

☆ Show the image of a Marabou stork and text on **CD** (file 10.2). See p.38 of the *Get Writing!* Book for this activity.

☆ Read the text. Say that you are going to highlight the most important facts in the text using the highlighter. Model reading the text and highlighting the first fact 'from Africa' using the highlighter tool on your whiteboard.

☆ Ask the children to read the rest of the sentence to find any other facts, TTYP and feed back: e.g. 'known as the "undertaker bird" because of its huge black cloak-like wings'. Ask the children to highlight the facts on their text as you go through the text together.

☆ Read through the text and check that you have highlighted all the key information.

☆ Click on the next screen and display the Marabou stork fact file template.

☆ TOL as you model writing notes under the headings.

☆ Ask the children to make their own notes in their *Get writing!* Books, p.38.

b) *Write about the Marabou stork and the Andean condor.*

☆ Ask the children to use their notes and their storybook *Vulture culture* to TTYP to find some similarities between the Marabou stork and the Andean condor. Popcorn feedback: *they have similar wingspans, they both have bald heads, they are both scavengers, they both nest on cliffs*, etc.

☆ Now ask the children to use their notes and *Vulture culture* to TTYP to find some differences between the Marabou stork and the Andean condor. Popcorn feedback: *they live in different places (Africa and South America), they lay different numbers of eggs, they have different coloured heads*, etc.

☆ Display **CD** (file 10.3). Tell the children you are going to use the notes to help you write about the Marabou stork and compare it to the Andean condor. See p.39 of the *Get Writing!* Book for this activity.

☆ Ask the children to TTYP and feed back: *What type of bird is the Marabou stork?* e.g. *scavenger What does it like to eat?* e.g. *dead animals, small animals like rats and doves.*

☆ TOL as you expand the description together, e.g.
The Marabou stork is a scavenger just like the Andean condor. It likes to eat dead animals and sometimes captures small animals as well.
Marabou storks and Andean condors are both scavengers, they eat dead animals, etc.

☆ Model writing the descriptions with some of their choices. Model re-reading for sense and punctuation.

☆ Ask the children to practise saying their first sentence.

☆ Rub out/cover up your writing and tell the children to write in their *Get Writing!* Books, using either their own ideas or yours, if they need the support.

☆ Celebration: Partner 1, think about what caption they would like to write for the Marabou stork. Partner 2, think about what caption they would like to write for the Andean condor. Ask the children to tell each other their caption. Can they say it back to their partner? Choose some children to feed back to the class.

Grey Storybook 11   *A celebration on planet Zox*

Introducing the story

light-headed   burning up   sweaty   aching all over

☆ Use these 'power words' when introducing the story during reading Activity 3. Write them on sticky notes so you remember to use them through the lesson/day, e.g. *I had a high temperature when I had a bad cold, I was burning up and I had a massive headache. I'm aching all over after all that exercise and I am sweaty and hot, too.*

See Blueprint lesson plans for **Activities 1, 2, 3, 4 (Spelling)** and **Activity 5 Hold a sentence** on pp.23–25.

Activity 6 Build a sentence

dizzy

✰ Ask the children to TTYP and think of words that mean the same as (synonyms for) *dizzy*. Offer words of your own.

✰ Ask the children when and where they might use the word. TTYP and feed back, e.g. *after a bump, when you spin around a lot, when you are excited.*

✰ Display the physical feelings/symptoms on **CD** (file 11.2) and drag and drop the words into the focus box. Model using each word so that the children are familiar with the meaning of each word (*light-headed, burning up, itchy, dizzy, terrible headache, sweaty, aching all over*).

✰ TOL as you try out an example of your own. MT/YT each time you develop it, e.g.
I was a bit dizzy after I bumped my head in the playground.
I felt quite dizzy with excitement after my team had won the match.

✰ Continue as for the lesson plan on p.146.

✰ Rub out/cover up your writing and tell the children to write their own sentence/s in their *Get Writing!* Books (p.41).

See Blueprint lesson plans for **Activity 7 Edit** on p.26.

Activity 9 Composition

a) *Write notes about how Clive feels.*

✰ Explain to the children that through role-play they will write a play about Cosmic Clive visiting the doctor at the astrohospital. They will write Clive's dialogue.
     Teacher role: space doctor   Children's role: Cosmic Clive

✰ Take on your role whole-heartedly throughout this activity so children adopt their role easily and enthusiastically. Make yours a calm and kind doctor who likes to get things exactly right. Be very deliberate and fussy when using MT/YT!

✰ Show the image of Clive on **CD** (file 11.3). See p.42 of the *Get Writing!* Book for this activity.

✰ Teacher in role as a space doctor: *Hello Clive, I hear you are feeling rather unwell. I am going to use my chart and write down your symptoms very carefully so that I can make the very best diagnosis and give you the right treatment so that you get better quickly.*
Now, I hear that the first thing you noticed was feeling lightheaded and dizzy. Can you think back to that first moment of feeling unwell and describe it to me?

✰ Ask the children to TTYP and feed back. Choose Two and write their ideas down next to Clive on screen, e.g. *First I felt a bit funny in my tummy, then I started to wobble, and before I knew it I fell down.*

✰ Ask the children to TTYP to discuss each question below and Popcorn the feedback. Paraphrase their answers adding additional information where needed. Write their ideas next to the relevant part of Clive's body.
Can you tell me how your legs felt before you fell over? e.g. *they wobbled like jelly, they started to ache.*
Can I look at your tummy? What do the spots feel like? When did they appear? e.g. *they appeared suddenly, they are very itchy, I've got millions of them.*
How does your head feel now? e.g. *I'm lightheaded, my brain feels like it's floating about.*
I'm going to look closely at your eyes… How do they feel? e.g. *all swimmy, I can't see straight, it makes me feel dizzy and sick.*
Open your mouth and show me your tongue. How does your throat feel? e.g. *dry, sore, like sandpaper.*
Lift your arms above your head. How do they feel? e.g. *stiff, achy, sore, itchy, tingly.*
Wriggle you toes. Any problems there? e.g. *they won't stop wiggling, they are sore, they are all achy.*

☆ Ask the children to practise saying their first set of notes.

☆ Rub out/cover up your writing and tell the children to write their plan in the boxes next to Clive in their *Get Writing!* Books p.42, using either their own ideas or yours, if they need the support.

b) *Write what Clive is saying to the doctor.*

☆ Show the image of the doctor leaning over and asking Clive a question on **CD** (file 11.4). See pp.43–44 of the *Get Writing!* Book for this activity.

☆ Tell the children that they are going to write a short play about Clive's hospital visit. The doctor's part has already been written and they only need to think about Clive's answers.

☆ Click on the next screen and show the first question that the doctor asks Clive in the speech bubble. Ask: *How did you feel before you fell over?* e.g. *my legs got all wobbly and I felt dizzy/I felt lightheaded and my legs turned to jelly* (mime).

☆ Ask children to use their notes to help them answer the question. TTYP and feed back using Choose Two or Paraphrase, e.g. *At first I felt dizzy, then suddenly my legs turned to jelly and I fell over.*

☆ Ask children to TTYP to try out different sentences out loud.

☆ Rub out/cover up your writing and tell the children to write their chosen sentence in the large speech bubble in their *Get Writing!* Books, using either their own ideas, or yours, if children need the support.

☆ Click through the screens and repeat the process with the questions below.
Can I look at your tummy? What do the spots feel like, and when did they appear?
Open your mouth and show me your tongue. How does your throat feel?
Wriggle your toes. Any problems there?

☆ Celebration: Say that the space doctor now has a good idea of what was wrong with Cosmic Clive: it is Planet Pixelitis and the worst symptoms are the itchy spots and wriggling toes. Can the children work together to tell Clive how to use the Pixelitis lotion and explain how often he can use it? Share their ideas orally.

Grey Storybook 12   *A very dangerous dinosaur*

Introducing the story

ferocious   devious   dangerous   deadly

☆ Use these 'power words' when introducing the story during reading Activity 3. Write them on sticky notes so you remember to use them through the lesson/day, e.g. *That was devious of the wicked witch to trick Sleeping Beauty into eating the poisoned apple. It would be incredibly dangerous to cross the road without looking. Fury, the wrestler, was ferocious in the wrestling ring but kind and sweet at home.*

See Blueprint lesson plans for **Activities 1, 2, 3, 4 (Spelling)** and **Activity 5 Hold a sentence** on pp.23–25.

Activity 6 Build a sentence

ferocious

☆ Ask the children to TTYP and think of words that mean the same as *ferocious* – synonyms. Offer words of your own.

☆ Ask the children when and where they might use the word. TTYP and feed back, e.g. *to describe: predators, a fight, their feelings.*

☆ TOL as you try out an example of your own. MT/YT each time you develop it, e.g.
The lion is very ferocious and can suddenly pounce with its teeth bared.
It was a tiny dog but it had a ferocious growl so I kept away.
I snarled at my brother ferociously when he tried to change the channel on the TV to watch sport!

☆ Continue as for the lesson plan on p.146.

☆ Rub out/cover up your writing and tell the children to write their own sentence/s in their *Get Writing!* Books (p.46).

*See Blueprint lesson plans for **Activity 7 Edit** on p.26.*

Activity 9 Composition

a) Design and describe your dinosaur.

☆ Drama: Tell the children that they are the Snatchosaurus. Ask them to act out sneakily taking the other dinosaur eggs and running away to greedily chomp on them.

☆ Show the image of the Snatchosaurus on **CD** (file 12.2).

☆ Ask the children to TTYP to describe what they are doing. Popcorn feedback: *sneaking, stealing, creeping up and running off, gobbling and chomping up other dinosaurs' eggs.* Ask them to help you write their ideas on the board.

☆ Ask the children to TTYP and consider what might frighten the Snatchosaurus. Popcorn feedback, e.g. *something ferocious/a bigger dinosaur/a fiercer dinosaur/a quicker dinosaur.* Click on the next screen and ask them to help you write their ideas on the board.

☆ Look at your notes and say that you think the Snatchosaurus would go away if we could design a really terrifying dinosaur.

☆ Click on the next screen (dinosaur outline). See p.47 of the *Get Writing!* Book for this activity.

☆ Ask the children to TTYP to help you describe and choose the different parts which you could add to make up a truly dangerous dinosaur to see off the devious Snatchosaurus.

☆ Ask them to help you write their ideas on the board as you focus on different dinosaur parts. Give the children options to choose from, e.g. *Does the new dinosaur have sharp, thin, spiky teeth like needles, or huge, vicious fangs? Is it covered in spines like a porcupine or is it scaly like a snake? Can it unleash a deadly stink like a skunk or does it have a ferocious roar like a lion?* Popcorn feedback.

☆ Use MT/YT to describe the teeth when you make your final choice, e.g. *its teeth are sharp and dangerous and will scare the Snatchosaurus.*

☆ Ask children to TTYP and feed back to think about what features their dinosaur will have and how their choice will terrify the Snatchosaurus.

☆ Model writing notes about the new dinosaur with some of their choices. TOL as you sound out each word. Model re-reading for sense and punctuation.

☆ Rub out/cover up your writing and ask the children to draw and write notes about their Catchasnatchosaurus in their *Get Writing!* Books.

b) Write a poem about Catchasnatchosaurus.

☆ Show the image of the Catchasnatchosaurus on **CD** (file 12.3). Explain that you are going to write a poem to describe this horrifying dinosaur to scare the Snatchosaurus!

☆ Ask the children to TTYP and feed back:
What does the Catchasnatchosaurus sound like? e.g. *it roars and howls, it snarls and growls, it gnashes its terrible teeth.*
Why does it make such terrible noises? e.g. *to scare the Snatchosaurus, to make the Snatchosaurous run away, to show that it is king of the dinosaurs!*

☆ TOL as you expand the description together: e.g. *snarl and growl.*
The Catchasnatchosaurus has ferocious snarls and terrifying growls.
Can you hear the terrible snarls? Can you hear the awful growls?
I can hear a hideous snarl and a deadly growl.

☆ Ask the children to TTYP to discuss the questions below to help you describe the Catchasnatchosaurus for the poem and Popcorn the feedback (add adjectives where needed). Ask them to help you write their ideas on the board:
How does it move? e.g. *clomps and bashes, runs as fast as lightning, stomps and pounds.*

Where could it hide? e.g. *behind rocks/in the swamp/in clumps of trees.*

What phrases could we use to scare the Snatchosaurus? e.g. *I'm big and bad, I'm angry and mad, I'm fed up with you, you devious egg snatcher! We dinosaurs say no to the Snatchosaurus!*

☆ Click on the next screen and say that you have discovered a fantastic chorus that will be part of the poem. Use MT/YT to share it with the children:

I'm huge and ferocious
I'm terrible and mean
Listen to my roars, Snatchosaurus
I'm fed up with your stealing.
You are devious and bad!

☆ Explain you are going to play around with the words and ideas they have come up with to write a line of poetry. Say you are going to use ideas from their descriptions of the Catchasnatchosaurus to make it sound really terrifying.

☆ TOL as you try out a few lines of poetry together that describe how the Catchasnatchosaurus moves, e.g.

I'm a pouncer and a smasher, I bash down trees with my huge dino-claws
I zip as fast as lightning and jump from tree to tree
I'm an enormous bulldozer that pushes trees aside

☆ Say the lines in different ways to make different rhythms, explaining the effects you are making, e.g. *If I say it fast it sounds like he is on a rampage, if I say parts slow then it sounds like he is creeping up.*

☆ Model writing lines with some of their choices. Model re-reading for sense and punctuation.

☆ Ask the children to practise saying the first lines of the poem.

☆ Tell children to write the first line of their poem in their *Get Writing!* Books.

☆ Repeat the above, exploring places the dinosaur could hide to jump out from and scare the Snatchosaurus (e.g. *behind boulders, in swamps and bushes*), and phrases to scare the Snatchosaurous away (see above). Choose words/phrases to repeat to give the poem rhythm, e.g.

I'll jump out of the bushes and roar into your ear
I'll explode out of the swamp and make you jump with fear

☆ Once you have written your lines, play around with the order until you are happy with the structure of the poem.

☆ Rub out/cover up your writing and tell the children to write the rest of their poems in their *Get Writing!* Books, using either their own ideas or yours, if they need the support. Encourage the children to continue editing and moving the lines around until they are happy with how it sounds.

☆ Celebration: In pairs choose one line of the poem and practise it together. Write it out and say it in unison to the class.

Grey Storybook 13   *The invisible clothes*

Introducing the story

proud   humiliated   embarrassed

☆ Use these 'power words' when introducing the story during reading Activity 3. Write them on sticky notes so you remember to use them through the lesson/day, e.g. *She is very proud of her wonderful picture. I was embarrassed when my dad did a dance at school!*

See Blueprint lesson plans for **Activities 1, 2, 3, 4 (Spelling)** and **Activity 5 Hold a sentence** on pp. 23–25.

Activity 6 Build a sentence

humiliated

☆ Ask the children to TTYP and think of words that mean the same as *humiliated* – synonyms. Offer words of your own.

☆ Ask the children when and where they might use the word. TTYP and feed back, e.g. *when they are embarrassed.*

☆ TOL as you try out an example of your own. MT/YT each time you develop it, e.g.
I was so embarrassed when the headteacher called me to her room and humiliated me when she told me off.
My mum humiliated me when she came to pick me up and called me 'bunnykins' in front of my friends!

☆ Continue as for the lesson plan on p.146.

☆ Rub out/cover up your writing and tell the children to write their own sentence/s in their *Get Writing!* Books (p.49).

*See Blueprint lesson plans for **Activity 7 Edit** on p.26.*

Activity 9 Composition

a) *Make notes about the Emperor before and after he is tricked.*

☆ Tell the children that following role-play activities, they will write sentences to compare how the Emperor feels, moves and thinks before and after he is tricked.

☆ Drama: Tell the children that they are the Emperor. Ask them to move around the room in a proud and important manner. Whenever they meet someone they need to sneer at them and push past rudely (without hurting anyone) to show how important they are.

☆ Show the image of the Emperor on **CD** (file 13.2). See pp.50–51 of the *Get Writing!* Book for this activity.

☆ Ask the children: *How would you describe how you moved when you were the Emperor?* Popcorn feedback: *I strutted, I strode, I pushed past people.*
How did you show you were important? Popcorn feedback: *I held up my head, I looked down my nose, I pushed people aside.*

☆ Ask the children to TTYP and discuss how the Emperor might feel when the tailor tells him that the cloth is magical and is invisible to stupid people. Popcorn feedback: *excited, special, superior, better than everyone else*, etc.

☆ Tell the children that they are trying the suit on for the first time. Ask them to mime putting on the clothes and moving around.

☆ Ask the children to TTYP to discuss the questions below in role as the Emperor and Popcorn the feedback. Ask them to help you write their ideas about how he feels, moves and thinks in the 'Before' section. Then ask them to make their own notes onto their Emperor in the *Get Writing!* Book.

☆ Use the heart, legs and thought bubble symbols on the next screen to help ask questions.
Heart: *How do you feel?* e.g. *excited, handsome, special, gorgeous.*
Thought bubble: *What are you thinking?* e.g. *Now I will know who is stupid, and I will show them how clever and important I am!… I will look stylish and everyone will look up to me.*
Legs: *How are you moving?* e.g. *strutting like a peacock* (mime), *striding, marching head up and chest out.*

☆ Click on the next screen (Emperor looking humiliated.) Drama: tell the children that they are going to imagine that they are the Emperor walking through the crowd, wearing nothing! At first they feel great but as time goes by they can hear what the crowd is saying and begin to feel differently.

☆ Get the children to make two rows facing each other. One row says what the Emperor is hearing and the other what he is thinking. Pass between the children turning to hear what they are saying, as you go down the line.

- ✩ Stop in the middle and change how you are walking: stoop and look more miserable. Say: *I am in a dilemma... Have I really got a beautiful robe on?*
- ✩ Continue down the line until you reach the end.
- ✩ Ask the children to TTYP to discuss the questions below in role as the Emperor and Popcorn the feedback. Click on the next screen and ask them to help you write their ideas about how he feels, moves and thinks. Model taking notes each time and ask them to make their own notes in the 'After' section of the chart in their *Get Writing!* Books.

  Heart: *How do you feel now?* e.g. *humiliated, stupid, shown up, embarrassed.*

  Thought bubble: *What are you thinking?* e.g. *I am a fool, everyone is laughing at me, why did I trust that man...? I'm not wearing anything at all!*

  Legs: *How are you moving?* e.g. *stooped and hunched up, shuffling.*

b) *Write a letter to a friend about the trick.*

- ✩ Tell the children that they are going to write a letter in role as the Emperor warning his friend about the villainous tailor who has tricked him. The letter is going to show how the Emperor has changed and what he has learned. See p.52 of the *Get Writing!* Book for this activity.
- ✩ Ask children to continue in role: TTYP, using their notes to help them to think about how they have changed by the end of the story. Ask them to TTYP and feed back using Choose Two or Paraphrase, e.g. *I was very proud and thought I was important but now I am ashamed and humiliated. Before I thought I was special and other people were stupid but now I know I was tricked and looked really silly.*
- ✩ Display **CD** (file 13.3) to show the letter writing frame. Model writing with some of their choices. Model re-reading for sense and punctuation.
- ✩ Ask the children to practise saying the first sentence of their letter.
- ✩ Rub out/cover up your writing and tell the children to write their sentence in their *Get Writing!* Books, using either their own ideas, or yours, if children need the support.
- ✩ Repeat the above, reflecting in-role about: what you hoped to find out when you wore the magical clothes; how it felt to walk through the crowd; what you were thinking as you walked through the crowd.
- ✩ For the final sentence ask the children to TTYP and discuss what advice the Emperor would give his friend so he doesn't get caught out. Ask children to TTYP and feed back using Choose Two or Paraphrase, e.g. *Whatever you do, try not to believe that you are cleverer than anyone else. If you are not careful you could be tricked too.*

Non-fiction Book 1 *A job for Jordan*

Introducing the book

> support   important   persuade

- ✩ Use these 'power words' when introducing the book during reading Activity 3. Write them on sticky notes so you remember to use them through the lesson/day, e.g. *I support a charity by collecting coins. The legs support the table – they keep it up! It is important to eat breakfast or else you will be hungry. Can I persuade you to share your chocolate with me...please?*

*See Blueprint lesson plans for **Activities 1, 2, 3, 4 (Spelling)** and **Activity 5 Hold a sentence** on pp.23–25.*

Activity 6 Build a sentence

persuade
- ✩ Ask the children to TTYP and think of words that mean the same as (synonyms for) *persuade*. Offer words of your own.

☆ Ask the children when and where they might use the word. TTYP and feed back, e.g. *to get their mum to let them have a special pudding, to stay up and watch something special.*

☆ TOL as you try out an example of your own. MT/YT each time you develop it, e.g.
How can I persuade you that the water is warm enough to swim in? I know, I'll jump in!
This advert is trying to persuade us to buy an expensive car.
If I promise to go to bed straight away afterwards, can I persuade you to let me stay up late and watch the film?

☆ Continue as for the lesson plan on p.146.

☆ Rub out/cover up your writing and tell the children to write their own sentence/s in their *Get Writing!* Books (p.54).

See Blueprint lesson plans for **Activity 7 Edit** on p.26.

Activity 9 Composition

Design a poster to raise money to train a guide dog

☆ Explain to the children that following a role-play they will plan and write a poster to raise money to train a guide dog puppy. You can use the Guide Dog website to help you get extra information for this role: **http://www.guidedogs.org.uk** Give the children time to read about the 'sponsor a puppy' scheme.

  Teacher role: a representative from the Guide Dog charity   Children's role: authors/designers

☆ Take on your role whole-heartedly throughout this activity so children adopt their role easily and enthusiastically.

☆ Show the image of a guide dog puppy on **CD** (file NF1.2). See p.55 of the *Get Writing!* Book for this activity.

☆ Teacher in role as representative from the Guide Dog charity: *Today you are going to help me by designing a poster that helps people to understand all about guide dogs and how important it is to train new puppies. You've read a book all about guide dogs so you can use the information in it to help me get together ideas for the poster.*

☆ Ask the children to TTYP and feed back: *What do you know about guide dogs?* e.g. *they are trained for more than a year, they wear a special harness, they help people with poor sight, they begin to get trained at 6–8 weeks, they do an important job, £1 a week will support a puppy to be trained.*

☆ Click on the next screen (guide dog information mind map) and ask the children to help you write their ideas.

☆ Ask the children to TTYP to discuss what they think is important to tell people about guide dogs and Popcorn the feedback e.g. *what they do, what they cost, how long the training lasts.*

☆ Click on the next screen (blank poster template). Say that they need to think of good words and phrases to persuade people that the Guide Dogs charity is worth helping. Focus on the images on the poster *(£1 coin, a puppy, a person with a guide dog, a person training a puppy)*. TOL as you build up some persuasive phrases that describe the different items with the children. Take their ideas as you write, e.g. *Only one pound a week helps to train a guide dog/guide dogs puppies have to be trained for more than one year/a guide dog is doing an important job! This cute puppy will soon have an important job...*

☆ TOL as you build up sentences with the children. Take their ideas as you write, e.g.
Sentence 1: Help support a puppy to learn to do an important job.
Support a puppy's training and change someone's life.
Sentence 2: Only £1 a week will train a puppy to become a guide dog.
For only £1 a week guide dogs will change a life.
Sentence 3: Every guide dog was a puppy once!
Each puppy needs over a year's training to become a guide dog.

☆ Each time use MT/YT to practise saying their sentences out loud using the children's ideas.

☆ Ask the children to write their chosen sentences one at a time on their poster.

☆ Celebration: Ask the Partners to choose their favourite sentence and rehearse saying it together and feedback in unison. Choose some examples as feedback.

Grey

Introducing the book

> weightless　gravity　bounce　glide

✰ Use these 'power words' when introducing the book during reading Activity 3. Write them on sticky notes so you remember to use them through the lesson/day, e.g. *If you go to the Moon there will be less gravity than there is on Earth. If you were weightless you'd float off up into the sky. I love to bounce on bouncy castles. The dancers glide smoothly about the dance floor.*

*See Blueprint lesson plans for **Activities 1, 2, 3, 4 (Spelling)** and **Activity 5 Hold a sentence** on pp.23–25.*

Activity 6 Build a sentence

gravity

✰ Ask the children when and where they might use the word. TTYP and feed back, e.g. *in science to describe why things fall down, when they talk about space.*

✰ TOL as you try out an example of your own. MT/YT each time you develop it, e.g.
If there was no gravity we'd all float about.
We stick to the Earth because we have gravity, which pulls us down.
In space there is no gravity and everything floats about, even water.

✰ Continue as for the lesson plan on p.146.

✰ Rub out/cover up your writing and tell the children to write their own sentence/s in their *Get Writing!* Books (p.57).

*See Blueprint lesson plans for **Activity 7 Edit** on p.26.*

Activity 9 Composition

a)	*Plan your poem about walking on the Moon.*

✰ Explain to the children that they are going to write a poem about walking on the Moon.

✰ Show the image of the astronaut walking on the Moon on **CD** (file NF5.2). See p.58 of the *Get Writing!* Book for this activity.

✰ Drama:

>	Teacher role: Mission Control　　Children's role: astronauts

✰ Take on your role whole-heartedly throughout this activity so children adopt their role easily and enthusiastically. Be very firm, you need exact descriptions and information. Be very deliberate and fussy when using MT/YT!

✰ Tell the children that they are astronauts and they are going to mime leaving their space shuttle and going on a moonwalk. Ask them to listen to your commands:
Right astronauts, this is Mission Control. I want you to open the heavy landing bay doors and push them open so that you can see the Moon.
Carefully step down the metal ladder holding on tightly, one step at a time, 5, 4, 3, 2, 1. You have landed on the Moon's surface. Look around you and note in your heads exactly what you can see… Look, can you see the Earth rising, a blue shining light…?
Now I want you to take your first Moon step… Your suit is very bulky so it is difficult to walk, take your time and get used to it.
It is time to try some Moon bouncing: push your body off the Moon's surface. How high can you jump? How does it feel? Do you notice any dust or Moon rock float up with you? I would like you to experiment with moving in this world…
Astronauts, this is Mission Control, your first experiment is complete, please return to the space shuttle… hold on to the ladder as you climb up and make sure the landing bay doors are firmly shut before you get out of your space suit.

☆ Click on the next screen and show the image of the Moon.

☆ Say you are gong to write your poem about walking on the Moon.

☆ Ask the children to TTYP to discuss the questions below and Popcorn the feedback. Ask them to help you write their ideas on the board. Then ask them to write notes on the planning page of their *Get Writing!* Books (p.58).

☆ Use the heart, eye, ear, legs and thought bubble symbols on screen to help ask questions.
    Legs: *How do you walk on the Moon? e.g. bounce, glide, fly, small jumps, hop.*
    Tell me exactly what your body does. Describe one step. e.g. you move slowly and carefully, it's like being in water, when you move your arms float up, you touch the Moon and you bounce up and glide off.
    Eye: *What did you notice as you walked on the moon? e.g. the darkness of the sky, the Earth above me, the grey cold Moon surface.*
    Ear: *What could you hear? e.g. Mission Control telling me what to do/my breathing/nothing/silence, etc.*
    Heart: *How did you feel? e.g. light and bouncy, like a bubble, far away, strange, tiny.*
    Thought bubble: *What did you think as you walked on the Moon? e.g. How far away I was, that Earth was a tiny speck, like a superhero…*

b) *Write your poem about walking on the Moon.*

☆ Click on the next screen (image of astronaut). See p.59 of the *Get Writing!* Book for this activity. Explain you are going to play around with the words and ideas they have come up with to write a few lines of poetry. First you will write about how it felt to leave the spacecraft. Say you are going to try to make an atmosphere of silence and slowness by repeating words to make a rhythm.

☆ TOL as you expand the description together of leaving the spacecraft: e.g. *float and bounce:*
    Step out slowly,
    Your arms float up slowly
    And then bounce up so slowly
    As if weightless
    I put my foot out into the darkness
    Then down towards the Moon's floor
    I bounced like a ball

☆ Ask the children to remember leaving the spacecraft and TTYP to practise their ideas with their partner. Choose Two for feedback.

☆ Model writing some lines of poetry with some of their choices. Model re-reading for sense and punctuation.

☆ Ask the children to practise saying their first lines of poetry about leaving the spacecraft for their poem.

☆ Rub out/cover your writing and tell the children to write their first lines in their *Get Writing!* Books, using either their own ideas or yours, if they need the support.

☆ Click on the next screens and repeat the process to add more lines, thinking about what you can see, hear, and your thoughts and feelings. Use the notes you have made to help you focus your writing, so that you have modelled three more stanzas of the poem.

☆ Celebration: Partners tell each other their favourite stanza of the poem and practise it together until they can say it in unison. Choose some children to feed back to the class.

Grey

Assessment

Children, in the main, learn to read at a quicker pace than they learn to write. Reading requires speedy decoding of print and understanding and interpreting someone else's ideas. On the other hand, writing requires careful formulation of one's own ideas and the encoding of these into print. Encoding requires segmenting words into sounds, scribing the sounds into graphemes, punctuating effectively, while remembering and adapting the idea at the same time.

Children must be allowed to progress through *Read Write Inc. Phonics* at the speed they can learn to read, even if their writing is slower to develop, so that they have speedy access to books that will drive their vocabulary growth, independently. A child may be reading the Blue books but have the same writing level as a child reading the Pink books. If a child is writing at a higher level than their reading, it is likely they are on the wrong reading book!

This assessment judges the effectiveness of the teaching on the success of the children's progress. If children are not making progress, they are assisted until they can. Praise and support is essential throughout. If a child has difficulty, it is assumed they are not doing this to irritate!

Children make the most progress through carefully planned modelling and oral rehearsal before writing; children must always rehearse their ideas out loud before they write.

Children need to be assisted at every stage: until they can articulate their ideas confidently and thoughtfully and can write their ideas down enthusiastically and reasonably quickly.

Use the key teaching points on p. 175–178 to deal with children's specific needs.

Children will complete *Read Write Inc. Phonics* at different levels of writing:
- ☆ some children will be able to articulate their ideas clearly with minimal scaffolding and assistance; others will need support all the way through primary school.
- ☆ some children may complete the *Read Write Inc. Phonics* programme with accurate spelling, others with predominantly phonically legal spelling.
- ☆ some may have beautiful joined writing; others may be printing with less-developed formation.

Expectations of reading progress

These expectations of reading progress are common to successful *Read Write Inc. Phonics* schools in challenging areas. Other schools may make speedier progress.

End of Reception
Speedy:	Pink Books
Steady:	Green Books
Slow:	Ditty Books

End of Year 1
Speedy:	Grey Books / *Read Write Inc. Comprehension*
Steady:	Blue Books
Slow:	Pink Books

Year 2
Speedy:	*Read Write Inc. Spelling* and *Read Write Inc. Comprehension*
Steady:	Finish Grey Books by end of term 1
Slow:	Grey Books by end of Year 2

Children with specific and profound educational needs will continue the programme into KS2.

Writing assessment Green to Orange Get Writing! Books

Base your assessment on the children's writing for *Get Writing!* Activities 8 and 9 as a culmination of the other reading and writing activities for each Storybook/Non-fiction Book. Write the date in the chart when a target is achieved. Use the key teaching points on pp.175–178 to develop children's writing. See p.179 for some examples of children's writing for *Get Writing!* Activities 8 and 9 at three different levels.

Child's name:													
Date started *Read Write Inc. Phonics:*													

Say the sentence

	Child:													
joins in with your sentence														
adds words														
adapts sentence														
holds a sentence														

Write the sentence

	Child writes:													
some key words of their sentence														
most words of their sentence														
all of their sentence														

	Child uses:													
a capital letter and full stop														
Set 1 consonant sounds, e.g. *stp w/ bst*														
Set 1 sounds, e.g. *stop will bust*														
Set 1 and some Set 2 sounds e.g. *stop will birst*														
phonetic spelling of Red Words, e.g. *yoo, mee*														
correct spelling of a few Red Words, e.g. *you, me*														
recognisable letter formation														
correct letter formation (most letters)														

Writing assessment Yellow to Grey Get Writing! Books

Child's name:

Date started Read Write Inc. Phonics:

Oral sentence building

Child:

- joins in with your sentence
- adds or changes words
- adapts/changes sentence
- holds the sentence, once constructed
- uses simple connectives – *first, next, then* (if appropriate)
- uses a range of synonyms for emotions, actions, atmosphere
- uses connectives to link sentences – *the next thing that happened, after that*

Writing

Child writes:

- most words of the sentence constructed orally
- all of the sentence
- the sentence, and reconstructs and amends sentence while writing

Child uses:

- a capital letter and full stop
- question/exclamation marks (if appropriate)
- Set 1 and Set 2 sounds, e.g. *stop will birst*
- some correct Set 3 vowels choices, e.g. *day/dai make/maik train/trane*
- correct spelling of a few Red Words
- mostly correct orientation and relative size

Key teaching points and marking for Green to Orange Get Writing! Books

The more enthusiastic and supportive you are, the more confident the children's writing will be. Praise and encourage children for offering their ideas as well as adding your own.

Make sure the children can say their sentence confidently before they write it. Praise the children as they write for:
- using the 'sounds' they remember to spell. Some words children will be able write correctly e.g. fed up, glum, limp, and for other words use spellings of sounds they know e.g. shufl (shuffle), hobl (hobble)
- saying the words in Fred Talk
- re-reading the sentence after each word to help remember the sentence
- using the 'power words' particular to the task
- using a full stop and a capital letter.

☆ Do not stay too long with one child – keep moving around.
☆ Talk very quietly as you walk around praising and helping the children.
☆ Make a note of poorly formed letters to practise in the next handwriting lesson
☆ Make a note of Red and Green Words to practise in your next Speeds Sounds lesson.
☆ Do not let anyone struggle – support the children at every stage!
☆ Write a short comment in the style and stage of handwriting the children are expected to use.

Key teaching points and marking for Yellow to Grey Get Writing! Books

The more enthusiastic and supportive you are, the more confident the children's writing will be. Praise and encourage children for offering their ideas as well as adding your own.

Make sure the children can say each sentence confidently before they write it. Praise the children as they write for:
- re-reading the sentence to check for sense
- using the 'power words' particular to the task
- using the 'sounds' they remember to spell
- using a full stop and a capital letter.

☆ Do not stay too long with one child – keep moving around.
☆ Talk very quietly as you walk around helping the children.
☆ Make a note of poorly formed letters to practise in the next handwriting lesson.
☆ Make a note of Red and Green Words to practise in your next Speeds Sounds lesson.
☆ Do not let anyone struggle – support the children at every stage!
☆ Always write a comment about how well the writing meets the purpose of the task. Make this positive!
☆ Underline, lightly, a few common Red and Green Words that you want the child to correct. Correct a few ambitious words that children have attempted.

Key teaching points: Green to Orange Get Writing! Books

Say the sentence

Child:	If not...
• joins in with your sentence	Check the child sits prominently in your line of vision. Start with a simpler sentence. Exaggerate key words with actions and facial expression. Repeat a few times. Praise the child as soon as he joins in.
• adds or changes words	Exaggerate your TOL as you add or change a word very deliberately. Praise the child for changing one word.
• 'holds' the sentence	Ask partners to decide the same sentence and practise it in unison. Ask partners to repeat their sentence to each other again, just before they write, in the same way as in the activity 'Hold a sentence'. Praise the partners who say the sentence very clearly in unison.

Write the sentence

Child writes:	If not...
• some key words of their sentence	Exaggerate how you read back the sentence after writing each word. Praise the children for writing down their full sentence.
• most words of their sentence	As above
• all of their sentence	As above

Child uses:	If not...
• a capital letter and full stop	Have fun with the punctuation mimes. Ask children to re-read their writing as though they were doing the 'edit' activity.
• Set 1 consonant sounds e.g. stp wl bst	Model very explicitly, using Fred Fingers, how you use the sounds you can hear to write the word using Set 1 vowel sounds. Note the sounds that need to be practised in the daily Speed Sounds lesson
• Set 1 sounds e.g. stop will bust	As above
• Set 1 and some Set 2 sounds e.g. stop will birst	As above, using both Set 1 and 2 vowel sounds.
• phonetic spelling of Red Words e.g. yoo, mee	Select 'Red Words of the day' that you want children to spell correctly. Focus on these for 'Hold a sentence'.
• correct spelling of a few Red Words e.g. you, me	As above
• recognisable letter formation	Note the letters that need to be practised in the daily class handwriting lesson.
• correct letter formation (most letters)	As above

Key teaching points: Yellow to Grey *Get Writing!* Books

Oral sentence building

Child:	If not...
• joins in with your sentence	Check the child sits prominently in your line of vision. Start with a simpler sentence. Exaggerate key words with actions and facial expression. Praise the child as soon as he joins in.
• adds or changes words	Exaggerate TOL as you add or change a word deliberately. Praise the child as soon as he changes one word.
• holds the sentence, once constructed	Ask partners to decide the same sentence and practise it in unison. Ask partners to repeat their sentences to each other again, just before they write. Praise the partners who say the sentence clearly in unison.
• uses simple connectives – *first, next, then* (if appropriate)	Exaggerate the connective and add the action. Use connectives as part of a narrative through the day e.g. *First of all* we put our coats on, *next* we wrap our scarves tightly round our necks... *Finally* we pull on our hats....
• uses connectives to link sentences – *the next thing that happened, after that, once there was...*	As above
• uses a range of synonyms for emotions, actions, atmosphere	Use particular synonyms throughout the day. Make the meaning clear by the facial expression. Use sticky notes to remind you. Write three words on your hand to use all day! Use MT/YT to copy these sentences – see p.8. Praise the children for using synonyms in their talk through the day. Touch the word on your vocabulary board as you say it. As children write, 'catch' interesting words from them and write them on the board with their name alongside.

177

Key teaching points Yellow to Grey *Get Writing!* Books

Writing	*If not...*
Child writes:	
• most words of the sentence constructed orally	Exaggerate how you read back the sentence after writing each word. Praise the children for writing down their full sentence.
• all of the sentence	As above
• the sentence and reconstructs and amends sentence while writing	Provide explicit modelling of how you change your ideas as you write, and after you write the sentence. Cross out words, write above them – do not rub out. Show excitement as you have a better idea. Praise the children for amending as they write.
Child uses:	*If not...*
• a capital letter and full stop	Have fun with the punctuation mimes. Ask children to re-read their writing as though they were doing the 'edit' activity.
• question/exclamation marks (if appropriate)	As above
• Set 1 and Set 2 sounds, e.g. *stop will birst*	Model very explicitly how you use the sounds you can hear to write the word using Set 2 vowel sounds. Note the letters that need to be practised in the daily Speed Sounds lesson.
• some correct Set 3 vowels choices, e.g. *day/ dai make/maik train/trane*	Choose a couple of words to model very explicitly how you use the Complex chart to make vowel choices. Emphasise the a-e, i-e, or o-e spelling choices EVERY week!
• correct spelling of a few Red Words	Select 'Red Words of the day' that you want children to spell correctly. Focus on these when you teach 'Hold a sentence'.
• mostly correct orientation and relative size	Note the letters/joins that need to be practised in the daily handwriting lesson.

Writing examples

The following are examples of texts written by children for the composition activities in the *Get Writing!* Books. There are examples from children at three different levels: a) being the lowest, c) being the highest.

Green *Get Writing!* Book, Storybook 7 *Chips*

What is Kim saying about chips?

a) i lv cips
b) i lik cruchee chips
c) my fvrit chips are cruche and crispe i lik vingr on mi chips and i lik hvg them

a) I wnt chps.
b) You can hav a cip.
c) ples dont tk mi chips wont ol the cips you cnt hav ene bicos then i wdnt hav ene

Purple *Get Writing!* Book, Storybook 9 *Billy the Kid*

What is Billy the Kid saying?

a) it is cross and hrbl
b) i thik the trol is horbl and nste and bad
c) the troll is cross and meen he haz a wrt on hiz noz and grin fs he iz smele i dont lik him

How does the troll feel?

a) i am fed up
b) i wish i woz not a trol i am cros
c) I am fed up and cross bcos i sit on the bidg oll dy i dont like it bing a trol

Pink *Get Writing!* Book, Storybook 2 *Tab the cat*

How did Meg feel when she got her cat?

a) Meg woz ver hap wen she got hr cat it wos tab
b) Meg wos rele glad wen she got her cat bcos she lict it a lot
c) Meg was reelee esitd wen she got her cat she luvd the cat was pleezd.

Orange *Get Writing!* Book, Storybook 6 *A good cook*

What would you cook?

a) i can cook jam trts
i can cook fish ad chip
i can cook psta

b) I can cook sweet choclet cayk
I can cook crunchee hot chips
I can cook chesee pasta

c) I can cook delishus choclet cayk
I can cook solty hot chips
I can cook chooee cheesee pasta.

Yellow *Get Writing!* Book, Non-fiction Book 2 *A mouse in the house*

Write about what a mouse likes to do.

a) Mice licke to run in the whel
Mice licke to gobl up nuts
Mice licke to get in the nest
mice stay in the caj

b) Mice like to zoom in the whel
mice like to chomp on nuts
Mice like to snugl in the sotf worm nest.
mice like to play in the cayg

c) Mice like to scurree and zoom on the wheel
Mice like to choo and chomp on nuts and seeds.
Mice like to snuggl in a worm coze nest
mice feel sayf in the cage.

Blue *Get Writing!* Book, Storybook 3 *Hairy fairy*

What does the Fairy Queen say a real fairy should be like?

a) A rel fairy shod hav silk her bt you hav spicy her.
A rel fairy shod hav a sprkly wond but you hav a durty wond.
a rel fairy shod hav glitry wings but you hav dull wings
A rel fairy shod hav a bootifl dress but you hav a messy dress

b) A real fairy shod have bouncy cleen hare but you have hare like a nest.
A real fairy shod have a majicul wond but you have a wonky wond.
a real fairy shod have bright sparcklin wings but you have filfy wings
A real fairy shod have a thrilly pink dress but your dress is durty and dull.

c) A real fairy should have beootiful hair but you have durty hair like a piel of twigs.
A real fairy should have a wand foll of wishes but your wand is brooken and can not maik wishes cum troo.
a real fairy should have light flutring wings that sparkul but your wings do not glit at orl.
A real fairy should wair a pritty flooty dress but you have a durty raggy dress that looks narsty.

Grey *Get Writing!* Book, Storybook 2 *The lion's paw*

You are Androcles. Write about what happened to you.

a) At furst I cud hardly stand up becos I was so scaird my hart was beating and my hands were wet with swet. The sunlight made it hard to see but I notised hewg shapes moving and heard terribel low growls licke thunder. I turned to the gard and wisperd, "this is it I am doomd.' As he gave me a hard push and I fell into the sunshine I new I wud die. But to my amaizment there in front of me was the lion from the cave. I put my hand on its head and it sat next to me. I was saved.

b) I could hardly stand and I trembulled all over with fear my heart beating like a runaway train. The crewl gard larfed at me, I beged him to let me go free but he just pointed at the prowlin shapes at the end of the tunnle and he said "soon you will be free when those monsters have finished with you!" My mouth was dry but I manedged to croak out the words 'if I shall die I will die bravely." So I walkt out into the ring towards the crowd and I strode bravely although I was terrifyed. I lookt around and saw a sea of faces all woching me. Then to my amaizment the lion from the cave came and sat by me and I kissd his por. The crowd calld out to let me go and I was overjoyd becos I new I was saved.

c) I could hardly beleaf the crewltee of my marster as I stood sweting with fear lisening to the bludthirsty roar of the crowd. My heart hammerd in my body and I was dizze with terror but I lookt the guard in the eyes and whispered, "I will die bravely." But as I got closer to the ring and I could see the prowling shapes of the enormus beasts I began to trembel with fear. 'This is it' I thort "This is the end." I stepped into the ring the sun blindid me and the crowd defened me. I waited for the ferce lions to strike me but nothing happened. Then I felt warm soft fur and herd purring... it was the lion from the cave. It came and sat next to me I pickt up his enormouse paw and kisst it. The crowd began to cheer, they wanted me to be set free I was overjoyed I new then I wood not die. Now I am free at larst.

Handwriting

Introduction

Teach handwriting as a discrete daily lesson. This will allow children to put all their energies into the physical process of writing. Plan whole class lessons for five to ten minutes every day, or at least four times a week, until children have a strong flowing joined style. A 'little and often' approach is more successful than one long weekly session. Make this a separate time from the phonics lesson; handwriting and reading often develop at a different pace.

The method outlined below can be adapted to suit any style. The reading and writing link is key to *Read Write Inc.* – children learn to print so they can read what they write. When they can write legibly and quickly, they are taught a joined style. The handwriting lessons focus on lower case letters.

Lessons are short and pacey with a clear purpose. Children articulate a mental checklist of pictures to visualize the shape of letters and joins before they start to write. This allows them to focus on their own formation without copying from the board or book.

What resources do I need to teach the handwriting lessons?

Children will need a table and chair, a sharp pencil, a plain exercise book for letter formation and a book with widely spaced lines. Teachers will need the blueprint lessons from this *Handbook*, a pen and a large writing board that can be seen by all children from their tables. The CD files contain checklists for letters, and example words.

The three stages of Read Write Inc. handwriting

Stage 1

a) Basic letter formation using mnemonics – start in Reception Term as soon as children can read Set 1 Speed Sounds quickly. Teach basic letter formation in this order:
    'Around' letters: c a o d g q
    'Down' letters: l t b p k h i j m n r u y
    'Curly' letters: e f s
    'Zig-zag' letters: v w z x.

b) Relative size of letters
    Progress to wide-lined paper.
    floating: a c e i m n o r s u v w x z
    tall floating: b d h k l t f
    or wet: g y j p q.

Stage 2

Letter formation with flicks – Year 1, Term 1.

Stage 3

Joining letters – Year 1, Term 2/3 onwards to Year 4.

These ages are approximate – older children with poor handwriting may need to start at Stage 1 or Stage 2.

There is one basic lesson with the sections: Demonstrate, Practise, Review. Use this structure with the other letter checklists which are provided on the CD. However, the formation of the letters and words should always be demonstrated by the teacher. Continually review what you have taught until children are successful.

Handwriting Stage 1

a) Letter formation

While children are reading Storybooks Green to Orange, refer to the letters by their sound, rather than using letter names.

The lesson plan

Children sit at tables where they can see the interactive whiteboard or board.

Check they are sitting in the perfect handwriting position. They should have their feet on the floor, and their chair pulled up (not too tightly). One hand should be holding the page while the other is used to write.

Example: g

1. Demonstrate

TOL as you use your mental checklist to write g.

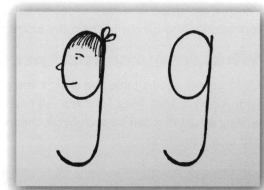

I must remember to:

✓ start at the girl's hair bobble
✓ go over the top her head
✓ go all round her face and under her chin
✓ go back to the bobble
✓ give her long straight hair
✓ curl her hair under her chin.

See the file named 'Handwriting Stage 1a' in the Handwriting section of the **CD** for checklists.

Repeat a few times using MT/YT.

Ask the children to TTYP to say the mental checklist. Take feedback and praise. Ask a partnership to tell you how to write g.

Repeat a couple more times until the children can say the mental checklist to each other.

2. Practice

Check again that the children are still sitting in the perfect handwriting position.

Rub out the picture and any letters from the board – the children must not copy.

Ask children to write one letter – slowly and carefully. (Do not ask them to draw the handwriting picture.)

Repeat getting quicker and quicker each time.

Go round the room praising what you see so others can hear – don't sit with one child.
Nice round chin there! Love the long straight hair. What a great curl.

3. Review – Spot the error

Write the letter on the board – make one error.

Ask the children to give you ticks for the things you have remembered, for example, you remembered to start at the bobble. Then say 'Spot the error'. Ask children to practise again.

On the next day, have a new focus letter, and review one or two previously taught letters.

Note: Get children learn to visualize the letter as a picture and not a written list. Do not write the list on the board, though you may need a sticky note to help you remember to begin with.

b) Relative size of letters

Once most children can form the letters well, introduce wide-lined books to teach them where to position the letters on the lines. Use the idea of a swimming pool to help the children visualize the size and position of letters.

Show the children how some letters float on the water, e.g.
a c e i m n o r s u v w x z

> Draw a sun in the sky, on the right-hand side, to remind the children which direction they should write in.

Some float on the water and almost touch the sky, e.g.
b d h k l t f

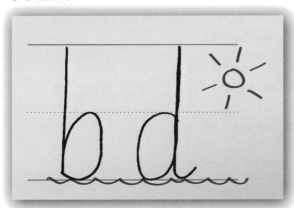

Some float on the pool, but a bit gets wet!
g y j p q

Use Demonstrate, Practise, Review on p.184 to combine letter formation with relative size by writing CVC words. Use the file called 'Handwriting letter activity' in the Handwriting tab on the **CD** to practise the position of letters with the children.

The lesson plan

1. Demonstrate

For example: write 'dog'.
Show how the dinosaur's head of 'd' reaches up to the sky.
Show how the small 'o' floats on water.
Show how the girl's hair on 'g' gets wet – look sad!

Ask the children to TTYP and say if the letter floats, floats and almost touches the sky, or gets wet.
Demonstrate how to write the letter in the children's wide-lined books.

2. Practice

Check they are sitting in the perfect handwriting position (see p.182).
Ask children to write 'dog' once – slowly and carefully.
Go through the letters with them: *does the letter float, reach the sky, or get wet?*
Repeat getting quicker and quicker each time.
Go round the room praising what you see so others can hear, for example:
Love your 'touch the sky' d.
What a great floating 'o' – just the right size.
Love the hair that's getting wet!
Comment on the letter formation too.
Well done – you remembered where to start the letter.
Repeat with one or two more words.
If you notice that children need further help in forming particular letters, return to the letter lesson.

3. Review – spot the error

Write the word on the board – make one error.
Ask the children to give you ticks for the things you have remembered. Then say 'Spot the error'.
Ask the children to finish with one fantastic word.

Review formation of the letters and follow the lesson plan above to practise writing the words on the file named 'Handwriting Stage 1b' in the Handwriting section of the **CD**.

Start this stage when children can print easily.

This is an intermediate stage between printing and joining; the style becomes more oval with exit flicks.

Grouping of letters

d c o a g and q, u and y, b and p are now taught using a different set of mnemonic pictures so that the relative size and shape can be established further.

These ten letters are important in determining the style of writing and need to be practised more than others. The following notes concentrate on these key letters.

Start by telling the children all about the six sisters, their grandads and the pets:
a d g c o q – the six sisters
Explain how the six sisters look exactly the same until their hairstyle is added.

Each is very fussy about their hairstyle.

- Annie likes to have a neat curl.
- Dina likes to have a neat curl and a ponytail on top.
- Gabi likes her hair to be straight with a gentle curl underneath. She gets her hair wet when she goes swimming and won't wear a swimming hat.
- Carina goes swimming and has her hair so short you can't see it at the back.
- Olivia has a simple fringe and a simple short cut.
- Queenie has the same haircut as Gabi, except she likes a sharp flick on her hair.

The six sisters live with their two grandads – Grandad Umberto and Grandad Yaseen. If they weren't bald you would see how much they look like the sisters!

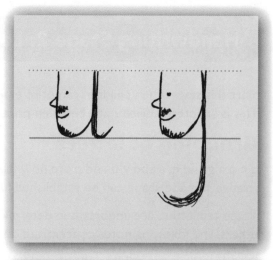

The six sisters have two dogs called Ben and Peter that look just the same – except that Ben has sticky up ears and Peter has floppy ones. The funny thing about the dogs is that they look a bit like the sisters – except they are always running off in the opposite direction (i.e. they are facing the opposite way).

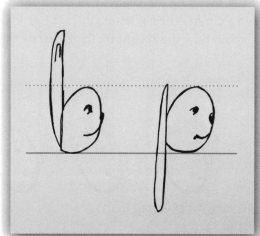

Explain to the children that they are going to learn how to write a d g c o q u y and b p using these pictures to help them remember the shape.

The lesson plan

Example 'd': Dina with a neat curl and a ponytail on top.

1. Demonstration

TOL as you remember the mental checklist to write the letter.
I must remember to:

✓ make Dina's head small and float on the pool
✓ start at the bobble (draw this in) – halfway between the water and the sky
✓ go all the way over the top of her head (colour in a fringe)
✓ curve down her face (draw in nose eyes and mouth)
✓ draw a nice round chin – sitting on the pool-line
✓ join the chin by her ear (draw in ear)
✓ draw back up to the bobble
✓ draw very straight, tall hair – up and then down
✓ curve her hair just at the line and draw a very straight flick (not too curly).

Ask the children to TTYP to say the mental checklist. Take feedback and praise.
Select a partnership to help you write another 'd' using the mental checklist. Let other children call out to help too.
Repeat a couple more times until the children can say the mental checklist to each other.

Note: Get the children to learn to visualize the letter as a picture and not a written list. Do not write the list on the board, though you may need a sticky note to help you remember to begin with.

2. Practice

Check again that the children are sitting in the perfect handwriting position.
Rub out the picture and letter from the board.
Ask children to write one letter – slowly and carefully. (Do not ask them to draw the faces.)
Repeat getting quicker and quicker each time.
Go round the room praising what you see so others can hear, for example:
Nice round chin there! Love the tall spiky hair! What a great curl.

3. Review

Write the letter on the board – make one error.
Ask the children to give you ticks for the things you have remembered. Then say 'Spot the error'.
Ask the children to finish with one fantastic letter.
Repeat, with d c o a g and q, u and y, b and p.

On the next day, have a new focus letter, and review one or two previously taught letters. Practise the different groups below. Compare the letters using the mental checklists. Follow the lesson plan above to teach the letter formation, see the 'Handwriting Stage 2' file on the **CD**, in the Handwriting section.

1. Sisters together e.g. dog, mad, lad
2. Sisters with grandads e.g. day, guy
3. Sisters with their dogs e.g. pop, bag
4. Sisters, grandads and dogs with l h t k
5. Sisters, grandads and dogs with i m n r j
6. Sisters, grandads and dogs with e f s
7. Sisters, grandads and dogs with w v x z

Choose common Red Words to practice writing in the new style.

Handwriting Stage 3 Joining letters

Learning to join letters slows down the speed of writing while children are learning, although speeds up writing when mastered. The aim is for children to learn how to join letters in Year 1 Term 3, and to start to use joins to their own writing during Year 2 and beyond.

The joins

There are *only two types of basic joins*: the arm join (diagonal) and the washing line join (horizontal).

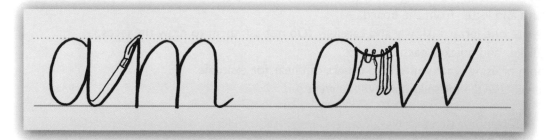

Each of these joins has three variations:
Arm join to small letters, e.g. am
Arm join to tall letters, e.g. al
Arm join to 'sister' letters, e.g. nd
Washing line join to small letters, e.g. ow
Washing line join to tall letters, e.g. wl
Washing line join to 'sister' letters, e.g. wa

Children learn two actions with three variations on each – six in all. Once these have been taught, practise them over and over until they can write them effortlessly in the handwriting lesson. When they can do this encourage them to apply it to their own writing (see p.189).

The lesson plan

Example: arm join to small letter

1. Demonstration

TOL as you show the children how you use the mental checklist to join a to n.
I must remember to:

✓ write 'a' carefully
✓ make the flick gentle – not too round, not too spiky
✓ sweep up the 'arm' join in a gentle curve
✓ make the down stroke of 'n' very straight

Repeat a couple more times until the children can say the mental checklist to each other.

2. Practice

Check they are sitting in the perfect handwriting position (see p.182). Rub out the join and letters from the board.
Ask children to write 'a join n' – slowly and carefully. (Do not ask them to draw the handwriting picture.) Repeat getting quicker and quicker each time. Go round the room praising what you see so others can hear, for example: *Good arm join there! Great flick!*

3. Review

Write 'a join n' on the board – make one error.
Ask the children to give you ticks for the things you have remembered. Then say 'Spot the error'.
Ask the children to finish with one fantastic 'a join n'.

Use this lesson plan to teach the joins on the 'Handwriting Stage 3' file in the Handwriting section of the **CD**. Once children can join all the letters, practise writing red words. There are examples of these in the 'Example red words' file in the Handwriting section of the **CD**.

Key teaching points

Be patient! If you praise the children for the progress they make they will gradually learn to have legible handwriting. It is vital that children understand that being a good writer is not the same as being a good handwriter.

There are some children, often boys, who have poor motor control. This is often because they spend little time doing activities that practice a strong pencil grip – drawing, colouring, doodling and writing messages. It is helpful if all children are encouraged 'to choose' these activities. Sitting with these children in the office and the home corner and playing with attractive pens and paper, as well as giving them extra support during the handwriting lesson, will help.

Some children manage to do beautiful handwriting during the lesson but do not transfer this skill to their own writing. How can this be achieved? When we can focus on one thing, we can do it better than when we are doing three things at once. Gently praise children who transfer this skill, once you know they are able to do this. Reminding children to do their 'best' handwriting is usually unproductive.

Tell older proficient writers that you use three speeds of writing.
Speed One: smart writing for letters and presentation – it's slow!
Speed Two: everyday writing that you use for others to read. You want it to be fast, but legible, so you can get your ideas down quickly. This is the style you all use most of the time.
Speed Three: the writing you use for notes that nobody else will ever read. Not very tidy but you can still read it!

It takes a long time to help children achieve a strong, flowing legible style that can be used for Speed Two writing. Most children either choose to revert to quick printing or a laborious style that appears to be like inscribing in stone.

Once children have learnt all the basic joins, emphasis should be placed on writing quickly and easily so that children will find it easier to join than use quick printing. Until this occurs, no amount of praising and chivvying will help.

Three suggestions that might help:

1. Choose children you are going to 'allow' to start using joining in their books. By giving permission, the children will see it as an accolade to start, rather than as a bind. Only choose children you know can join quickly in the handwriting lesson.
    Other children often start to use the joins by choice!

2. While children are starting to use joins ask everyone to write the first line in joined writing and then continue the rest by printing. The next day, increase this to two lines and so on.

3. Get children to use Speed 1 when they sometimes write the 'hold a sentence' in the *Get Writing!* lessons. Tell them that they must use the joins. You will be able to check this as you walk round. Start slowly on the first day and then increase your speed. Ask the children to tick every word that they have joined. Give lots of praise.

Installing and using the CD

The CD contains resources to help you make teaching writing fun, engaging and straightforward.

When using the PowerPoint CD files, ensure that you press F5 or select 'Slide show mode', so that you can enjoy the full functionality. If you want to annotate the files or model writing with your whiteboard pen, ensure that you lock the screen before doing so.

All the files you need when teaching writing using the *Get Writing! Handbook* are included on the CD, and the resources are editable so that you can adapt them to suit the needs of your class.

- For every 'Edit' activity there is an accompanying file on the CD. On a PC click 'Edit' to highlight the errors one by one, and 'Reveal' to show the corrected sentence. The Edit files are always the first file in a Storybook section, i.e. File 1.2, 2.1, 3.1 in Green are all 'Edit' files.
- There are files on the CD for each writing composition activity. These contain colour images from the Storybooks, as well as photos, sound effects, animation and drag and drop activities. You can use them to generate ideas, discussion, and to model taking notes, planning and writing longer sentences. These files are clearly referenced by name in the lesson, e.g. 'Display CD (file 1.2) to show the image of the noisy bus'.
- There are 'Word bank' files, which contain lists of Power words.
- There is a Handwriting section, containing resources you will need to teach handwriting.
- There are achievement certificates to celebrate children's progress.

Installing the CD on a PC

To install *Read Write Inc. Get Writing!* CD on your PC:
1. Start your computer as usual. If you are already logged in, exit any other applications that you are running. Make sure you have administrator rights on the computer.
2. Insert the CD-ROM into your CD drive.
3. The installer should 'auto-run'. If it does not start automatically, then navigate to the root directory of the CD-ROM and run **Setup.exe** to start the installation process.
4. Follow the instructions on screen. When the licence screen appears, if you accept the software licence terms, select the **I accept** radio button and then select **Next**.
5. When the final screen appears, select **Finish**.

Installing the CD on an Apple Mac

To install *Read Write Inc. Get Writing!* CD on your Apple Mac:
1. Start your Apple Mac as usual. If you are already logged in, exit any other applications that you are running. Make sure you have administrator rights on the computer.
2. Insert the CD-ROM into your CD drive.
3. If the installer does not open automatically select the *Get Writing!* icon and then select **Install Get Writing.app**.
4. Follow the instructions on screen. When the licence screen appears, if you accept the software licence terms, select the **Agree** button and then select **Install**.
5. When the final screen appears, select **Quit**. It is now installed in your applications folder.

Location and installing on a network

If you follow the default installation, *Read Write Inc. Get Writing!* CD will install locally on your machine (in the Program Files folder of your PC). It is possible to install the software onto a network drive. Select the location you wish when you are prompted to confirm the install location.

Getting around the software

Click on the tabs to access resources linked to the books in each colour level. A second set of tabs will allow you to access the content linked to the book title on the tab. After the tabs for the colour levels, there are also tabs for Handwriting, Word banks and Achievement certificates.

Simple Speed Sounds chart

Consonants: *stretchy*

f	l	m	n	r	s	v	z	sh	th	ng
										nk

Consonants: *bouncy*

b	c	d	g	h	j	p	qu	t	w	x	y	ch
	k											

Vowels: *bouncy*   **Vowels:** *stretchy*

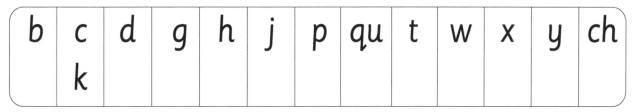

a	e	i	o	u	ay	ee	igh	ow

Vowels: *stretchy*

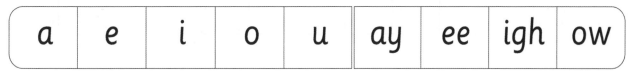

oo	oo	ar	or	air	ir	ou	oy

Complex Speed Sounds chart

Consonants: *stretchy*

f	l	m	n	r	s	v	z	sh	th	ng
ff	ll	mm	nn	rr	ss	ve	zz	ti		nk
ph	le	mb	kn	wr	se		s	ci		
					c					
					ce					

Consonants: *bouncy*

b	c	d	g	h	j	p	qu	t	w	x	y	ch
bb	k	dd	gg		g	pp		tt	wh			tch
	ck				ge							
	ch											

Vowels

a	e	i	o	u	ay	ee	igh	ow
	ea				a-e	y	i-e	o-e
					ai	ea	ie	oa
						e	i	o

oo	oo	ar	or	air	ir	ou	oy	ire	ear	ure
u-e			oor	are	ur	ow	oi			
ue			ore		er					
ew			aw							
			au							